Marketing the Sports Organisation

M

Marketing and the world of sport overlap in two main ways: in the marketing of sports related products and services, and in the use of sports to market a broader range of products and services. *Marketing the Sports Organisation* introduces the most effective marketing methods and tools available to sports organisations, and offers practical, step-by-step advice for sports organisations in the use of relationship-marketing techniques.

Comprehensive and innovative in its approach, the book includes:

- A practical framework for implementing relationship marketing throughout the product and service range
- An in-depth examination of tools and methods that increase the value of the product for the consumer
- A genuinely international approach, applicable in all countries
- Detailed international case studies from the world of sport.

Offering a thorough introduction to first principles in sports marketing, and focused throughout on best practice, this book is essential reading for all students of sport and business marketing, and for all professionals seeking to improve their sports marketing activity, in both commercial and non-profit environments.

Alain Ferrand is Professor of Marketing at the University of Poitiers, Director of the Business and Research Centre (CEREGE), Director of the Masters in Sport Organisations Management conducted in French, and an Associate Professor at the University of Turin and the Scuola Dello Sport, Rome (Italian Olympic Committee – CONI Servizi).

Scott McCarthy has been Chief Executive of the British Judo Association since 2002. Before that he was Chief Executive of the Irish Basketball Association and spent ten years as a Foreign Service Officer for the United States Department of State.

Marketing the Sports Organisation

Building networks and relationships

Alain Ferrand and Scott McCarthy

Routledge
Taylor & Francis Group

LONDON AND NEW YORK

First published 2009
by Routledge
2 Park Square, Milton Park, Abingdon, Oxon OX14 4RN

Simultaneously published in the USA and Canada
by Routledge
270 Madison Ave, New York, NY 10016

*Routledge is an imprint of the Taylor & Francis Group, an informa
business*

© 2009 Alain Ferrand and Scott McCarthy

Typeset in Garamond 3 by
Swales & Willis Ltd, Exeter, Devon
Printed and bound in Great Britain by
The Cromwell Press, Trowbridge, Wiltshire

British Library Cataloguing in Publication Data
A catalogue record for this book is available
from the British Library

Library of Congress Cataloging-in-Publication Data
A catalog record for this book has been requested

ISBN10: 0–415–45329–1 (hbk)
ISBN10: 0–415–45330–5 (pbk)
ISBN10: 0–203–89303–4 (ebk)

ISBN13: 978–0–415–45329–5 (hbk)
ISBN13: 978–0–415–45330–1 (pbk)
ISBN13: 978–0–203–89303–6 (ebk)

To my family, my friends, the MEMOS community and all my students.
Alain Ferrand

To my family, friends in the MEMOS network, and colleagues within British sport.
Scott McCarthy

To Alberto Madella.

Contents

Figures

Tables

Foreword

I am delighted to comply with the authors' request to write a preface for their book on the management of networks and relationships among sports organisations. In fact, this ground-breaking work is a direct result of a network that I have had the honour and pleasure of coordinating for nearly 10 years: the MEMOS program (Executive Masters of Sport Organisations Management). Alain Ferrand has been the lecturer in charge of the MEMOS marketing module since its creation in 1995, and Scott McCarthy graduated from the Masters course in 2005.

Over the years, the lecturers and graduates of the MEMOS program have gradually built up a vast network within the Olympic Movement – a system of organisations that contribute towards the holding of the Olympic Games: the National Olympic Committees (NOCs), the International Sports Federations (IFs), the national sports federations and clubs, the International Olympic Committee (IOC) and the Organising Committees of the Olympic Games (OCOGs). All these organisations and others – such as local, regional and national public authorities – are stakeholders within the Olympic System.

One major factor behind the renewed success of this System, since its foundation by Pierre de Coubertin in 1894 until the present, could be explained by an intuitive application of relationship marketing even before the theory was advanced by Berry in the early 1980s. The massive event that the Games have become could not, in fact, be organised without the close cooperation of an entire series of stakeholders that depend on each other but that all derive benefit from their contributions. The IOC depends directly on the OCOG which is constituted following the election of the host city of the Games, at which the competitions are sanctioned by the IFs and the athletes are provided by the NOCs and national federations of each country. In return, all these organisations share the Olympic marketing revenues, mainly from television broadcasting rights, sponsoring and merchandising related to the Games. Their joint market is far superior thanks to these relationships, which are ancient, yet constantly renewed from one Olympiad to another.

This System has gradually succeeded in structuring world sport by its involvement in the organisation of national, continental and world champion-ships held throughout the year under the aegis of Olympic values. There are few disciplines that escape the Olympic System apart from the major North American professional sports. Nevertheless, it is a system that is currently under considerable pressure from a whole series of new actors, such as national and transnational governments, local or international sponsors, and profes-sional teams or athletes' leagues that wish to develop the sports market and achieve a substantial profit from it – whether of a tangible or intangible nature.

Several of these new challenges are illustrated in this book by means of cases studies, for the most part prepared by MEMOS graduates. They demon-strate that nothing is more practical than a good theory – that of relationship marketing – to position the sports organisations of the twenty-first century in an efficient way in relation to their objectives of development on a social and environmental level, and not just on one of economics alone.

Jean-Loup Chappelet
MEMOS Program Director
Professor, IDHEAP Swiss Graduate School of Public Administration
Lausanne
Switzerland

Preface

When I was asked to write the preface for the book, three thoughts came to my mind. The first one brought me back to those days during the first MEMOS edition in 1995 where I met with Alain Ferrand, the co-author of this book.

I had just started a year earlier at the International Basketball Federation, FIBA, and was very fresh in enthusiasm and curiosity, but lacking in knowledge and experience in sport organisations. I therefore gladly enrolled in the first MEMOS edition, wanting to fill in those gaps, and the experience was indeed very enriching. Besides and beyond what we learned, it created the first alumni group which today is an extensive network of MEMOS graduates that spans over all five continents and possesses a wealth of experience and know-how. It is therefore not a surprise that 13 years later, this book is written with the contributions of MEMOS graduates and I feel very privileged to have been asked to write these few introductory notes.

The second most immediate thought concerned the task at hand and the book's objective to help sport organisations '. . . increase the relationship, constellation and functional values with their internal and external stakeholders . . .'. I suddenly had to ask myself whether I had slept through the marketing session in MEMOS 13 years earlier! How complicated all this had become.

I have a very pragmatic view on marketing. Marketing is about Action: doing what is right, efficiently and rapidly, as only results count.

Undoubtedly, when I started at FIBA and was confronted with marketing, the concept seemed straightforward, similar to the transactional approach readers will find out about later in this book and mainly concentrating on generating resources from marketing partners. In fact, it was even simpler as ISL, the best-known marketing agency around for many years, was ready to invest and guarantee sufficient funds for FIBA to operate. There was no real exchange of services, except that FIBA was to deliver the events, which we mastered almost blindly.

But with the growing 'commercialisation' of sports over the past 10–15 years, greater financing requirements have emerged as well as greater competition. FIBA has not escaped from this trend and has slowly realised that marketing agencies can be valuable partners, but also an obstacle for development if the terms of the relationship are purely based on transactional marketing. The agencies' interests in investments are typically short-term versus the right-holder's long-term interests.

Interestingly and well-fitted to the subject of this book, sports marketing agencies base their competitive advantage on the number of accounts that they manage, both of rights (acquired from right-holders) and of commercial partners (interested in those rights). In other words, they use in a very efficient way, solid network- and relationship-based marketing. A Federation, which sells its rights out to an agency, could easily remain isolated in such a scenario and on the margin of those networks, thus unable to build upon them directly and independently should it need to do so.

Over the years 2000 and 2001, FIBA had to decide to jump into the cold water: we were no longer working exclusively with agencies and had to immediately develop in-house marketing and commercial capabilities. The sports business market at the time was digesting the ISL bankruptcy and the slump in television rights for sport in Europe. Commercial partners and potential sponsors were also becoming more and more sophisticated, evaluating every partnership very carefully in strategic terms and calculating their return on investment with precision.

We had to learn that they were less interested in simple transactional marketing. They required efficient value-creation chains, innovative ideas and positive differentiation from other right-holders. They also expect to tap into the Federation's network and relationships to reach their potential customers.

This requires in turn a Federation that is highly professional, re-organised from top to bottom and that delivers more value to its partners. I am certain that as competition grows for the same dollar and customer, this applies across the whole spectrum of sport organisations.

The third and last thought brings me to the changes that occurred and are ongoing in FIBA from those early days of 2000 until today:

- Alignment of the FIBA family to a vision, mission and long-term objectives
- Re-branding of the whole FIBA family
- Re-organisation of the administrative structure to include a strong team of in-house professionals in communication, marketing, television and new media
- Improvement of standards for delivery of events worldwide to reach top sport properties quality
- Re-enforcement and improvement of regulatory framework
- Involvement of 213 national federations as key stakeholders in growing and developing the sport in particular through technology and transfer of knowledge.

In essence, it was, and still is, about creating an efficient institutional (internal) network of our membership, which can be used within the system for each others' benefit and growth. Strategic and/or commercial partners want to use this network for their benefit. Both aspects – internal and external – are necessary to grow the sport and to find the resources necessary for this growth.

Institutional re-organisation and internal motivation is difficult as members are coming from the most disparate corners of the world and, in an international federation setting, tend to be far from the centre and not as developed. Here, internal relationship marketing with a lot of positive communication, transparency and tangible benefits are required on a permanent basis.

But it is far more difficult to convince external partners of the certain and added value that such institutional networks can bring to them. Following the Saint Thomas principle, only real experience will build the necessary trust and create value for your product in your partners' eyes.

Therefore, in addition to the networks, another priority is to clearly define the product and the brand you want to promote. Consistency over time, together with perfect organisation and professional management of events has thus been an important pillar of FIBA's recent developments. After achieving high organisational quality standards in our key events, the focus has now shifted to more comprehensive communication and public relations strategies. In professional terminology, the marketing-mix is now shifting to achieve further growth.

The developments over recent years have thus been very important for FIBA. Similarly, other sports organisations have evolved and are now commonly using terminology from the corporate world, such as stakeholders, customers, partners, social networks and relationships, branding, product development, etc.

A more recent trend, which cannot be contained and perfectly suits sport, relates to the latest technology developments. These add another layer of complexity – and costs – but also of opportunities for the world of sport. The development of new media and digital technology in general is still in its infancy, but rapidly growing in sport as the US experience testifies. We should not expect to exchange the analogue dollars (e.g. traditional television rights) for digital pennies (e.g. broadband video platforms) too soon, but certainly we need to adapt our internal processes to the technology trends and needs now. As costs diminish and technology permeates all our internal activities and processes, it will become simpler to create value out of digital assets. But one should not forget that the use of technology is already instrumental today in widening your own network and tying-in your fans, athletes and partners alike. They all have something in common on which any sport organisation can build upon: the passion for your sport.

In conclusion, it is essential for sports organisations to invest in human

Acknowledgements

Quite aptly, given its theme of managing networks and relationships, this book is the fruit of a collective project that began in 1984, during the first edition of the Executive Masters in Sports Organisation Management (MEMOS). The MEMOS programme was set up by the International Olympic Committee and Olympic Solidarity to increase the managerial skills of professional and volunteer managers working within national and international sports organisations. Today, the MEMOS network includes more than 300 graduates throughout the world. The governance and implementation of this programme is the responsibility of a network of universities and organisations belonging to the Olympic family. It is a learning community that enables administrators, sports-organisation managers and respected academics in the sports-management field to compare, combine and capitalise on their experiences.

The idea for this book arose at the 9th edition of the MEMOS and stemmed from a collaborative project between a university lecturer who has had the privilege of teaching at every edition of the MEMOS and the Chief Executive Officer of the British Judo Association. It has been enriched by contributions from Andreu Camps i Povill, Bob Gambardella, Jeffrey Howard, Clement Mubanga Chileshe, Patrizia Marchesini, Joanne Mortimore, Denis Mowbray and Alexis Schaffer, all MEMOS graduates, whose case studies have greatly widened the book's international outlook. The two authors have also incorporated invaluable contributions from their networks of colleagues, including Nick Bitel, Stuart Dalrymple, Donna Kaye, Sylvie Montagnon, Monica Paul and David Stotlar. We would also like to thank Valentina Calvani and François Vermeulen, whose MEMOS projects contributed to the conception and production of this method.

We would also like to extend a special thank you to Paul Henderson, whose professionalism and diligence are reflected in his excellent translation of the original French texts.

Produced as a collaborative project involving a network of very different people who share a number of values – commitment, friendship, solidarity, tolerance and respect – the writing of this book embraced the spirit of relationship marketing, a spirit we hope to share with our readers.

Abbreviations

BJA	British Judo Association
COIB	Belgian Olympic and Inter-federal Committee
CNOSF	French National Olympic Committee
CONI	Italian Olympic Committee
CRM	Customer Relationship Management
CSR	Corporate social responsibility
FFVB	French Volleyball Federation
FIBA	International Basketball Federation
FIFA	International Federation of Football Associations
FIVB	International Volleyball Federation
IOC	International Olympic Committee
NF	National Federation
NGB	National Governing Body
NOC	National Olympic Committee
OCOG	Organizing Committee of the Olympic Games
OG	Olympic Games
RFU	Rugby Football Union
UCI	International Cycling Union
UEFA	Union of European Football Associations
RM	Relationship Marketing
VANOC	Vancouver Organizing Committee for the 2010 Olympic and Paralympic Winter Games

Introduction

The history of sports marketing can be traced back to the 1870s, when tobacco companies placed cards of baseball players in packs of cigarettes to boost sales and develop brand loyalty. Ever since its creation, in 1894, the International Olympic Committee (IOC) has depended on partnerships with the business community to develop the Olympic Games and the Olympic movement. Some 20 years later, in 1903, the sports newspaper *L'Auto* created the 'Tour de France' so it would have a major sports event to cover during the month of July, which was a very quiet period in the sporting calendar. One of the first examples of an amateur athlete being used for public relations or advertising was in 1936, when Adidas gave Jesse Owens free shoes during the Berlin Olympics. Today, marketing partners are an integral part of the Olympic system.

The formalisation of tools and methods for sports marketing is, however, a relatively recent development and the first manual dedicated to sports marketing, by Mullin, Hardy and Sutton, was not published until 1993. Now there are several specialist academic journals and professional reviews, especially in North America, Europe and Asia. The American Marketing Association's Academic Resource Center lists three: the *International Journal of Sports Management and Marketing*, the *International Journal of Sports Marketing & Sponsorship*, and *Sports Marketing Quarterly*.

Sports marketing defined

According to Mullin *et al.* (2007: 11), 'sports marketing consists of all the activities designed to meet the needs and wants of sport consumers through exchange processes. Sports marketing has developed two major thrusts: the marketing of sports products and services directly to consumers of sport, and the marketing of other consumer and industrial products or services through the use of sports promotions'.

This definition concurs with the classic Kotlerian notion of marketing based on exchange, in which marketing is defined as 'a social and managerial process whereby individuals and groups obtain what they need and want through creating and exchanging products and value with others' (Kotler and Armstrong, 2001: 6). Shank (2005: 3) also stressed this connection, maintaining that 'sports marketing is the specific application of marketing principles and processes to sport products and to the marketing of non-sports products through association with sport'.

Thus defined, sports marketing affects 'consumers' (i.e. participants, spectators, corporate partners and non-profit partners), who have an interest in the 'products' (i.e. personal training, competitions, events, sporting goods and sports information) that have been put on the market by 'producers and intermediaries' (i.e. sponsors, media, agents, equipment manufacturers). This resembles Porter's (1985) 'value chain' model, in which marketing and sales are regarded as primary activities and are part of 'market interrelationships'. In Porter's model, the specificity of sports marketing derives from the combination of these three elements.

Consumers

Consumers are the people who consume or use sports products and services. For clarity, they are best referred to here as 'end users'. The main limit of this approach for sports organisations is that many exchanges, such as those involving sports event volunteers and the actors in social marketing programmes (e.g. FIFA's 'Football for hope' programme), are not monetarised. In other words, there are customers and non-customers. As a result, sports organisation marketing involves a heterogeneous mix of characteristics and motivations.

Products and services

The relationship between products and services is still subject to debate; however, it can be said that the division between the two entities is becoming increasingly blurred, as product manufacturers start to offer associated services (e.g. the Nike+ community, which allows runners to compare their races with other community members) and services require the use of physical objects (e.g. fitness training requires equipment). In addition, some sporting-goods manufacturers also distribute their products (e.g. Nike Town) and some distributors manufacture sports equipment (e.g. Decathlon). As Normann and Ramirez (1998) have pointed out, a product or a service corresponds to an offer that has value for the 'consumer'. It is the result of a number of actions carried out by different actors. Mullin et al. (2007: 17) defined a product as 'any bundle or combination of qualities, processes and/or ideas that a buyer expects will deliver satisfaction'.

On the basis of this definition, the term 'offer' is used here to describe 'a product or a service, anything of value to a "customer", [that] is created through a collection of activities by different actors made available in one way or another to the "supplier" bringing value to the customer' (Normann and Ramirez 1998: 27). From an operational point of view, it must be remembered that consumers and users expect products and services to satisfy a need or provide a benefit. Grönroos (2000: 3) maintains that consumers buy the benefits linked to these products and services: 'They buy offerings consisting of goods, services, information, personal attention and other components'.

Offers are complex wholes composed of tangible and intangible elements that provide consumers and users with a wide range of benefits (functional, affective, emotional, psychological, social, hedonistic and aesthetic). Functional benefits are derived from the ability of a product or service to meet utilitarian and/or physical needs. Thus, children belonging to a football club want to improve technically and tactically, and to take part in competitions. The service provided by the club also delivers benefits that are social (group membership, make friends, etc.), affective (generate emotions), hedonistic (give pleasure, joy, etc.) and aesthetic (sense of beauty, enhance personal expression, etc.). According to Holbrook (1999), these benefits are experiential because the value can only be derived from experiencing the situation and this experience provides emotional, symbolic and socio-cultural benefits.

The above analysis can be used to differentiate between products and services by plotting the characteristics of an offer along two axes (Figure I.1). The first axis shows the tangible and intangible characteristics of the offer; the second shows the nature of the benefits to be obtained (i.e. functional or experiential). An offer is described as a 'product' if it primarily consists of tangible elements; it is described as a 'service' if it mostly consists of intangible elements.

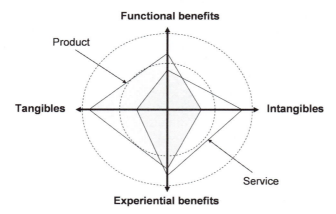

Figure I.1 Differentiation between products and services.

Producers, distributors and intermediaries

In general terms, a producer can be defined as a person or an organisation that produces, or contributes to the production of (e.g. as an employee or an investor), goods or services. Products may then require distribution to their end-users. The situation in the sports sector is complex because it contains a large number of actors of different sizes and with different statuses (i.e. companies, associations, freelancers). Some of these organisations are profit making but the sector is dominated by non-profit organisations. For example, an international federation, such as FIFA, whose mission is to develop the game of soccer and to contribute to building a better future, acts in partnership with its 208 member associations, each of which is in relation with all the affiliated clubs in its own country. This forms a vast 'distribution network' with local, national and international connections. The system also includes intermediaries, such as players' agents – independent third parties who act as mediators during negotiations.

The structure of the sports industry

The structure of the 'sports industry' is complex. Classically, models of the industry take into account variables, such as end goals (i.e. profit or non-profit) and missions (i.e. develop products, organise events, etc.). In very general terms, the industry can be divided into four sectors (Figure I.2):

- *Sports organisations* provide services that allow participation in sport and activities directly linked to entertainment provided by sport (e.g. clubs, federations, etc.).
- *Providers* supply products and sports equipment (e.g. equipment manufacturers).
- *Service organisations* support participation in sports (e.g. information, health, marketing).
- *Private or public organisations* use collaborations with sports organisations to achieve their strategic and marketing objectives. They can be partners (e.g. local authorities) or clients (e.g. sponsors).

The organisations directly responsible for competitive or recreational sport form the heart of the sports industry. Sports events can be organised by associations or companies. Sports events can also provide entertainment, in which case they also involve other parties, such as spectators, the media and sponsors. They may be profit oriented (e.g. professional soccer clubs) or non-profit bodies (e.g. sports federations). They mostly provide services. Participation in sport requires facilities, equipment and associated services. The dynamics of this system are directly related to the relationships between its members.

Figure I.2 The sports industry and its related sectors.

What is a sports organisation?

Robinson *et al.* (2007) have proposed a general classification of sports organisations based on four characteristics:

1   The people who make up an organisation and the relationships between these people
2   The rules that govern an organisation
3   The objectives and end goals an organisation pursues
4   The resources at an organisation's disposal.

Slack and Parent's (2006: 5) very general definition describes a sports organisation as 'a social entity in the sports industry; it is goal-directed, with a consciously structured activity system and a relatively identifiable boundary'. This wide-reaching description covers any group of people with a juridical personality that is directly involved in one or more sectors of the 'sports industry'; hence, such very different players as Nike, the International Association of Athletics Federations, the American sports magazine *Sports Illustrated*, and America's Cup organisers AC Management can be regarded as sports organisations.

Sport is a social phenomenon involving a large number of very different parties; however, sport's front-line is occupied by sports organisations whose mission is to develop participation in sport and directly associated activities. This includes associations, such as the International Volleyball Federation, companies that organise events, such as AC Management, and non-profit organisation committees, such as the Vancouver Organizing Committee for the 2010 Olympic and Paralympic Winter Games (VANOC).

The International Volleyball Federation's (FIVB) mission is 'to govern, manage and communicate all forms of Volleyball and Beach Volleyball worldwide. It aims to develop Volleyball as a major world media and entertainment sport through world class planning and organisation of competitions, marketing and promotional activities'. AC Management, an independent company created by Team Alinghi (winners of the 31st America's Cup) and the Société Nautique de Genève (SNG), was mandated to manage the organisational and commercial aspects of the 32nd America's Cup. Its mission is to move the event forward through professional and permanent organisation. The company's management insists that its objective is to respect the Cup's heritage and to work closely with participants, the host city, its partners and the media in order to provide an exceptional and innovative event and to share it with the public. The Vancouver Organizing Committee for the 2010 Olympic and Paralympic Winter Games (VANOC) was set up to support and promote the development of sport in Canada by planning, organizing, financing and staging the 2010 Olympic and Paralympic Winter Games. Its mission is to touch the soul of the nation and inspire the world by creating and delivering an extraordinary Olympic and Paralympic experience with lasting legacies. Its vision is to build a stronger Canada whose spirit is raised by its passion for sport, culture and sustainability.

Combining these considerations leads to a narrower definition of a sports organisation to be an entity with a juridical personality whose main mission is to contribute to increasing participation in sport and developing activities directly linked to sport. This is the definition that has been used for this book. Sports organisations carry out their actions within a network of stakeholders.

Sports organisation marketing must be aimed at all stakeholders

As was highlighted above, it is important to take into account the dynamics of the relationships between the different parties who make up this system. For example, a club will develop relationships with its members, the authorities of the town in which it is located, its regional league, its federation and the local media, etc. Accepting Freeman's (1984: 46) definition of stakeholders as 'any groups or individuals who can affect or are affected by the achievement of the organisation's objectives', all the people and organisations that have a relationship with a club are stakeholders in that club. From a marketing point of view, strategic choices must be made about which of the stakeholders to engage and satisfy. Thus, the IOC focuses on both its internal network (i.e. Olympic family) and its external network (i.e. candidate cities, sponsors, media).

Traditionally, sports marketing has been considered from a transactional point of view, in which the exchange of value, e.g. exchanging sports services for money, is the core phenomenon. According to this view, marketing is planned and implemented to create and facilitate the exchange of products and services for money. Consequently, 'the major focus of marketing programs has been to make customers buy, regardless of whether they are new or old customers' (Grönroos, 2000: 20). This type of approach is often referred to as transaction marketing with a business focus.

However, many sports organisations have adopted a relationship-marketing approach. For example, a club may use relationship marketing to develop its relationship with its supporters, as in the case of AC Milan's Cuore Rosso Nero programme. AC Milan's official online community unites people who share the same passion for the 'Rossoneri'. Registration is free and personal data are used to personally tailor the services the site offers each fan. Its services include a 'mobile blog' (fans can publish photos on the Rossoneri site by sending them to mms@acmilan.it or mobileblog@acmilan.it from their cell phones); My Panini (fans can take a digital photo and create their personal Panini sticker); a chat room (using acmilan.com, fans can chat with current and past Milan players); a download facility (photo and video gallery, desktop wallpaper and screensavers for PCs); a contact page (to request information on a number of different topics: tickets, player autographs, sponsorship opportunities, accreditation and interviews) and e-cards.

AC Milan has also introduced a number of programmes based on collaboration with partners, such as the regional authorities, sponsors and the media. The AC Milan Youth Programme is a coordinated programme of events and activities aimed at actively involving boys and girls under the age of 18. It covers all AC Milan's Youth Sector teams, all associated teams belonging to Galassia Milan and AC Milan Soccer School, as well as Milan Junior Camp, Sunday Camp and many other purely entertainment events, such as the Mgeneration Park and Milan Party. Its objective is to meet the expectations of kids who are new to soccer and to promote a positive life model.

These two examples illustrate how AC Milan has approached relationship marketing. The first example shows relationship marketing with a market orientation, as its objective is to build loyalty by strengthening the club's relationship with its supporters. The second example shows relationship marketing with a network orientation because it is based on collaboration between several parties. Both examples are based on the notion 'that it is not exchanges *per se* that are the core of marketing, but that exchanges take place in ongoing relationships between parties in the marketplace – and now also in the virtual marketplace facilitated by the internet' (Grönroos, 2000: 22). Relationships between parties or stakeholders are the core phenomenon and marketing is about managing the relationship between organisations, customers, suppliers and other partners organised in a network.

The relational approach suits the situation and goals of sports organisations better than a transactional approach. Sports organisations are necessarily network based because they operate in a system formed by numerous stakeholders. Their goals may be economic (generate income), social (e.g. generate positive interactions between individuals or groups) or environmental (e.g. to minimise the environmental impact of sports events). The foundation of the system is the sport itself, with various bodies involved in the furtherance and development of that sport. Sport has two main service areas: participation in sport, which includes training and competition, and sports events.

The rationale of this book

The main objective of this book is to present, in an in-depth and innovative way, a framework for implementing relationship marketing. This framework includes network- and market-oriented methods and tools that enable sports organisations to design and develop offers that provide targeted stakeholders with greater functional and experiential value. Sports organisations provide a wide variety of services, from leadership, governance, management, development, entertainment and control to educational materials and other retail products, all of which would benefit from greater emphasis on relationship-marketing principles. This would allow sports organisations to enhance their relationship value by developing existing offerings and by introducing new initiatives.

In short, this is a 'how to think' and 'what to do' book.

The structure of the book

Chapter one describes the conceptual bases of relationship marketing and stakeholder theory, highlighting the strategic and operational consequences that affect the marketing of the services provided by sports organisations. This is followed by an analysis of the system in which sports organisations operate and the presentation of a model based on managing relationships in the three sub-systems (i.e. market, network and internal). The chapter ends with a discussion of key challenges facing marketers.

Chapter two looks at strategic issues concerning relationship marketing. If an organisation is to achieve its goals and fulfil its mission through relationship marketing, it must ensure that decisions concerning its marketing strategy are based on a coherent, clear and integrated process capable of differentiating the varying requirements of the market, network and internal sub-systems. This process should include the systematic analysis of opportunities and threats in the environment and the market, and it should pay careful attention to the organisation's distinctive competences. Through systematic analysis, the sports organisation will be able to make decisions and take actions that will engage and satisfy targeted stakeholders.

Chapter three focuses on the issues surrounding the introduction of a relationship-marketing strategy. Strategic decisions relating to marketing and relationship-marketing strategies have to be implemented. The method is applicable to all three sub-systems (i.e. market, network and internal) they focus on. Before implementing a relationship strategy, specific strategies should be chosen for each sub-system, taking into account variables such as sports organisation resources and competencies, the environment, targeted stakeholders and the extended marketing mix. This chapter also illustrates and explores methods organisations can apply in order to improve their relationships, constellation and functional value through relationship marketing and to give their stakeholders greater experiential value. Case studies and examples from a number of international sporting bodies are used to consider practical strategies for each of the three relationship sub-systems. In practice, combing these three aspects of relationship marketing provides benefits for sports organisations.

The final chapter illustrates how these three types of relationship strategy (i.e. market, network and internal) are combined in the case of the British Judo Association (www.britishjudo.org.uk). The BJA is a national federation that manages a single sport. The case study is structured as follows: current situation, presentation and diagnosis, analysis and recommendations.

Chapter 1

Relationship marketing for sports organisations

Theoretical foundations and challenges

Following the 1996 Atlanta Olympic Games, the Belgian Olympic and Inter-federal Committee (COIB) created the Olympic Health Foundation (OHF). The OHF's objective is to 'make an objective, positive and relevant contribution to the development of a healthy lifestyle amongst the largest sections of the population, focusing on young people aged six to eighteen'. In order to spread its message, the foundation works closely with a number of key partners, such as parents, teachers, doctors, dieticians, nutritionists and public bodies. Initiatives introduced by the foundation include:

- The 'Sport à l'école' (Sport at school) scheme, which provides financial support for sport in primary and secondary schools through the sale of promotional objects.
- The 'Fou de Santé' (Mad about health) project, which is aimed at 8–12 year old primary school students, their teachers and their families. It provides 4,000 classes with educational materials about physical activity and healthy eating habits, together with free healthy breakfasts or snacks.
- The 'Olympicnic', which is a fun day for children and families that promotes Olympic values, in particular physical activity and healthy eating habits.
- 'Olympisme et Jeunesse' ('Olympic spirit and youth'), which is a project week for schools that teaches young people about the Olympic Movement. It is held every Olympic year.
- The OHF science prize, which recognises master's and bachelor's degree projects that investigate the relationship between regular physical activity and health.

Aimed at all Belgian children and their families, the OHF's programme is a social marketing operation that produces both functional benefits (by highlighting the links between physical activity, good eating habits and health) and socio-emotional benefits. Its success has been reinforced by the involvement of high profile partners, such as Nestlé Céréales (health orientation), Coca Cola Belgique-Luxembourg, Winterthur Assurances, Delhaize Le Lion,

Belgacom, Union Nationale des Mutualités Libres, VRT, RTBF, VUM-Groep, Roularta-Group, Le Soir and Kinepolis, all of which have signed the charter and become OHF partners. Thus, the OHF has adopted a relationship-marketing approach to the implementation of its programme and strategy, which involves a large number of partners and is network-oriented.

The first part of this chapter presents the underlying principles of relationship marketing, together with the relevant tenets of stakeholder management, which are rooted in systems theory. The marketing actions of a national sports organisation (Swiss Olympic) are then analysed in order to highlight the benefits that sports organisations can gain by adopting a relationship-marketing approach. The chapter concludes with a general analysis of the challenges sports organisations must overcome when implementing relationship-marketing strategies.

Theoretical foundations

Originally developed in the commercial world, relationship-marketing and stakeholder management strategies are increasingly being adopted by sports organisations to implement their actions through networks. The principles underlying relationship marketing and stakeholder management are recognisably systemic, however, these approaches were initially based on practical experience rather than theory. Nevertheless, by defining the concepts underlying relationship marketing and stakeholder management, it has been possible to open up new managerial perspectives. These theoretical concepts are presented below.

Relationship marketing

Relationship marketing is generally associated with Customer Relationship Management; however, it covers a range of actions based on different theoretical foundations.

Origins of relationship marketing

Researchers (e.g. Berry and Parasuraman, 1993; Christopher *et al.* 1991; Sheth and Parvatiyar, 2000) agree that a new marketing approach has recently emerged. It is based on the notion 'that it is not exchanges *per se* that are the core of marketing, but that exchanges take place in ongoing relationships between parties in the marketplace – and now also in the virtual marketplace facilitated by the internet' (Grönroos, 2000: 22). Relationships between parties or stakeholders are the core phenomenon; therefore, managing the relationships between the organisations, customers, suppliers and other partners that form a network is a key aspect of marketing.

Arndt (1979) and Flipo (1999) have shown that many markets have a relational structure based on commitments between highly motivated parties with complementary long-term outlooks. According to Bruhn (2003), relationship marketing has various origins. Bagozzi (1975) was the first person to define marketing as a renewed process of exchanges between a buyer and a seller. The evolution of commercial relationships can be divided into a number of phases. Berry (1983) has identified these phases for the service sector, which is the sector that has seen the most significant contributions in this field (Gummerson, 1987; Grönroos, 1990, 1994).

According to Möller and Halinen (2000), relationship marketing finds its roots in four strands:

- Business marketing, in terms of the interactions between parties and the network approach
- Distribution channels in marketing
- Services marketing
- Direct and database marketing.

The relational approach suits the environment and goals of sports organisations (i.e. clubs, national and international federations, etc.) better than a transactional approach, as the systems in which sports organisations operate consist of multiple networks made up of numerous stakeholders (Figure 1.1).

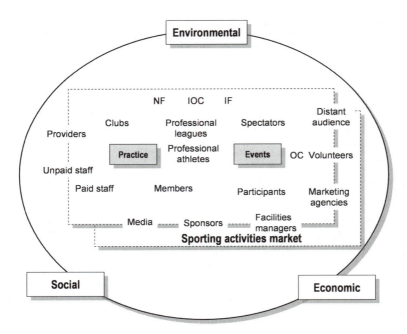

Figure 1.1 The sporting activities market and its environment.

Their goals may be economic (e.g. to generate revenues), social (e.g. to generate positive interactions between individuals or groups) or environmental (e.g. to minimise the environmental impact of sports events). The core of the system is the sport itself, surrounded by various bodies involved in the furtherance and development of that sport. Sport can be divided into two main service areas: sporting practice (including training and competition), and sporting events.

The sporting activities market is open and in constant interaction and interrelation with its environment, which is composed of specific stakeholders with similar economic, social or environmental goals (Figure 1.2).

As the issues facing sports organisations are often very complex, it can be difficult for an organisation working in isolation to achieve its goals. Therefore, sports organisations need to join forces with other parties in order to optimise their impact on their environment. They must determine which parties have matching or complementary goals (not necessarily the same goals) and identify ways in which they can work together (Figure 1.3).

Definition of relationship marketing

Relationship marketing has been defined in a variety of ways by different authors. Most of the approaches limit themselves to the supplier–customer dyad, although some consider multiple stakeholders. Christopher *et al.* (1991); Kotler (1992); Morgan and Hunt (1994) and Gummerson (1999) have gone

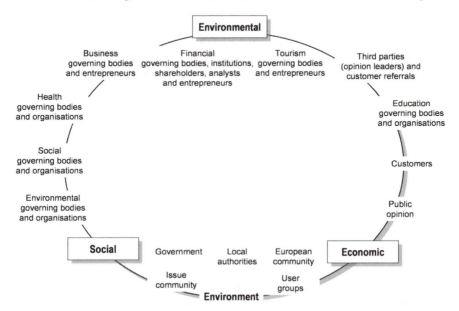

Figure 1.2 External stakeholders in the sporting activities market.

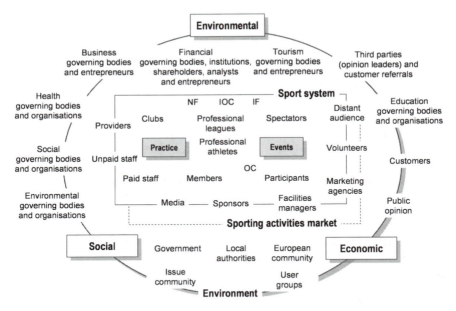

Figure 1.3 The sports activities system.

beyond simple supplier – customer interactions to consider marketing relationships as being embedded in a network of multi-relationships. We will follow Gummerson's (2006: 3) definition of relationship marketing as 'marketing based on interaction within networks of relationships'. As these relationships occur within groups of stakeholders, relationship marketing aims to 'identify and establish, maintain and enhance and, where necessary, terminate relationships with customers and other stakeholders, at a profit, so that the objectives of all the parties involved are met; and this is done by mutual exchange and fulfilment of promises' (Grönroos, 1994: 9). It is important to remember that marketing also concerns not-for-profit (or non-consumer) relationships, which constitute a large proportion of the relationships developed by sports organisations, as these organisations often adopt social marketing programmes and work with volunteers.

What is a relationship?

The concept of a relationship, which lies at the heart of relationship marketing, is quite large and requires definition. According to Hinde (1979), a relationship is a series of interactions between two parties with each interaction contributing to the evolution of the relationship. Grönroos (2000: 33) considers that 'a relationship has developed when a customer perceives that a mutual way of thinking exists between customer and supplier or service provider'. This touches upon the concept of empathy, which is an important dimension in the perceived quality of a service. Hinde (1995) has identified four conditions that can be used to describe relationships in inter-personal terms:

1 A relationship involves reciprocal exchanges between entities that are both active and interdependent (interaction). Hence, this concerns all the stakeholders that interact within sports systems.
2 A relationship has an end goal, and this end goal gives purpose to the people and the organisations involved. In a marketing context, this purpose is essentially related to the objectives and culture of each stakeholder.
3 Relationships can represent varied realities because they concern different dimensions and they take different forms, thereby procuring a variety of benefits for the participants. These benefits can be functional, affective, emotional, psychological, social, hedonistic or aesthetic and sports organisations must deliver benefits in both functional and experiential ways.
4 A relationship is a process-based phenomenon that evolves through series of interactions and in response to fluctuations in the environment (temporality). Hence, a competitive situation can produce a cooperative relationship. For example, Brussels wanted to set up a body to promote and manage the activities of the Roi Baudouin Stadium in order to maximise use of the stadium for non-sporting activities and to ensure Brussels City Council's offer matched the demand from private firms. Therefore, the council decided to confide these promotional and managerial tasks to a specially created body, called 'Prosport', who work closely with the council's sports department (which owns and runs the stadium), events organisers, sports associations and economic partners. Upstream, Prosport uses this network to obtain finance (e.g. via partnerships with private companies), to organise non-sporting events (e.g. concerts, conferences, exhibitions, seminars, etc.), and to develop the concept of stadium visits. Downstream, it uses the network to support local sports policies (e.g. aiding initiatives by Brussels' sports clubs, etc.) and to advertise Brussels' image via the major sports events that are held within the city (www.prosportevent.be/ prosport.html).

Each relationship has a content that procures benefits for the parties involved. Long-term development contributes to the formation of links of different types:

• Commercial links are based on the notion of exchange and the construction of relationships that provide economic benefits (e.g. the relationship between a professional sports club and its sponsors). This relationship may or may not be formalised by a contract.
• Functional links are related to the use of a product or service.

- Social links can be analysed within the framework of Durkheim's sociology, defined as 'the link that connects the individual to social groups (e.g. family ties, community ties) or to society in general, and that allows the individual to be social, to integrate into society and to extract elements of his/her identity' (Lewi, 2005: 152). This social link is one of the cornerstones of the sports system that helps integrate people into society (e.g. social function). The link can also be tribal or community-based, as in the case of professional football team supporters' clubs or certain groups of motorcyclists.
- Emotional links produce emotions that hopefully will be positive. This is a fundamental element for sports organisations.
- Semantic links give purpose to the product or the service and to its use and consumption.

Hence, a relationship has an end goal, a form (i.e. formal or informal), a content (i.e. functional and experiential benefits), a frequency and an intensity. Peppers and Rogers (2004: 36) have pointed out that the relational dynamic leads to changes in behaviour by the parties involved. The process is an iterative one that leads to the establishment of a relationship of trust based on the reliability, durability and integrity of the other party and the belief that one's actions serve the common good and will produce the desired positive effects. This requires a commitment to the relationship that progressively increases the importance of the relationship for both partners.

However, relationships also have a number of constraints and disadvantages. First, there is the risk of failure by one or more partners. For Hakansson and Snehota (1995) relationships evolve continuously and it is difficult to predict what their final outcome will be (indeterminateness). Consequently, resources must be committed to build relationships (resource demanding), even though committing these resources may prevent an organisation seizing other opportunities (preclusion from other opportunities). In addition, an organisation may unexpectedly find itself part of a network of relationships when it enters a partnership (unexpected demand).

What type of relationship?

Most research has focused on drawing up a typology of relationships rather than on defining what constitutes a relationship. Examples include Morgan and Hunt (1994), who outlined four categories of relationship, Gummerson (2006) who identified 30 types of relationships in the marketing field (the 30Rs) that he grouped into market relationships (i.e. suppliers, customers, competitors, other actors in the market) and non-market relationships, which have an indirect impact on market relationships. Also, Christopher *et al.* (1991) who developed the five markets model (referral, internal, influence, supplier and employee recruitment).

A comparative analysis of the different conceptions of relationship marketing allowed Möller and Halinen (2000) to distinguish two basic types of relationship-marketing theory; market-oriented and network-oriented. The former deals with fairly simple exchanges and assumes a market environment, whereas the later examines complex relationships and assumes a network-like business environment (Figure 1.4).

These two types of relationship marketing depend on a third type: internal marketing, that is to say, the application of marketing principles within an organisation. In the case of sports organisations, internal relationship marketing ensures that an organisation's goals and philosophy are shared by its entire staff, whether they are paid or volunteers. Once again, practice came before theory, as a large number of organisations had already introduced an internal marketing approach before there was any significant body of research into the subject (Christopher *et al.*, 1991). In recent years, a small number of articles on internal relationship marketing have been published but the discrepancy between practice and theory remains.

These three types of relationship marketing (market-oriented, network-oriented and internal) are defined below.

Market-oriented relationship marketing

Most sports organisations focus their relationship-marketing actions on the market sub-sector. Furthermore, the recruitment of new consumers, users and volunteers often monopolises efforts and resources to the detriment of the loyalty-building process. This can result in the 'leaking bucket effect', in which membership increases more slowly than expected due to the addition of new members being offset by the loss of old members. For example, a sports club that attracts 20 per cent new members every year will double its membership in five years if it only loses 5 per cent of its existing members.

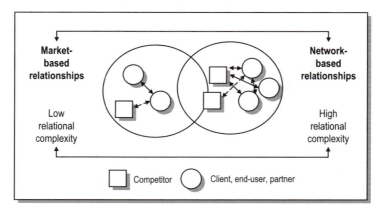

Figure 1.4 The two types of relationship-marketing theory.

However, if its loss rate is 15 per cent, its membership will only increase by 27 per cent. Therefore, it is extremely important to build loyalty. Palmer (1994: 573) summarised this strategic issue as follows: 'successful marketing should focus attention not just on how to gain new customers, but on how to develop loyalty from those that an organisation has previously and expensively gained. It is about seeing a relationship from the customers' perspective and understanding just what they seek in a relationship'.

Christopher *et al.*'s (2004) 'relationship marketing ladder' shows how the relationship between a company and its consumers evolves. Table 1.1 shows the six rungs on this ladder, with each rung representing a stage in the construction of a strong relationship between a sports organisation and its stakeholders. It is important to remember that this ladder describes commercial relationships and that depending on the situation the progression does not necessarily have to continue as far as the partner stage. An advocate's relationship with an organisation may be rational (based on the quality of the service provided), as well as emotional. If that advocate is an organisation, the relationship must be considered within the framework of a co-marketing operation.

Customer Relationship Management is a strategy that allows organisations to develop lasting relationships with their clients. According to Peelen

Table 1.1. The relationship ladder of loyalty

Steps	Status	Example in sport (Arsenal Football Club)
6	Partner	Partners that actively collaborate with you by committing resources to obtain common objectives (e.g. O_2, with whom Arsenal develops specific information packages for mobile phones and podcasts)
5	Advocate	People and organisations with whom you have established an emotional link and who actively support and promote you, notably by word of mouth (e.g. Arsenal's fan clubs, which carry out actions to support and promote the club)
4	Supporter	People and organisations with whom you have established an emotional link and who support you in a non-active way (e.g. that segment of the club's fans that have a strong emotional attachment but are not necessarily in the stands each week)
3	Client	People and organisations with whom you regularly carry out commercial transactions (e.g. regular spectators at the Emirates Stadium)
2	Customer	People and organisations with whom you have carried out a single commercial transaction (e.g. Japanese spectators who went to watch a match during the club's tour of Asia)
1	Prospect	People and organisations belonging to the marketing target group with whom you would like to create a relationship (e.g. Arsenal + Japanese football fans)

Source: Adapted from Christopher *et al.* (2004).

(2005), it involves managing four fundamental and closely linked components; customer knowledge, relationship strategy, communication and individual value proposition (Figure 1.5).

For example, a marathon organisation committee collects information in order to find out more about the participants (e.g. benefits sought, place of residence, how far and how often they run, communication methods used, etc.). This information can be used to develop a personalised service that will best meet the participants' needs (e.g. hotel packages, race, finish-line photos and tourist visits) and may lead the committee to provide an individualised offer that will ensure the desired benefits are obtained (i.e. functional, emotional, social). Asking participants to provide feedback on the quality of the service delivered and on possible improvements can help create a lasting relationship between participants and organisers, especially if it is carried out as part of a loyalty-building strategy. In this case, loyalty can be built through operations such as posting results tables for each edition of the event on the marathon's website so individuals can see how well they did, and printing personalised T-shirts showing the number of times a person has run that marathon. To do this, organisers must solicit the opinions and needs of individual participants; however, this is a complex task that requires planning and organisation, as well as technological resources. The London Marathon, for instance, has set up a CRM system for participants.

Key account management

Key account management, which is CRM applied to business-to-business situations, can be used to manage both commercial and non-commercial relationships. Kempeners and Van Der Hart (1999: 311) have defined key account management as 'the process of building and maintaining relationships over an extended period, which cuts across multiple levels, functions

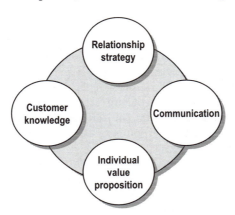

Figure 1.5 Relationship-marketing cornerstones (adapted from Peelen, 2005).

and operating units in both the selling organisation and its carefully selected customers (accounts) that contributes to the company's objectives now or in the future'. For sports organisations, this involves judiciously choosing the stakeholders most important to the organisation's strategic objectives, and then creating and developing long-term relationships with these stakeholders by defining and introducing cross-functional processes for servicing accounts. The UEFA Champions League has adopted key account management for its six main sponsors. Relations with these sponsors are managed by a team of several people working in conjunction with Team Marketing A.G. In this case, the cross-functional processes concern marketing, communications, logistics and safety. This enables the Champions League to deliver a high quality service that combines personalisation, empathy, reliability and responsiveness; however, it is very costly in terms of human resources.

Network-oriented relationships

A network can be defined as a group of nodes (or poles) that are interconnected by links or channels that allow the flow of forces, energy or information. The nodes can be single-unit points or complex sub-networks. The network approach is based on general systems theory, according to which systems have end goals and the dynamic interactions of their components are organised as a function of the objectives to be achieved. Le Gallou's (1992: 54) definition of a system can be applied to the study of a wide variety of complex objects: 'A system is an ensemble that forms a coherent and autonomous unit of real or imaginary objects (i.e. material elements, individuals, actions, etc.) that are organised to achieve a goal (or a set of objectives, end goals, projects, etc.) via the interplay of relationships (i.e. mutual interrelations, dynamic interrelations, etc.), and operating within a certain environment.' It is a global unit of interrelationships between elements, actions and individuals.

Sports organisations work in conjunction with a number of different stakeholders and the relationships between these various stakeholders form a network. Figure 1.6 shows the network of stakeholders built up by the Olympic Health Foundation. In this case, the main focus is on social marketing aimed at changing the behaviour of Belgium's children and their families. The Belgian Olympic and Inter-federal Committee (COIB) has created links with strategic partners who have the same objectives. The dialogue through which these links are established corresponds to the communication dimension of relationship marketing.

The map of OHF's stakeholders and their interactions shows that OHF is at the heart of the network and the partners, doctors and teachers also occupy central positions. OHF's relationship-marketing strategy is built around this network, which was built through dialogue with stakeholders and through action programmes that provide value for all the members of the network.

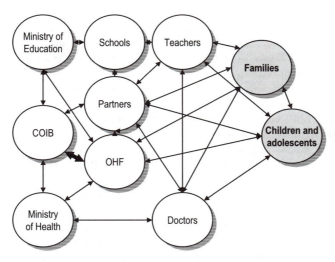

Figure 1.6 Relationships between stakeholders in the OHF network.

The value of a relationship depends on the benefits obtained by each partner. Network-oriented relationship marketing goes much further than the horizontal and unidirectional relationships contained within the notion of value chain. Normann and Ramirez (1998) refer to the creation of a 'value constellation'. They recognised that, 'instead of "adding" value one after the other, the partners in the production of an offer create value together through varied types of "co-productive" relationship'. Designed in accordance with this idea, collaborative programmes involve the co-production of value. When designing this type of offer, it is imperative to ask 'how different actors' activities are to be configured for optimum value creation: who does what, when, where, and with whom?' Hakansson and Snehota (1995) identified three important characteristics: 'activity links', which concern a group of activities on which the partners work together (i.e. marketing, technical and administrative aspects); 'resource ties', which are related to the provision and sharing of technical, human, financial and knowledge-related resources; and 'actor bonds', which are linked to the relationships between the people and stakeholders who work together.

Internal relationships

Whether they are market-oriented or network-oriented, relationship-marketing actions can only be designed and implemented by human resources working within the organisations concerned. Sports organisations mostly deliver services and the staff members in contact with clients or users are part of that service. For a sports club, the delivery of services to its members is mostly the responsibility of the club's manager, as the manager is responsible for training, for coaching during competitions and for providing information about the life of the club, etc. The perceived quality of a service is linked to the behaviour of the people who deliver that service. These people represent the organisation in the eyes of the consumer and they are therefore part of the marketing process (Zeithaml and Bitner, 2003).

Sports organisations differ from most commercial organisations in that they employ both volunteers and paid staff, whose interactions and relationships form an internal network. Ballantyne (1997: 51) has defined internal networks as 'open organisational systems within host organisations whose members are connected to each other by choice, and through complementary patterns of cyclical activity, for the legitimate purpose of creating and circulating knowledge to the host organisation'. Consequently, it is essential to manage the human factor within organisations. Human resources management can achieve this by taking into account the principles of relationship marketing and the goals of the organisation's marketing actions.

Managing organisations' internal relationships according to marketing principles has led to the development of internal marketing, which has been defined as 'a relationship development process in which staff autonomy and know-how combine to create and circulate new organisational knowledge that will challenge internal activities which need to be changed to enhance quality in marketplace relationships' (Ballantyne, 1997: 44). According to Zeithaml and Bitner (2003: 319), the end goals of internal marketing are 'enabling promises' and 'the activities that management engages in to aid the providers in their ability to deliver on the service promise: recruiting, training, motivating, rewarding and providing equipment and technology'. Applying the principles of relationship marketing enhances the internal marketing process.

Internal marketing affects all the forms of marketing within an organisation. Its aim is to improve an organisation's internal communication, and its knowledge of its stakeholders. Internal marketing also focuses people's attention on the activities and relationships that need to be changed in order to improve global performance. All the members of an organisation must be conscious of the fact that they and their unit are in contact with stakeholders and that they must contribute to defining what needs to be done to improve service quality and consumer satisfaction. In order to do this, they must work towards the success of the mission and the achievement of the organisation's objectives, and organise themselves in such a way as to best manage all the interactions with the organisation's stakeholders. These interactions are referred to as 'moments of truth'.

In his case study of the bank ANZ, Ballantyne (1997) identified three relationship development modes.

- Energising refers to the commitment of the staff to consumers: 'seeking and receiving the willing commitment of staff to work towards a given goal within or outside the boundaries of their job description'.

- Code breaking concerns 'consumer consciousness' and the will to resolve the consumers' problems: 'translating known customer requirements into an agenda for detailed changes in production or delivery systems with new 'know-how'.

- Border crossing involves 'dealing with dysfunctional processes which cross departmental borders by circulating new knowledge across the borders'. Even though there is a hierarchy within most organisations, internal communication must be managed transversally in order to find solutions.

Dunmore (2002), working from an operational perspective, has highlighted the importance of an integrated approach to internal marketing strategies, which must take into account the following seven dimensions:

1   Vision, mission, values, positioning and personality
2   Corporate strategy
3   Processes, service standards and measures
4   Knowledge management
5   Internal communication
6   Human resources strategy
7   Integrating internal, interactive and external marketing.

Summary and conclusion

Every sports organisation operates in an environment in which it is necessary to take into account the exchanges between the stakeholders. In addition, an organisation's marketing actions must be oriented towards three sub-sectors of its environment: the market, the network and the organisation itself.

Möller and Halinen (2000) have shown that relationship marketing is based on business marketing from the point of view of the interactions between stakeholders, the network-oriented approach, distribution channels, the marketing of services, and direct and database marketing. As relationship marketing requires organisations to take into account networks and the interactions between parties, certain aspects of this approach can be analysed in terms of stakeholder theory.

Sports organisations must develop relationships with their stakeholders, and these relationships vary in nature (multi-dimensional) and constantly evolve through an iterative process. This evolution involves the following stages:

- *Start*, which involves creating an initial interaction or volunteer involvement
- *Development*, which involves an increase in the frequency of interactions, an increase in involvement and the development of trust

- *Established relationships*, which make fewer demands on both parties and offer much higher rewards
- *Decline*, which may consist of a gradual deterioration in the relationship, or a sudden exit on the part of one party.

The relationship between two parties can be characterised according to a number of dimensions (Figure 1.7). They are:

- Linked benefits (i.e. functional, social, emotional, psychological)
- Loyalty, which is by nature functional and emotional
- The status of the parties, which can evolve from client to partner
- The type of exchange (i.e. B to C, B to B or network)
- The distance of the exchange (i.e. intimate, face-to-face, distant, no contact)
- Trust and involvement
- The resources provided by the partner (i.e. financial, technical, human, time).

How the components of a relationship evolve depends on the dynamic of that relationship. For example, trust can be built up gradually, social benefits may be added to functional benefits, and a sponsor's status may change from client to partner, etc. Figure 1.8 shows the combination of these dimensions.

Stakeholder theory

Stakeholder theory, like relationship marketing, is based on systems theory. It has enabled managers to move from an organisation-based approach, in

Figure 1.7 The dimensions of a relationship between two parties.

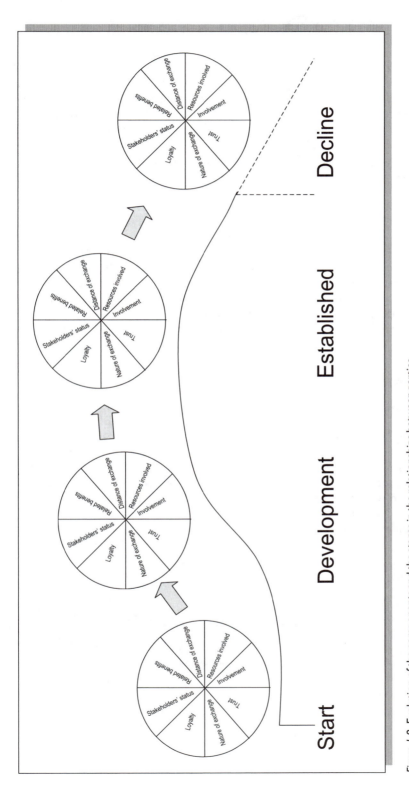

Figure 1.8 Evolution of the components and the stages in the relationships between parties.

The circular diagrams each contain the following components: Resources involved, Involvement, Trust, Nature of exchange, Loyalty, Stakeholders' status, Related benefits, Distance of exchange.

Stages (left to right): Start, Development, Established, Decline.

which stakeholders are seen as entities that have to be managed solely for the benefit of the organisation, to a network-oriented vision that focuses on relationships and processes. The aim of stakeholder theory is to bring together organisations and their stakeholders by considering their mutual interdependence as well as their power. Popularised by Freeman (1984), stakeholder theory identifies and models the persons and groups that really count for an organisation. In addition, it describes and recommends methods management can use to give due regard to the interests of those groups. Freeman's work was carried out from a strategic perspective that Mintzberg *et al.* (1998) assigned to the power school.

Stakeholder theory, which is based on an analysis of the relationships between the parties within networks and of the processes that enable organisations to engage key stakeholders, can be used to enhance the relationship-marketing approach. Pesqueux (2006) has highlighted the numerous conceptual debates surrounding stakeholder theory. Minvielle (2004) considered it to be a 'frontier object' that can be appropriated by different theoretical and managerial frameworks. This section presents the different definitions of the concept of stakeholder, and then examines how the different theoretical streams contribute to the strategic and operational aspects of relationship marketing.

What is a stakeholder?

In a recent article, Friedman and Miles (2006) noted that definitions of the concept of stakeholder vary widely. Some definitions, notably the one proposed by Freeman (1984), are very broad in that they use verbs such as 'affect', 'impact', 'influence' and 'interact' in their widest sense. Other definitions are very narrow and only take into account stakeholders that affect an organisation's strategic objectives. The decision of whether to adopt a broad definition or a narrow definition is important (Figure 1.9), because this decision determines which parties are considered stakeholders. In this book, the term 'stakeholder' is used in a very broad sense to denote any person or entity that has a relationship with the sports organisation in question. These stakeholders make up the sports systems described at the beginning of the chapter.

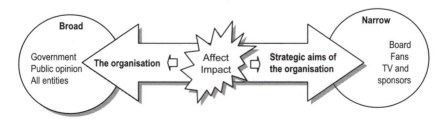

Figure 1.9 Broad versus narrow definition of a stakeholder.

Mercier (2006) noted that there is confusion between individuals and groups when defining the concept of stakeholder. In fact, an individual can belong to several different groups, for example, as a volunteer, a spectator and the manager of a sponsor company. Martinet (1984: 87) uses the expression 'ubiquitous stakeholder' to describe this situation.

The four facets of stakeholder theory

An analysis of the literature led Donaldson and Preston (1995) to suggest that stakeholder theory was developed on the basis of its descriptive accuracy, instrumental power, and normative validity. They also pointed out that stakeholder theory also has a bearing on management and the actions of managers.

Viewed descriptively, a sports organisation can be considered a constellation of cooperative and competing interests that have intrinsic value. Organisations have stakeholders and their activities have an impact on these stakeholders; therefore, it is necessary to analyse all the relationships in the vast network formed by an organisation and its stakeholders. This is one of the basic principles of relationship marketing. For example, when the International Motorcycling Federation chooses a host city for the Enduro World Championships, it must take into account the interests of the national federations, the teams, the riders, the media, the local authorities of the candidate areas and the spectators, as well as environmental bodies, which are hostile to this type of event as it damages the environment. Gummerson (2006) has proposed the terms cooperation, competition, institutions and regulations to describe the relationships between stakeholders in a market-oriented environment.

The instrumental facet considers the link between managing stakeholder relationships and organisational performance. Organisations that introduce stakeholder management systems tend to achieve better results; however, good results can only be achieved if appropriate partners are chosen and an effective network is built. This is the domain of relationship marketing. OHF, for example, chose its partners on the basis of how well their marketing objectives converged and on how complementary the resources were that each could provide for implementing actions. These two conditions are critical in order to create a value constellation.

It is possible to go further in this approach by analysing the interactions within sports organisation networks. Rowley (1997) analysed the density of a network and the centrality of each party by mapping stakeholders and their interactions. Figure 1.10 shows the relationships between the different parties involved in organising Eurobasket Women 2007, which was held in the Italian city of Chieti. By combining network density and stakeholder centrality it is possible to identify four categories of stakeholder:

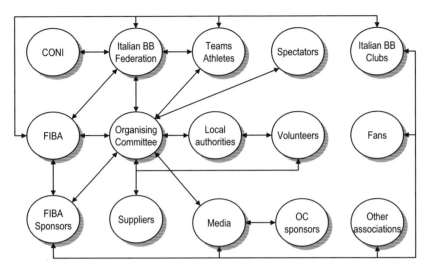

Figure 1.10 The stakeholder network for EuroBasket Women 2007.

- *Compromisers* occupy a central position in dense networks: e.g. the Euro-Basket Women 2007 organisation committee
- *Commanders* occupy a central position in wider networks: e.g. FIBA Europe, which holds the rights to this event
- *Subordinates* occupy a peripheral position in very dense networks: e.g. the Italian National Olympic Committee
- *Solitaries* occupy a peripheral position in low-density networks: e.g. fans, who follow the event through the media.

In order to carry out a more in-depth analysis of the dynamics of these relationships, Friedman and Miles (2002) drew up a model based on the theory of social change and differentiation. They showed that the actions, perceptions, cognitions and attempts made by people to influence the ideas and actions of others are shaped by social structures (i.e. roles, opportunities, power differentials) and cultural systems. Based on the proposition that the organisation–stakeholder relationship brings out ideas, centres of interest and cooperation, they drew up a typology of the relationships between organisations and their stakeholders. This typology was established by bringing together two dimensions: the compatibility of a relationship in terms of culture, ideas and interests, and the type of relationship (necessary or contingent). Table 1.2 illustrates the resulting four categories with reference to EuroBasket Women 2007.

- Necessary compatible relationships occur when the parties have something to lose. The associated logic is protectionist or defensive. The local

Table 1.2 Stakeholder configurations and associated stakeholder types

	Necessary	Contingent
Compatible	Organising committee Sponsors Local authorities	Italian basketball clubs Other associations
Incompatible	FIBA Sponsors	Badly behaved fans

Source: Adapted from Friedman and Miles (2002).

authorities and the organising committee's sponsors, which provided most of the resources required for organising the event, fall into this category.

- Necessary incompatible relationships occur when stakeholders have opposing ideas or interests and are therefore forced to take into account the position of others. The logic here is one of concession leading to compromise. This category describes the sponsors of FIBA, who block certain product categories, thereby reducing the local organising committee's pool of potential sponsors.
- Contingent compatible relationships occur when stakeholders have converging ideas or interests without a direct or contractual relationship between the stakeholder and the organisation. This type of relationship creates opportunities for collaboration. The contingent compatible category includes Italian basketball clubs not directly associated with the event but which may be involved in event-related programmes, for example, those based around the theme of sport and health.
- Contingent incompatible relationships occur when stakeholders have opposing ideas and interests but no formal links. This category includes badly behaved fans, who need to be controlled or kept away from the event.

Relationships can be formalised or totally informal; however, given the importance of marketing and brand rights, the relationships between stakeholders are increasingly defined in the form of contracts. Figure 1.11 shows the position of sports events in the Olympic system.

These relationships are not fixed and the status of certain stakeholders can change. As mentioned above, FIBA's sponsors, which play a dominant role in the system, can be a source of conflict as they often block the best product categories. When this occurs, an organisation committee's sponsorship options are reduced and it becomes necessary to seek sponsors from product categories further removed from their event. To get around this type of situation, it is possible to create peripheral events whose rights belong to the local organisation committee and which are open to the sponsors of the international federation. Giving FIBA's sponsors the opportunity to

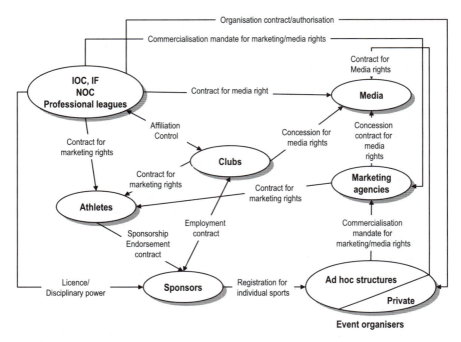

Figure 1.11 Stakeholders in the sports event market (adapted from Melero and Durand, 2005).

participate in the event moves them into the necessary compatible category (Figure 1.12).

The instrumental perspective focuses strongly on value creation. In a relationship-marketing context, value must be viewed in its widest sense by considering, for example, the benefits for the spectators, the sports organisations and the partners that provide resources, etc.

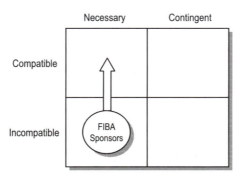

Figure 1.12 Illustration of a possible change in the status of the FIBA's sponsors with respect to EuroBasket Women.

The normative aspect of stakeholder theory describes an organisation's duty to define and take into account the philosophical and moral frameworks in which it operates. Normative theories take account of societal ethics and are based around the premise that every society has legitimate practices (norms or standards of behaviour) and ideals, and that actions must be taken based on the notion of good. A corollary of this is the need for the governance of an organisation to consider the legitimacy of its stakeholders' interests in order to do (or not do) something because it is the right (or wrong) thing to do. When viewed from a normative perspective, each group, within the bounds of its legitimacy, deserves consideration. This notion leads to the concept of corporate social responsibility (CSR).

Based on work carried out during a period of strong economic growth, Bowen (1953) stressed that companies have social responsibilities. According to the UK's Institute of Directors (2002), 'CSR is about businesses and other organisations going beyond their legal obligations to manage the impact they have on the environment and society. In particular, this could include how organisations interact with their employees, suppliers, customers and the communities in which they operate, as well as the extent to which they attempt to protect the environment'. Andrioff and Marsden (1999) have shown that companies can have a ripple effect on society (like a stone thrown into a pool of water), first impacting the stakeholders that are closest to them, and then those that are further removed. This impact is economic, environmental and social.

Most sports organisations have missions that naturally draw them towards the notion of CSR and they often set up social marketing programmes. 'Social marketing is the application of marketing concepts and tools to programmes designed to influence the voluntary behaviour of target audiences where the primary objective is to improve the welfare of the target audiences and/or the society of which they are a part' (Andreasen, 1994: 109). Hence, the primary mission of the Union of European Football Associations (UEFA) is 'to oversee the development of European football at all levels and to promote the principles of unity and solidarity'. The International Volleyball Federation's (FIVB) mission is 'to manage and communicate all forms of Volleyball and Beach Volleyball worldwide. It aims to develop Volleyball as a major world media and entertainment sport through world class planning and organisation of competitions, marketing and promotional activities'. Both UEFA and the FIVB, like numerous other sports organisations, have social marketing programmes.

As well as becoming increasingly business oriented, many professional football clubs are also making greater commitments to social marketing programmes. For example, the Fundació Futbol Club Barcelona (created in 1994) is a cultural charity that mainly operates in Catalonia. Its main aim is the non-profit promotion of the sporting, cultural and social dimensions of Barcelona Football Club within the sporting and cultural community in general. In Italy, the AC Milan ONLUS Foundation was set up to promote social welfare, education, training and sports instruction in Italy and abroad. It is also actively involved with disadvantaged minorities.

These programmes reinforce the community's bonds with a club and legitimise its social-welfare actions. They also help bridge the gap between a club's business focus and its social values, that is to say, solidarity and working for the welfare of others. Fundació FC Barcelona has become a key player in the social-welfare field through its numerous cultural and social activities.

Some of the stakeholders in sports systems, for example, local authorities and certain sponsors, have social objectives. These stakeholders are becoming increasingly aware of the importance of CSR and are becoming involved in social marketing programmes. This was the case for the 'Noi 2006' volunteers programme for the Turin Winter Olympics, in which the local authorities (i.e. Turin City Council and the Province of Turin) worked alongside the foundation created to organise the Games, the Turin Olympic Games Organisation Committee (TOROC). Figure 1.13 shows the network of stakeholder relationships that was built up around TOROC.

Donaldson and Dunfee's (1999) theory of integrative social contracts provides a possible foundation for stakeholder analysis. According to this theory, company managers have an ethical obligation that leads them to contribute to the well-being of society. They must satisfy their stakeholders' interests without violating the principles of distributive justice. There is a moral contract between society and a company, and this is recognised in so far as it serves the company's interests.

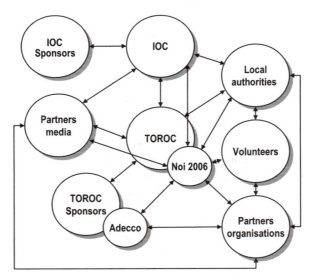

Figure 1.13 The relationships between the main stakeholders in the 'Noi 2006' programme (adapted from Ferrand and Chanavat, 2006).

The managerial aspect of stakeholder theory examines the drawing up of strategic and operational recommendations relating to stakeholder management. Freeman (1984) has described a six-stage process for stakeholder management: identify the stakeholders, explain behaviour, analyse behaviour, formulate a generic strategy, apply the strategy, and create specific programmes for stakeholders (Figure 1.14).

Friedman and Miles (2006) have added 'issue identification' (defining the desired issue of the strategy) and 'stakeholder salience' (the importance of the stakeholders in the system) to this list. Frederick *et al.* (1988) have proposed a six-stage process for conducting stakeholder analyses: map stakeholder relations, map stakeholder coalitions, assess the nature of each stakeholder's interest, assess the nature of each stakeholder's power, construct a matrix of stakeholder priorities, and monitor shifting coalitions. Without entering into a detailed discussion of the scope and limitations of these two processes with respect to relationship marketing, it can be pointed out that they, like all managerial processes, follow the sequence: diagnosis — strategy formulation — strategy implementation, and that neither mentions evaluation of the result. Chapter two will present a stakeholder management method for sports systems that is consistent with the principles of both relationship marketing and stakeholder theory.

Stakeholder theory and relationship marketing

Although the theoretical debate surrounding stakeholder theory has tended to focus on the strengths and weaknesses of the various points of view, this, as Friedman and Miles (2006) quite rightly pointed out, is not the most important issue. In fact, relationship marketing is much more likely to be advanced by combining different approaches than by defining their scope and limits. The approach preferred here situates all three aspects of stakeholder theory (normative, instrumental and descriptive) on the same level. The interaction between these aspects, which serves as a base for the managerial approach, is illustrated in Figure 1.15.

Thus, from a managerial point of view, a sports organisation must design and implement a relationship-marketing programme that brings together the descriptive, normative and instrumental facets. This can lead to dilemmas in terms of stakeholder recruitment, as the different facets may vary in the

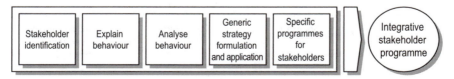

Figure 1.14 The six phases of the stakeholder management process (adapted from Freeman, 1984).

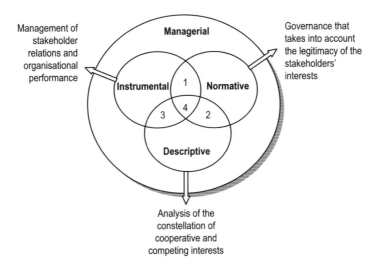

Figure 1.15 Relationship between the four aspects of stakeholder theory.

strategic importance they accord to each stakeholder. Consequently, managers must find compromises and define priorities. Table 1.3 illustrates this point with reference to some of FC Barcelona's stakeholders (players, sponsors, media, supporters, Catalans, disadvantaged communities). Supporters are the only stakeholders to be considered 'very important' by all three facets of stakeholder theory. In contrast, disadvantaged communities are 'very important' according to the normative facet but 'unimportant' according to the instrumental facet.

This strategic analysis must also take into account the sports organisation's desired end goals, which may be commercial, social or environmental. In its widest sense, CSR can be considered to embrace both environmental protection and social issues, thus, relationship marketing can be considered in terms of the managerial framework shown in Figure 1.16.

This model is based on a sports organisation's network of internal and external stakeholders. It includes the cooperative and competitive relation-

Table 1.3 Importance given to FC Barcelona's stakeholders by the different aspects of stakeholder theory (1 = 'unimportant', 5 = 'very important')

	Players	Sponsors	Media	Supporters	Catalans	Disadvantaged communities
Descriptive	5	5	5	5	5	2
Instrumental	5	5	5	5	3	1
Normative	3	2	2	5	5	5

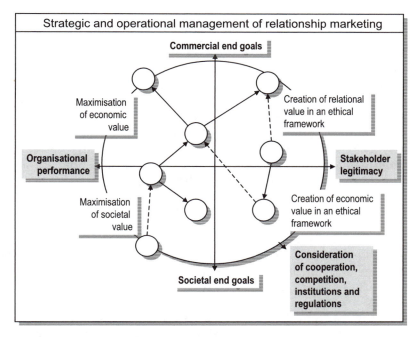

Figure 1.16 Marketing end goals in relation with the different aspects of stakeholder theory.

ships between stakeholders, as well as institutions and regulations (descriptive approach). The basic model has been refined by the addition of two further axes: the end goals (i.e. commercial and/or social) and the stakes that affect organisational performance (instrumental aspect), and the legitimacy of the stakeholders (normative aspect). These two axes define four sectors, each of which corresponds to one orientation of a sports organisation's marketing actions.

- A sports organisation seeks to maximise economic value when it combines commercial ends with organisational performance. This is the strategy adopted by the FIVB for the SWATCH FIVB World Championships. The FIVB set up a relationship-marketing programme directed towards the players, sponsors, local promoters, the media and the public.
- A sports organisation seeks to maximise social value when it combines organisational performance with society-oriented objectives. This is the case for Olympic Solidarity, an International Olympic Committee body responsible for managing and administrating the share of the Olympic Games television rights that is allocated to each National Olympic Committee (NOC). Olympic Solidarity helps continental and national

Olympic committees develop sport by organising, in conjunction with organisations in each country, a wide range of programmes designed to meet their specific needs and priorities.

- Economic value is created in an ethical framework when commercial objectives are combined with consideration of the legitimacy of stakeholders.

- Finally, sports organisations can create relational value in an ethical framework by working towards a social end goal while taking into account the legitimacy of its stakeholders. For example the British Olympic Association's National Olympic Academy brings together individuals from various sporting backgrounds to share information about and discuss current issues affecting the Olympic Movement and sport, both nationally and internationally.

The relationship-marketing approach required by this managerial framework is primarily network-oriented; however, it must also take into account the other two orientations. An organisation's strategic choices about which stakeholders to recruit are network-oriented when they take into account the positions stakeholders occupy in the system, as well as their strategic and marketing objectives. The organisation must then design and implement programmes that provide value for each stakeholder. The market-oriented approach requires organisations to analyse the competition and to choose the stakeholders with whom it is advantageous to create and/or develop long-term relationships. A similar approach should be taken to internal marketing: identify the people to involve and then train them so they can deliver quality services. It is also a management process in which marketing actions are adapted in response to changes in the network and in the relationships between the network's stakeholders.

The market and network sub-sectors are the focus of a sports organisation's external strategies. For Tabatoni and Jarnioux (1975: 67–8), these strategies 'define the relational modes with the environment: they identify the target groups or, better, the correspondents the organisation is addressing; the support and the relational mode (i.e. transactions, information, personal or institutional ties, etc.); the desired intensity of these relations; and the acceptable degree of asymmetry (domination effect); the degree of cooperation permissible in the definition of the relational modalities'. Internal marketing is an internal strategy that applies strategies to relationship modes within the organisation.

The marketing challenges facing sports organisations

Every sports organisation is part of a system consisting of a number of interacting stakeholders. In such contexts, the objective of relationship marketing is to create value through exchanges within this network. The following section looks at how theory can be put into practice by examining the benefits relationship marketing has provided to Swiss Olympic and by identifying the main marketing-related challenges facing sports organisations.

Swiss Olympic

Swiss Olympic is both Switzerland's National Olympic Committee and an umbrella organisation, under private law, that represents Swiss sports federations for both Olympic and non-Olympic disciplines. It was formed on 1 January 1997 when the Swiss Sports Association (SSA) merged with the Swiss Olympic Committee (SOC) and integrated the National Committee for Elite Sport (NCES). The 82 federations within Swiss Olympic represent 27,000 sports clubs with 3.2 million members. The largest federations are subdivided into regional and cantonal federations. One in three Swiss people belong to a sports club. Taking into account people who belong to more than one club, 2 million Swiss belong to at least one sports club.

Swiss Olympic carries out a number of actions.

- It facilitates the promotion of sport in society as a factor that improves quality of life and health, and it encourages the population to do sport regularly.
- It encourages top-class sport aimed towards international competition.
- It represents the interests of those areas of Swiss sport governed by private law in their dealings with the public, the authorities and national and international organisations.
- It supports and coordinates the activities of its member federations and carries out higher-level tasks according to the principle of subsidiary responsibility.
- It supports and encourages the Olympic movement and its objectives in Switzerland.
- It is a member of Olympic organisations and other international organisations.

As Table 1.4 shows, Swiss Olympic obtains more than 50 per cent of its funding from lotteries (Sport-Toto) and 28 per cent from public funds (Confederation). It is trying to diversify its sources of finance, most notably by developing commercial actions associated with its emblem.

Table 1.5 shows how these funds are used. The operating costs of Swiss Olympic's four divisions (sport, development and training, finance and organisation, marketing and communication) account for a third of this revenue and 44 per cent is directed directly to the national federations and their members.

Table 1.4 Sources of funding for Swiss Olympic (2004 financial year)

Source of funding	%
Advertising revenue	2
Financial result	3
Events revenue	3
Other	3
Sports aid	8
Confederation contribution	28
Sport Toto	53
Total	100

Source: Swiss Olympic.

The marketing of Swiss Olympic

In August 2002, having decided to no longer outsource its marketing, Swiss Olympic's executive council created an in-house marketing division that is divided into four departments:

- Project promotion (one manager and two staff)
- Public and media relations (one manager and two staff)
- Events (one manager and three staff)
- Sponsorship (one manager and three staff).

Table 1.5 Use of Swiss Olympic's financial resources (2004 financial year)

Use of financial resource	%
Contribution to federations	44
Sports expenditure	11
Development and training expenditure	9
Marketing and communication expenditure	7
Contributions to athletes	7
Fight against doping	6
Finance and administration expenditure	6
Olympic Games	4
Allocation of funds for national sports facilities	3
Other	3
Total	100

Source: Swiss Olympic.

Marketing functions within Swiss Olympic

Marketing is closely associated with fulfilling the organisation's mission and assuring its development. This marketing provides three types of benefit.

Increased efficiency for Swiss Olympic's projects

Swiss Olympic's projects (i.e. ethics in sport, 'Cool and Clean', fight against doping, etc.) must be neither a goal in themselves, nor a way of paying lip service to the fulfilment of a precise statutory mandate. They must bring tangible results, and lead to a better understanding of a problem and to changes in behaviour.

Development of the basic principles of cooperation in the world of sport

Effective marketing should raise the profile of Swiss Olympic and its projects with key stakeholders (i.e. federations, political and economic world) and strengthen cooperation with and between its partners.

Willingness to seek new sources of finance

New partners (i.e. public, sponsors, patrons, etc.) need to be found in order to obtain financial resources for new projects and to develop existing projects to benefit Swiss sport. The aim is to improve the profile, image and credibility of Swiss Olympic and its projects.

Given these objectives, the goals of the marketing and communication department are:

- to develop Swiss Olympic's profile
- to build a harmonious image of Swiss Olympic
- to manage its brand and market the exclusive rights to the Swiss Olympic rings and brand names
- to ensure targeted communication for its various projects
- to develop marketing platforms to generate extra income.

Swiss Olympic's stakeholders

Swiss Olympic's internal and external stakeholders are shown in Table 1.6.

Among these stakeholders, special mention must be given to:

- The Swiss Sports Aid Foundation, which gives financial support and encouragement to top-level Swiss athletes, as well as to young talents. It also fulfils a primordial social role by actively promoting sporting models

Table 1.6 Swiss Olympic's internal and external stakeholders

Internal stakeholders	External stakeholders
President	IOC
CEO	Confederation
Executive committee	Sport TOTO (lotteries)
Sport parliament	Media
Staff	Swiss states sports department
	Sports events organisers
	Swiss Sports Aid Foundation
	International sports organisations
	Sports clubs (22.600)
	Athletes
	Sports federations (82)
	Sponsors
	Medical centre
	Federal Sports Commission
	Tenero Sports Centre

for young people. However, it would like the Swiss sporting world to more fully recognise its status as a foundation, rather than just an organisation 'at the service' of Swiss Olympic.

- The objective of Sport-Toto, which organises sports betting, is to collect funds to support amateur sport, youth sport and recreational sport. Since it was founded in 1938, Sport-Toto has given 1.6 billion Swiss francs to sport, making it the number one benefactor in this field.
- The Federal Sports Commission (FSC) is responsible for sport throughout Switzerland. It is an extra-parliamentary commission composed of representatives of the national government, the cantons, local councils, schools, sports federations and the research field, together with other partners from the world of Swiss sport. It is responsible for the aspects of sport that are regulated under public law and forms a link with the areas of sport that are governed by private law.
- Swiss Olympic's relations with the 82 national sports federations are generally good; nevertheless, each federation has its own needs and expectations. Swiss Olympic works with the federations to reinforce policies for top-class sport (following the model adopted by other countries, such as France) by establishing national career-development programmes (sport/study, training, professional retraining, etc.) for elite sports people.

Types of marketing action

The marketing department has been organised in such a way as to allow it to create and carry out different types of marketing action. The 'Swiss Olympic' brand is managed by the brand marketing and communications director, who works in consultation with the other departments and reports to the executive council. Each of the department's four sections is responsible for one type of action.

Communicating a single identity for the Swiss Olympic brand

In order to give Swiss Olympic a unitary image and to ensure it is clearly perceived as the high authority for Swiss sport, the organisation has developed a coherently structured, modular and forward-looking visual identity that communicates its values as well as its professionalism. The title 'Swiss Olympic Association' and the graphic charter have been accepted by the International Olympic Committee. By communicating in English, Swiss Olympic has a greater international impact and a single name, rather than four names, one for each of the country's official languages.

Swiss Olympic's brand identity was designed to cover two aspects of sport: elite sport and performance, and leisure sport and social responsibility. The ideals most commonly associated with performance are determination, concentration, enthusiasm, dynamism, will to win. Social responsibility is related to willingness, cooperation, values, serving humanity, social commitment, openness and ethics.

Development of sponsoring programmes

The sponsoring department is responsible for marketing Swiss Olympic's brand and projects. It aims to involve a maximum of 12 'leading partners', between 12 and 15 'partners' and between 20 and 25 'suppliers'. It also manages partnerships for projects, such as the Gigathlon, the Swiss Olympic Team, and Fairplay, and develops co-marketing strategies with certain partners (e.g. Parex, which distributes promotional articles). In addition, it looks for advertisers for Swiss Olympic's official magazine, *Swiss sport*, and for the Swiss Olympic Team Guides. The sponsoring department is also responsible for ensuring partners respect their contractual obligations.

'Swiss Olympic Marketing' has three levels of partner for each of its four lines of action: the Olympic team, social marketing campaigns, projects and events (Figure 1.17).

The contributions made by 'Swiss Olympic Leading Partners', 'Swiss Olympic Partners' and 'Swiss Olympic Suppliers' can be either financial or 'value in kind', that is to say, the supply of products or services. Collaboration is often closer when the partners commit human and technical resources, rather than just financial resources.

Some partner companies support Switzerland's best athletes by contributing to Olympic projects run by individual sports federations. Through an exclusive marketing programme, companies can invest in training for selected athletes: the 'Swiss Olympic Team'.

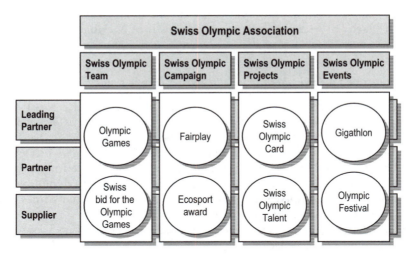

Figure 1.17 Partnership levels and associations with the activities of Swiss Olympic.

The project promotion department

The project promotion department is responsible for drawing up the management and development bases for the Swiss Olympic brand. As well as providing advice on promotion, it runs the internet site (www. swissolympic.ch) and it designs and implements projects in the fields of development and training, elite sport and sports events. Swiss Olympic's projects cover a wide range of activities, including:

- Fitness and health (Cool and Clean)
- Sports ethics (Fairplay)
- Elite sport and the next generation of top sportspeople (Swiss Olympic Talents)
- Sports medicine (Label Swiss Olympic medical centre)
- Supervision of professional training for athletes (Swiss Sport School)
- Training sports specialists (sports manager diploma, Swiss Olympic coaches, etc.)
- Promoting Olympic values (Olympic Spirit for Kids, Swiss Olympic Academy).

The events department

Swiss Olympic's events policy is an integral part of the organisation's marketing mix. The idea was originally inspired by the French model, which included organising 'Olympic Parks' and 'Olympic Lunches' to promote sport, especially the Olympic Games and Paris's bid for the 2012 Games. The events staged by Swiss Olympic are designed to bring the brand to life by creating a link with specific sections of the public through the provision of experiential benefits. Swiss Olympic events are directly financed by sponsoring. 'Leading partners' are solicited first, even though these events are not included in their contracts. Whether or not a leading partner decides to take part, its product category remains protected.

The events department is responsible for events marketing. In this respect it:

- designs, plans and organises events (e.g. Gigathlon, Swiss Olympic Parks (see below)
- helps organisations plan and run major international sports events held in Switzerland
- provides 'Swiss Olympics Partners' with advice and support for the organisation of sports events.

Public and media relations department

The public and media relations department is responsible for designing and implementing promotion actions to support the marketing strategy. The primary aim is to raise the brand's profile and promote its identity. It also supports Swiss Olympic initiatives with precisely targeted promotion actions in the press (e.g. in 2005 Swiss Olympic sent out 30 press releases and organised around 20 press conferences). In addition, it creates links with partners through events and public relations operations. It also produces the magazine 'Swiss Sport'.

Perception of Swiss Olympic by the Swiss public

In March 2006, ISOPUBLIC carried out a survey of a representative sample of the population of Switzerland to obtain quantitative and qualitative data about Swiss Olympic. The results for unprompted awareness (Table 1.7)

Table 1.7 Prompted and unprompted awareness of Swiss Olympic and other sports organisations based in Switzerland (%)

	Unprompted awareness	Prompted awareness	Difference
FIFA	31	97	+66
Swisski	16	87	+71
Swiss Football Federation	15	82	+67
IOC	9	85	+76
Swiss Olympic	5	60	+55

Source: Adapted from ISOPUBLIC, 2006, www.isopublic.ch

show the weakness of the Swiss Olympic brand compared with some of Switzerland's national federations.

Although half the people questioned appreciate Swiss Olympic, the organisation obtained lower sympathy scores than the IOC and Aide Sportive Suisse, which topped the table even though its score fell 7 per cent between 2003 and 2006 (see Table 1.8). However, Swiss Olympic did obtain slightly higher sympathy scores than organisations such as Swisski and the Swiss Football Federation.

Swiss Olympic's brand image corresponds to the large number of terms with which it is associated. ISOPUBLIC's study showed that 21 per cent of respondents associate Swiss Olympic with the Olympic Games, 17 per cent associate the organisation with Olympic disciplines and 80 per cent associate it with Olympic values (including: peace and bringing together peoples in sporting competitions = 28 per cent, friendship, feeling of belonging = 8 per cent). These results show that Swiss Olympic is associated with terms and values that correspond to the identity it wishes to communicate. However, this image is neither sufficiently nor spontaneously present in people's minds.

The strengths and weaknesses of Swiss Olympic's marketing strategy

Vermeulen (2006) analysed Swiss Olympic's marketing strategy and stressed its strengths and weaknesses.

The strengths of Swiss Olympic's marketing strategy

- Marketing actions are designed to serve Swiss Olympic's social and commercial objectives. The organisation tries to achieve the necessary balance between its business and social objectives. Its desire to develop synergies between its social and commercial responsibilities is manifest in its projects and events.

Table 1.8 Sympathy scores for Swiss Olympic and other sports organisations based in Switzerland (%)

	2006	2003	Change
Aide Sportive Suisse	66	73	-7
IOC	55	51	+4
Swiss Olympic	45	44	+1
Swisski	41	55	-14
Swiss Football Federation	40	44	-4
FIFA	38	35	+3

Source: Adapted from ISOPUBLIC, 2006, www.isopublic.ch

- Swiss Olympic markets its brand in such a way as to promote its goals and the values on which its actions are based. Its 'corporate identity' gives it a clear direction and identity for all its programmes and projects.
- Marketing that is both market- and network-oriented.
  - Swiss Olympic uses aggressive marketing to recruit sponsors and to create links with its event's policy. This enables it to increase the financial resources at its disposal for its actions.
  - Swiss Olympic's marketing also has a network orientation, based on the implementation of collaborative projects involving stakeholders such as sports federations, regional authorities and sponsors. For example, it organised 'Olympic Parks 2006' in partnership with four Swiss ski resorts, in order to promote the Turin Olympic Games and to strengthen support for the Swiss Olympic Team. Other events, such as the Gigathlon (www.gigathlon.ch), have been organised with similar objectives. Gigathlon is a major event that Swiss Olympic has organised since 2002, when, as part of Expo.02, the organisation formed a partnership with Expo.Games.02, the media and sponsors to organise the Swisspower Gigathlon Expo.02. The Gigathlon is a long-distance relay event that combines five disciplines: swimming, cycling, running, in-line skating and mountain biking. Its objective is to encourage Swiss people to give themselves clear sporting objectives and to meet the challenge of competition.

The weaknesses of Swiss Olympic's marketing strategy

- Environmental concerns are not clearly formulated, even though this is a very important issue in Switzerland and an integral part of Swiss Olympic's social responsibility. Swiss Olympic should follow in the footsteps of other sports organisations (e.g. IOC, IAAF, etc.) and set up relationship-marketing programmes involving public and private partners. This would allow the development of synergies between its social and economic objectives, and improve its sympathy ratings with the public.
- Swiss Olympic's approach to the market sub-sector is still essentially transactional, as is shown by the absence of a CRM programme. Furthermore, it has insufficient human resources to introduce high-quality key account management for all its sponsors. It should be remembered that the objective is to find 12 'leading partners', 12–15 'partners' and 20–25 'suppliers', i.e. a total of 44–52 partners, all of whom demand a reliable, personalised service, as well as reactivity in case of a problem. In addition, there is no systematic evaluation of stakeholders' expectations or the perceived quality of the services provided; therefore, there are no facts on which to base decisions.
- Marketing in the network sub-sector should be strengthened by increasing the number of programmes and stakeholders, and by developing

the ways in which these stakeholders are involved. Swiss Olympic has developed very few programmes that involve and create value for its stakeholders. A notable exception is the Gigathlon, venues for which are chosen in partnership with the regional authorities, the federations of the relevant disciplines (i.e. swimming, cycling, athletics), associations, and even sponsors and the media. In order to build this network of relationships, stakeholders must provide human, material and technical resources, as well as financial resources. Partnership priorities should also be defined by evaluating the legitimacy of the event's stakeholders and analysing whether or not they have convergent strategic and marketing objectives.

- Swiss Olympic undertakes no or very few internal marketing operations. As stated above, internal marketing provides a foundation on which other marketing actions, whether they are market- or network-oriented, are based. Internal marketing actions should be developed to ensure that all Swiss Olympic's paid and volunteer staff share a commitment to the organisation and to the achievement of its objectives. Quality procedures should also be defined in order to improve internal communication and knowledge of the different stakeholders, most notably with respect to causes of satisfaction and dissatisfaction.

- Swiss Olympic is not an experiential brand because it is primarily seen as a provider of organisational and social benefits. This is coherent, as the communicated identity does not include socio-emotional components. In the introduction we stressed the fact that sports organisations must provide socio-emotional benefits and that this is a key factor in success. This would require the addition of a second, functional/experiential axis in Swiss Olympic's identity and the organisation of fun events that bring together sport and entertainment as part of a network-oriented relationship-marketing programme. This was done by the 2007 Winter Universiades in Turin, which adopted the slogan 'Crazy for You'.

- Awareness of the Swiss Olympic brand is extremely low and levels of brand sympathy are not increasing. These indicators show the weakness of the organisation's marketing: Swiss Olympic does not have the means for a 'pull-type' strategy based on powerful media campaigns. Top-class sports people and sponsors need to be engaged in a relationship-marketing strategy in order to increase Swiss Olympic's media impact through press relations or advertising financed by sponsors. In such a situation, it is necessary to develop more strategic partnerships in order to increase the number of marketing operations that provide both functional and experiential benefits by systematically branding the experience.

This analysis of the strengths and weaknesses of Swiss Olympic's marketing strategy can be used to identify actions that would increase its impact. The recommendations listed below involve relationship marketing, brand marketing and experiential marketing.

- In the market sub-sector, move from a transactional to a relational approach in order to engage key stakeholders (i.e. sports organisations, local authorities, sponsors, media, athletes, public opinion, etc.)
- Design and implement relationship-marketing strategies for the market, network and internal sub-sectors
- Design and implement a consistent branding strategy
- Increase the functional and experiential value of its brand and offerings
- Link the brand with stakeholders' experiences.

Marketing challenges for sports organisations

The marketing challenges facing sports organisations can be summarised in the form of six recommendations:

1   Sports organisation marketing should become more relationship-oriented rather than transaction-oriented.
2   Sports organisations should implement relationship-marketing strategies in each of the three sub-sectors (market, network and internal).
3   Sports organisation offers should involve key stakeholders in the creation of a value constellation.
4   Sports organisation marketing programmes should balance commercial, social and environmental objectives.
5   Sports organisation marketing should create both functional and experiential value.
6   Sports organisations should link their brand with their stakeholders' experience.

Each of these recommendations is explored in more detail below.

Sports organisation marketing should become more relationship-oriented rather than transaction-oriented

Sports organisation marketing should strive to move towards a relational approach and away from a transactional approach (Figure 1.18). That is to say, organisations must build long-term relationships with strategic stakeholders (market sub-sector) and develop relationships between these stakeholders by involving them in collaborative programmes (network sub-sector).

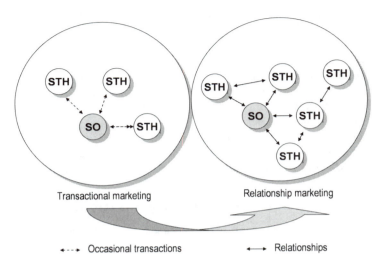

Transactional marketing   Relationship marketing

←--→ Occasional transactions   ←—→ Relationships

Figure 1.18 Sports organisation marketing shift (STH = stakeholder).

Sports organisations should implement relationship-marketing strategies in each of the three sub-sectors

Relationship-marketing strategies for the market and network sub-sectors can only be designed and implemented if an organisation manages its internal relationships effectively. Many organisations underestimate the important supporting role marketing can play in increasing overall efficiency. Internal marketing sets the stage for the implementation of marketing actions in the market and network sub-sectors. It is an ongoing process that occurs within organisations that have introduced functional processes that align, motivate and empower employees at all levels. Internal marketing includes recruitment, training, motivation and productivity. Sophisticated marketing relationships with employees, members, fans, and all other stakeholders are essential to maximise productivity in any sports organisation.

Consequently, relationships with key stakeholders should be developed through market- and network-oriented actions that are supported by an internal (organisation-based) marketing process involving the creation and exchange of value. This requires a strategy for managing all three sub-sectors (market, network and internal, Figure 1.19).

- Relationships in the market sub-sector constitute the classic type of relationship between a sports organisation and each of its stakeholders. These relationships provide the foundation for commercial and non-profit

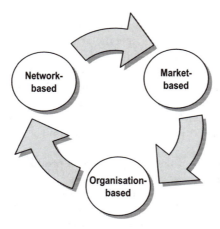

Figure 1.19 The three categories of relationship.

exchanges and interactions. They are stimulated by competitors and other parties operating in the market.

- Relationships in the network sub-sector form the platform on which market relationships are based. These relationships focus on stakeholders' alliances, competition and institutional regulations[1] in the sports organisation environment.
- Relationships in the internal sub-sector are intra-organisational. They can have a strong influence on external relationships.

Sports organisation offers should involve key stakeholders in the creation of a value constellation

Sports organisations promote specific values; however, the intrinsic characteristics of their services and products are filtered by the subjective perception of the stakeholders for which they are intended. According to Normann and Ramirez (1993: 66), the 'focus should be on the value-creating system itself, within which different economic actors – suppliers, business partners, allies, customers – work together to co-produce value'. In order to achieve this goal, sports organisations and their stakeholders must work together to facilitate the creation of new forms of value by new players. This involves managing four important areas:

- The stakeholders involved
- The convergences between their respective objectives
- The joint programmes that will enable these goals to be achieved
- The resources mobilised by partners.

The sports organisation is at the centre of the resulting network. Each stakeholder involved in a programme provides resources and skills that will be used to design and implement a specific action aimed at creating value for targeted stakeholders. Thus, stakeholders are sources of both benefits and resources. As sports organisations are parts of networks, competition is between networks, rather than between individual organisations.

This approach to relationship marketing enables sports organisations to renew and diversify their offers and to deliver greater value to their stakeholders. Most notably, this allows an organisation to:

- Create, in conjunction with its partners, a product and services portfolio for its stakeholders (e.g. sporting holidays abroad, supporters clubs, etc.)
- Develop merchandising products in conjunction with sports equipment companies or bestow the right to develop such products under license
- Design sponsorship programmes associating sports organisations, sponsors, media, events, patrons and funding partners
- Develop tailor-made training programmes in conjunction with partners, in order to promote sporting skills and to provide alternative services to its membership
- Implement sports event marketing as collaborative programmes in a complex system
- Run social marketing programmes aimed at improving peoples' quality of life in a given region.

Sports organisation marketing strategies should balance commercial, social and environmental objectives

A large majority of sporting organisations are becoming increasingly focused on commercial objectives (e.g. increasing the number of members and potential revenues). This commercial focus creates a real problem for both non-profit and for-profit organisations, as it is difficult for a club or a national federation to optimise income from their marketing activities while preserving their social base. It can lead to conflict between their values and the 'business' culture they have to develop. In addition, all types of sports organisations, whether they are for-profit or non-profit, create social marketing programmes in an attempt to alleviate the social problems within their environment. This involves applying marketing concepts and methods to create and implement programmes that will influence the behaviour of the organisation's target groups and that will improve the well-being of the groups to which these organisations belong (Andreasen, 1994). Waddock and Graves (1997) have proposed a 'good management theory' that suggests there is a link between corporate 'social' performance (CSP) and overall performance.

Sports organisations have to overcome the environmental challenges posed by certain sports (e.g. mountain biking) and by the construction of sports facilities. Major sports events can also have a significant environmental impact; an impact that organisation committees must do their utmost to minimise. For example, TOROC carried out a number of environmental protection actions, including registering with the EU eco-management and audit scheme (EMAS), launching green procurement programmes and promoting the EU Eco-label for tourist accommodation in the Olympic region. Consequently, other organising and bidding committees for the Olympic Games and other major sports events are considering joining EMAS and the EU Eco-label. Sports organisations are starting to clearly embrace the paradigm that environmental issues are intertwined with social/cultural and socioeconomic issues.

Sports organisation marketing should provide both functional and experiential benefits

According to Holbrook (1999: 5), consumer value is 'an interactive relativistic preference experience'. It is interactive because the consumer interacts with the offer by consuming it; it is preferential because it embodies a preference judgement; it is relative because it requires comparison between this experience and another; and it is experiential because value, which may involve emotional, symbolic and/or socio-cultural benefits, can only be obtained by experiencing the situation.

Hence, sports organisations should deliver experiential value that generates emotional, symbolic and socio-cultural benefits (while not neglecting functional benefits). For example, a judo club must satisfy its members' functional expectations (improve technique, obtain a higher ranking belt), while developing social bonds and the feeling of being part of a community with shared values (such as friendship, courage, sincerity, honour, modesty, respect, self-control and courtesy) and bringing pleasure and positive emotion to its members' lives. Paying members also expect a reasonable level of customer service from their sports body. This experiential value should be a focus of all three marketing sub-sectors.

Sports organisations should link their brand with their stakeholders' experience

Technically, a brand is simply a trademark that helps to differentiate the goods and services of one organisation from those of another. In reality, brands are much more than that: they create a relationship with their customers based on their experiential value (Ferrand and Torrigiani, 2004). Smith and Wheeler (2002) described two strategies for creating a Branded Customer Experience. The first strategy aims at 'experiencing the brand', which is a 'pull strategy' used by sports organisations with the highest levels of appeal. This strategy should allow a sports organisation to deliver on its promises, i.e. the

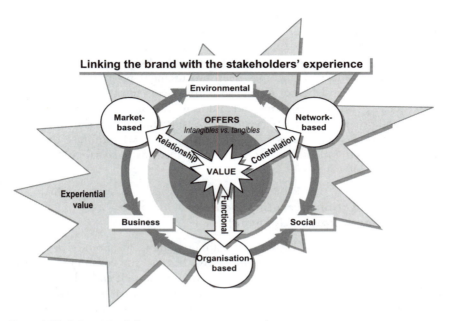

Figure 1.20 A framework for sports organisation marketing.

value it undertakes to deliver to its fans. 'Experiencing the brand begins with the brand and its desired values, turns these into a promise for target customers, and delivers the promise in a way which brings the brand alive' (Smith and Wheeler, 2002: 10). Nevertheless, fulfilling promises requires good sporting results, effective teamwork, strong communication and quality management.

The second strategy, which relies on branding the experience, tries to create a unique experience for targeted customers and then brands it accordingly. This process starts with the consumers and what they desire and value. This type of 'push strategy', which is used by clubs with less appeal, could involve organising friendly events in order to create a unique experience and then developing a brand to reflect that experience. The two strategies have the same goal, which is to link the brand with the experience.

Figure 1.20 presents a framework for sports organisation marketing that encourages sports organisations to provide better relationship (market sub-sector), constellation (network sub-sector) and functional (internal sub-sector) value. Organisations should offer experiential value for all their stakeholders by linking the brand with the experience(s) they provide. Furthermore, marketing should build relationships within a network and inside the organisation, pursuing business, social and environmental goals. As these relationships are organized in a system whose dynamics are related to the exchanges between its constituent elements, sports organisations should take a systemic approach that analyses and manages the value constellation.

Chapter 2

Strategic analysis for relationship marketing

Managers often associate strategy with military manoeuvres. In his 'Art of War', the Chinese general Sun-Tzu (544–496 BC) advised that when assembling troops a general must ensure they occupy an advantageous position, as this is a vital condition for success; although he admitted that this is much more difficult than might be thought. Sun-Tzu also realised that success depends on combining one's own resources with those of one's allies, and then ensuring the cohesion of the whole – a result that can only be achieved through the skilful management of the relationships within the system. In business management, drawing up a strategy forces an organisation to identify the fields in which it wants to be present and to allocate the resources needed to ensure it maintains and develops its presence in those fields (Detrie *et al.*, 2005). This can be achieved in two ways:

1 By increasing market power in the competitive field(s) targeted by the organisation (i.e. Porter's approach). In order to do this, an organisation must analyse its competitors' strengths, and then choose one or more segments in which to dominate or avoid these competitors.
2 By developing resources and competencies that are superior to those of its competitors. This will result in the emergence of distinctive competencies in marketing, as well as in human and financial resources, which will give the organisation an advantage over its highest performing competitors.

Relationship marketing can help sports organisations strengthen their market power and build their resources and competencies. The relational approach should be applied to all the sub-strategies an organisation uses to achieve the goals set out in its 'corporate' strategy. An organisation's corporate strategy should identify the sectors in which it should be present and from which it should withdraw in order to create a balanced business. For example, the French Volleyball Federation's (FFVB) corporate strategy was to be present in the sports, leisure and education sectors of the general sports market and, more particularly, in the volleyball and beach volleyball markets. To achieve this, the FFVB adopted a business strategy that defines ways of gaining competitive advantages in each of these sectors. The federation decided that efforts to differentiate itself from its competitors should focus on five main areas: increasing name recognition, attracting new players and spectators, education, feminising the sport and by opening up to establish new partners. In order to implement the different strands of the competitive strategy, each of the FFVB's departments (marketing, human resources, finance, etc.) had to draw up appropriate functional strategies. The marketing strategy is a key component of this strategy, as marketing can increase the number of registered players, media exposure, events, etc., thereby generating new resources that can be used to boost the impact of the FFVB and its member clubs.

The FFVB's overall objective – to occupy a competitive or dominant position in the fields in which it has chosen to develop – is shared by all organisations, including the FFVB's competitors. Consequently, success requires creating and maintaining competitive advantages over these competitors. Adopting a relational approach to the network, market and internal aspects of marketing can help achieve this, as relationship marketing enables organisations to design and deliver offers that give targeted stakeholders better value than the offers provided by their competitors. The first part of this chapter shows the benefits to be obtained by taking a relational approach to strategic marketing; the second part describes a methodology that allows sports organisations to structure the process of making strategic choices.

The relational approach to strategic marketing

The principles of relationship marketing should be an integral part of the methods and tools of strategic marketing. This section presents the strategic marketing cycle and explains the advantages to be gained from applying the principles of relationship marketing.

Strategic marketing: method and tools

Aaker (2001) used the term strategic marketing management to describe 'a system designed to help management both precipitate and make strategic decisions, as well as creating strategic vision'. Strategic marketing involves a proactive process that allows organisations to analyse changes in the market and consequently identify new opportunities and take medium-term decisions. Strategic marketing is directly linked to an organisation's overall strategy, as it involves analysing changes in the target market and evaluating the attractiveness of current or potential segments as a function of its resources and competencies. These analyses can then be used to draw up a development strategy.

Strategic marketing also forms the basis for operational marketing, which consists of short-term strategies and actions related to the offer, promotion, distribution and price. Operational marketing has been defined as 'an active approach to the conquest of existing markets. Its action horizon is short- and medium-term. It is the classic central approach, centred around the achievement of a turnover objective and it is based on tactical means derived from the product, distribution, price and publicity policies' (Lambin, 2002: 124). In short, strategic marketing focuses on analysis; operational marketing focuses on action. The two parts of this process are illustrated in Figure 2.1.

This cyclical and iterative approach, which is an integral part of an organisation's strategic cycle, allows objectives and resource allocations to be modified according to final and intermediary results. Chappelet (2004) has proposed a simple, pragmatic model of the strategic management cycle that was directly inspired by the ideas on designing strategy originally developed during the 1970s at Harvard Business School. The model describes a cyclical process of Analysis → Vision → Action → Control → Analysis, based on the questions: Where are we now? Where do we want to be? Are we getting there? and How do we get there? (Figure 2.2).

However, the strategic management and strategic marketing cycles do not follow the same timescale, as the strategic management cycle is medium- to long-term, and the strategic marketing cycle is medium-term. Nevertheless, the two cycles can be superimposed, as shown in Figure 2.3.

Applying the principles of relationship marketing to strategic marketing

According to the principles of relationship marketing, marketing can be viewed in terms of three complementary and interdependent sub-systems: network, market and internal. Consequently, sports organisations must implement actions aimed at each of these sub-systems.

A sports organisation's relational strategy should cover the end-users

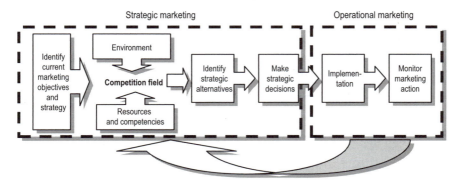

Figure 2.1 The phases of strategic and operational marketing.

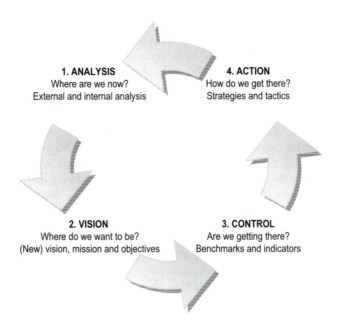

Figure 2.2 The strategic management cycle (adapted from Chappelet, 2004).

within its market, the stakeholders it will have to engage in its programmes, and its relations with the people inside the organisation. The analysis of Swiss Olympic's marketing actions showed the benefits a sports organisation can gain by adopting a relationship approach. This analysis allows a number of recommendations to be made about how Swiss Olympic should develop its marketing actions:

- Engage key stakeholders (i.e. sports organisations, local authorities, sponsors, media, athletes, public opinion, etc.) by moving from a transactional approach to marketing to a relationship-marketing approach
- Design and implement relationship-marketing strategies for each of the three sub-sectors: market, network and internal
- Design and implement a consistent branding strategy
- Create a value constellation and provide both functional and experiential benefits by involving key stakeholders in offers and programmes
- Link the brand with stakeholders' experience.

Strategic decision-making should be based on the following general process:

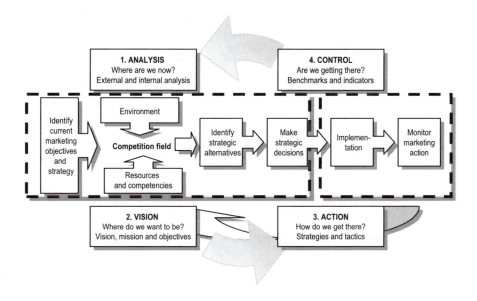

Figure 2.3 Superimposing the strategic and marketing cycles.

First, a diagnosis should be carried out to ascertain the benefits to be obtained from adopting a relationship-marketing approach. If these benefits are considered desirable, the organisation must decide which relationship strategy to adopt (Figure 2.4). This decision will also have a bearing on the structure of the system the organisation should introduce in order to meet its objectives.

What are the bases for the organisation's marketing actions?

The answer to this fundamental question depends on the corporate strategy, as marketing actions must be consistent with an organisation's mission, values and vision. They must also be consistent with its functional strategies, most notably in the areas of human resources and quality management.

Which relationship strategy?

This decision is at the heart of relationship marketing. It must be taken with respect to each of the three complementary and interdependent sub-systems mentioned above. The relationship-marketing strategy will influence the

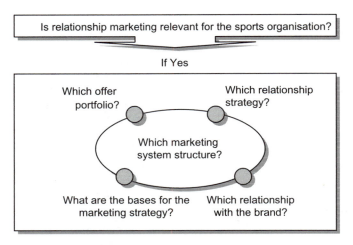

Figure 2.4 Strategic decisions concerning relationship marketing.

choice of marketing targets with which the organisation will develop a relationship (market sub-system), the strategy for engaging and retaining stakeholders (network sub-system) and the internal stakeholders to involve (internal sub-system).

Which offer portfolio?

According to Marion *et al.* (2003), an offer is a complex whole composed of tangible and intangible elements that are likely to be valued by the client. Offers are the elements on which exchanges between stakeholders are based. Organisations can design their offers independently, notably through the use of specific methods such as Customer Relationship Management, or they can develop them in collaboration with one or more of their stakeholders. Whichever offer-creation process is used, it must always take into account the expectations of end users and be developed with the idea of furthering the relationships.

What type of relationship should be developed with the brand?

A brand is a set of associations (Ries, 1998) that give an identity to a product or service in the eyes of the consumer (Kapferer, 2000). Aaker (1991) viewed brands in terms of the equity they can provide an organisation. Here, brands are viewed in terms of the relationships they enable an organisation to build and develop with its internal and external stakeholders.

Which structure for the marketing system?

Answering these questions will lead an organisation to make a number of closely linked strategic decisions. In order to produce a system that will create a 'value constellation' within its stakeholder network, an organisation's actions must be coherent with all these strategic decisions. This value is based on experiential benefits. The large number of components and the relationships between these components combine to make the resulting system of relationships highly complex. The methodology presented here enables sports organisation managers to answer this strategic question on the basis of a precise diagnosis.

Principles for drawing up a relationship-marketing strategy

This section presents a methodology managers can use to answer the five questions listed above.

What are the bases for the organisation's marketing actions?

A sports organisation's marketing strategy must respect its mission, vision and values, as these are both the foundation stones on which its actions are based and a means of expressing its relationship orientation. This is the case for the Sport North Federation, which was set up in 1976 to promote and develop amateur sport in Canada's Northwest Territories. Sport North was formed for two reasons:

1   The government of the Northwest Territories could no longer provide all the services required by organised sport without enlarging its staff.
2   The sporting community in the Northwest Territories was sufficiently organised and experienced to handle its own affairs.

Today Sport North consists of 27 territorial sports organisations and three partner organisations. It is responsible for providing programmes and services for organised sport in the Northwest Territories.

Sport North laid out the foundations on which its actions are based in its 2004–2009 strategic plan. The federation aims 'to enrich the lives of all Northwest Territory residents through sport' and its mission statement, which defines its purpose, is: 'Sport North represents the Territorial Sport Organizations of the Northwest Territories. We are dedicated to the development of sport at every level of participation in the Northwest Territories' (Sport North Federation Strategic Business Plan 2004–2009: 16). An organisation's mission helps ensure its stability and development over time; however, its strategic decisions and internal evolution, together with its

Table 2.1 Sport North's values

In our relationship with our stakeholders	In working with each other and in maximising our performance
• We respond to the needs of our clients • We consult with stakeholders and endeavour to reach common understandings • We are open and transparent in the process of allocation of resources • We listen and communicate openly • We accept full accountability for our decisions and actions	• We strive for excellence through cooperation and teamwork • We make the most of every opportunity to be innovative and to be leaders in our field • We listen and communicate openly • We accept full accountability for our decisions and actions • We value the well-being and diversity of our staff

environment, may result in this mission being modified. In order to accomplish its mission, Sport North has clearly chosen a relationship orientation that takes into account its internal and external stakeholders. Its strategic plan specifies that the federation takes 'a two-pronged approach in how we relate with our stakeholders and how we work with each other' (Table 2.1).

In fact, if value is defined as 'an enduring prescriptive or proscriptive belief that a specific end state of existence or specific mode of conduct is preferred to an opposite end state or mode of conduct for living one's life' (Rokeach, 1973: 73), this mission statement must be regarded more as a set of guiding principles than a list of values. An organisation's values can only be a reflection of personal values that are shared by the members of that organisation. Sport North's stated values, which include reliability, trust, teamwork, search for performance, involvement, reactivity, consideration of others and focusing on consumers and stakeholders, are coherent with a relationship approach.

An organisation's vision statement provides a clear indication of where the organisation wishes to go. Sport North's vision statement is: 'Sport North Federation will be the recognized leader in sport development and will ensure that opportunities in sport, based on fair play, are accessible to all residents of the Northwest Territories' (Sport North Federation strategic business plan 2004–2009: 31). The word 'recognized' was added to this statement to stress the importance of increasing the federation's recognition for its work developing sport in the province. In addition, as Chappelet (2004: 10) has pointed out, 'vision refers to shared values that are implied and to an ideal that is difficult to attain and as such, often not expressed'.

Sports organisations carry out their missions and achieve their visions by striving to meet a number of permanent objectives. Sport North has set itself seven goals that will guide the way it addresses the issues it faces and the demands of its stakeholders. These goals conform nicely with the priorities of Canadian sports policy:

1   Sport North Federation is financially self-sufficient
2   Sport North Federation operates efficiently and effectively, maximising programme spending and minimising administrative requirements that clients have to perform in being accountable to the Sport North Federation
3   Sport North Federation has an ample, strong, committed, and trained volunteer base throughout the Northwest Territories
4   Sport North Federation has strong brand equity among athletes, volunteers and the general public, as the sport council for the Northwest Territory
5   Sport North Federation brings sport to all populations, regardless of age, gender, physical ability etc., in the Northwest Territories
6   Sport North Federation supports both the development of a broad base of recreational athletes and a strong core of elite, competitive athletes
7   Sport North Federation has demonstrated, and promotes the link between participation in sport, and mental and physical wellness.

Sport North's mission, vision and end goals form the foundations on which its actions are based. They demonstrate its commitment to developing relationships, which is a product of its history and culture, and which was strengthened by the analysis carried out for its 2004–2009 strategic plan. However, when the plan was being drawn up, it was noted that the federation's policy of always consulting its stakeholders on important decisions had lapsed and that it tended to work too much in isolation, thereby weakening the validity of its strategic recommendations. As a result, all parties with a direct interest in the project, including the general public, partners, federation members and politicians, were invited to express their views and ideas on the key issues confronting the organization and the future direction of sport in the Northwest Territories. This consultation confirmed the benefits to be obtained by applying the principles of relationship marketing.

For change to happen, it must first be stimulated internally by pushing forward a mission, a vision and objectives. An organisation's mission 'is particularly important in non-profit organisations whose goal is not to share profits and who work to a large extent with volunteers and donors who it must continue to motivate' (Chappelet, 2004: 12). It enables internal stakeholders to understand the general sense behind a sports organisation's actions. According to Dunmore (2002: 35), 'the vision should provide a common picture for the people within an organisation as to where the organisation is heading and connect them to it, linking the external environment to internal resources'. However, it would be naïve to think that issuing a mission statement will suddenly cause employees and volunteers to change their behaviour and the organisation to adopt a relationship approach. Such change requires action in other fields, such as human resources management, and the introduction of internal marketing. Vision, mission and values are also important in the market because a sports organisation must clearly communicate the foundations of its actions in order to situate its sector of activity, its objectives and its values. This enables an organisation to differentiate itself from its competitors and to create a competitive advantage. A sports organisation's brand or brands must also reflect its relationship approach.

Which relationship strategy?

For an organisation to achieve its goals and fulfil its mission through the use of relationship marketing, its relationship strategy must be designed and implemented according to a coherent, clear and integrated decision-making process that includes a systematic analysis of the opportunities and threats in its environment and market. This process must also take into consideration the organisation's distinctive competencies. The systematic analysis should allow the organisation to make decisions and take actions that will enable it to engage and satisfy targeted stakeholders.

From a strategic point of view, it is logical to first consider a sports organisation within its network of stakeholders, then in its market, and then to take into account internal aspects. Relationship marketing in the network sub-system requires an organisation to determine who its stakeholders are and how they are connected. These connections have an impact on the market sub-system because they can be used to create competitive advantages. Within the market sub-system, relationship marketing can be used to define strategies for managing the maturity and content of the relationships with targeted stakeholders. Finally, when applying the principles of relationship marketing to the internal sub-system, an organisation must take into account its own culture, as only by doing this will it be possible to define the resources required to successfully implement its market and network strategies.

Implementing relationship marketing is a complex and iterative process. The following discussion starts by looking at relationship marketing within the network sub-system, as this aspect allows an organisation to situate itself within its network and therefore to define its market approach.

Analysis of the organisation's environment, competitors and current stakeholder networks (and relationship quality)

Analysis of the market environment should include all the key market players, including competitors, distributors and suppliers, as well as the customer groups in the wider macro-marketing environment. It is very important for an organisation to develop its knowledge and understanding of its stakeholders and the network in which it operates. This involves analysing the descriptive, instrumental and normative elements of stakeholder theory outlined in chapter one. The descriptive element requires a sports organisation to analyse the cooperative/competitive and influence/dependence relationships between it and its stakeholders. The instrumental element builds on the results of the descriptive analysis to evaluate the convergence between stakeholders' marketing strategies and the resources and competencies that need to be mobilised in order to improve the organisation's performance. Finally, the normative element encourages the organisation to take into account its stakeholders' legitimate interests when developing its marketing strategy.

The Italian organisation CONI Servizi provides a good illustration of this approach. CONI Servizi is a fully state-owned company that was created in 2002 when the Italian government decided to restructure the National Olympic Committee (CONI) in order to separate the committee's non-commercial actions from its commercial activities. The new company immediately had to face a huge challenge: to develop a high quality and competitive service offer, while significantly reducing costs, and then to implement a complete re-organisation and process improvement plan that would also involve major staff cuts.

The central focus of a market study is the analysis of the stakeholders in the market and the dynamics of their interactions, as these parameters are the basis for an understanding of the market as a whole. Godet's (2001) MACTOR (Matrix of Alliances and Conflicts: Tactics, Objectives and Recommendations) method provides a powerful tool for identifying which strategic stakeholders to engage in specific programmes in order to build a strong portfolio of high quality products and services. The approach presented here applies the principles of relationship marketing to the network sub-system in order to create a 'value constellation' in which value is co-produced by stakeholders who work together to achieve a common goal. An organisation's ability to develop and maintain strong relationships with their key stakeholders improves the chances that relationships will continue.

Studies of the interaction between stakeholders, which involves combining the descriptive and instrumental facets of stakeholder theory, can be facilitated by using the MACTOR method to analyse the balance of power between stakeholders and to study their convergences and divergences with respect to a number of issues and associated objectives. MACTOR is a decision-making tool that can be used to design a policy of alliances in a network-oriented relationship-marketing strategy. It is fully applicable to an organisation's overall strategy; however, it must be adapted in order to meet the specific needs of marketing strategies. MACTOR software converts stakeholder relationship analyses into clear charts and graphs that can be used to draw up hypotheses about the evolution of the stakeholder network. Thus, it is a valuable decision-making tool that can help organisations manage alliances and competition. MACTOR software can be downloaded free of charge at www.3ie.fr/lipsor/MACTOR.htm.

Calvani (2007) applied seven of the stages of the MACTOR method to CONI's strategic marketing decision-making process.

1. IDENTIFY THE ORGANISATION'S CURRENT AND POTENTIAL STAKEHOLDERS

CONI Servizi operates in a network of stakeholders that can be grouped into the following categories:

CONI Servizi departments
Stakeholders who provide services related to sports facilities:
- Sports Facilities Consulting (SFI)
- Olympic Training Centres and Foro Italico Park (OTC)
- School of Sport and Sports Science Institute (SDS)
- CONI Servizi Board (CS BOARD)
- Coninet (CONINET).

CONI departments
Stakeholders who deal with sports organisations to promote participation in sport at every level:
- Olympic Preparation (OP)
- Press Office (PO)
- Peripheral Network and Sports Promotion (T&P)
- CONI Local Sports Facilities Consultants (LSFC).

CONI Servizi commercial partners
- Official Suppliers and Sponsors (SUPPL).

Clients
Stakeholders who are the main users or targets of the sports-facility related services provided by CONI Servizi. These clients also use competing services. They cover two different markets:
- Italian market:
  - Professionals: engineers and architects (PROFESS)
  - Public sports facilities owners and managers (PA)
  - Private sports facilities owners and managers (PRIVATE)
  - National Federations (NF) and Clubs
  - General public or users (CUSTOMER).
- International market:
  - International Federations (IFs) and Teams
  - National Olympic Committees (NOC)
  - International Olympic Committee (IOC).

2. CREATE AN IDENTITY CARD FOR EACH STAKEHOLDER SHOWING ITS MISSION, GOALS, PROGRAMMES, NETWORK AND RESOURCES

CONI Servizi used documents, existing data and interviews with managers to determine the mission, objectives, on-going programmes, networks (internal and external), type and scope of relationships, and resources of each internal

Table 2.2 CONI Servizi's internal and external stakeholders

No.	Stakeholder name	Abbreviated name
1	Sports Facilities Consulting	SFC
2	Coninet	Coninet
3	School of Sport	SDS
4	Press Office	PO
5	Olympic Preparation	OP
6	Peripheral Network and Sport Promotion	T&P
7	Local Sports Facilities Consultants	LSFC
8	Public Administration	PA
9	National Federations	NF
10	Private Owners and Managers	Private
11	Architects and Engineers	Profess
12	General Public	Customer
13	Official Suppliers	Suppl
14	CONI Servizi Board	CS board
15	Olympic Training Centres and Foro Italico Park	OTC

and external stakeholder. Table 2.3 presents this data for Sports Facilities Consulting.

3. IDENTIFICATION OF STRATEGIC GOALS AND ASSOCIATED OBJECTIVES

By compiling (e.g. through interviews) and comparing stakeholder objectives, an organisation can determine the convergences and divergences between stakeholders. Table 2.4 presents the objectives of CONI Servizi's stakeholders. These objectives have been grouped into six strategic goals:

Table 2.3 Sports Facilities Consulting

Dimensions	Characteristics
Mission	• To generate revenues from sports facility consulting and training activities and from the exploitation of the CONI Servizi brand through commercial partnerships with leading companies in the sports facilities sector • To create social value and culture by improving the quality of sports facilities in general, thereby promoting participation in sport in high-quality and safe conditions
Objectives	• To generate revenues • To improve the quality of sports facilities • To increase awareness of the CONI Servizi brand in order to make it the reference for sports facilities in Italy and to position it better in the European market

(Continued overleaf)

Table 2.3 Continued

Dimensions	Characteristics
Programmes	• *CONI Servizi Official Supplier.* A programme that offers suppliers use of the brand and other value added services in exchange for a fixed sum or a percentage of market revenues • *Training.* A set of 14 courses and seminars was designed in conjunction with the School of Sport, in order to develop sports facility management and generate revenues. One of the more ambitious projects is the creation of an e-learning platform in collaboration with Coninet • *Consultancy.* A consultancy offer mainly related to sports event security management and sports betting management • *The National Sports Facilities Observatory.* Aims to monitor the sports facilities network by creating a national database • *The creation of a 'quality certification' for sports facilities.* CONI Servizi intends to launch a specific quality certification programme for the equipment, management and maintenance procedures at Italian sports facilities • *CONI Awards for Sports Facilities.* Biennial prizes for projects that are outstanding in terms of their quality, economic and environmental sustainability, safety, functionality and innovation. The prizes are awarded in consultation with public bodies and private companies • *Spazio Sport Review.* A technical–scientific quarterly journal covering the world of sports facilities, with in-depth reports and illustrations. The journal covers design innovations, fixed and mobile equipment, and important initiatives in town planning and the architectural and technological aspects of sport. • *Sports facilities website: http://impiantisportivi.coni.it*
Relationships and networks	• School of Sport is an 'internal strategic partner', as it works very closely with Sports Facilities Consulting to organise the CONI Servizi training courses programme • Olympic Training Centres is an 'internal functional partner', as it supplies the facilities where many Sports Facilities Consulting activities take place (i.e. training courses) • Peripheral Network is an 'internal functional partner', as it publicises and promotes CONI Servizi activities within Italy • Official Suppliers are 'external clients', 'external suppliers' and 'strategic partners', as they pay to use and exploit the CONI Servizi brand in their promotional campaigns (external clients), they provide CONI Servizi with their products/services (external suppliers), and they plan joint operations with CONI Servizi (strategic partners) • Local Sports Facilities Consultants are 'internal clients', as they are the internal targets of the technical training courses • Olympic Preparation has a non-commercial relationship with Sports Facilities Consulting
Resources	• Sports Facilities Consulting employs 11 people

Source: Adapted from Calvani (2007).

1   To generate revenues
2   To increase the value of the brand
3   To develop the network
4   To increase brand awareness and improve its image
5   To design new services
6   To improve the quality of services and of facilities.

Each stakeholder has a position with respect to each objective; therefore, it is necessary to determine what this position is in order to analyse the convergences and divergences between stakeholders. MACTOR asks stakeholders to state whether their position with respect to each objective is favourable, not favourable or neutral. Stakeholder positions are noted as follows:

- (1) stakeholder 'X' is in favour of objective 'J'
- (-1) stakeholder 'X' is not in favour of objective 'J'
- (0) stakeholder 'X' has a neutral or indifferent position regarding 'J'.

Table 2.4 Objectives of the stakeholders in the CONI Servizi network

No.	Objectives	Abbreviation
1	To generate revenues from consultancy and training work	$cons&trai
2	To generate revenues from brand exploitation	$brand exp
3	To strengthen the relationship network and strategies between CONI and CONI Servizi	linknoc/cs
4	To enhance the quality of sports facilities	>qual sf
5	To increase CONI Servizi brand awareness	>Cs brand
6	To generate revenues from managed sports facilities	$sf
7	To enhance the ICT services offer to sports operators	ICT offer
8	To develop knowledge, competencies and sports education	>know
9	To enhance the training course offer	>tr off
10	To promote CONI's image in Italy and abroad	CONI image
11	To strengthen the relationship network and develop collaborative strategies with official sponsors	>netsp
12	To strengthen and spread participation in sport and increase facility usage	>practice
13	To strengthen and broaden the partnership network with CONI Servizi and other suppliers	>netCSsupp
14	To increase business through exploitation of the CONI Servizi brand	$CSbrand
15	To keep prices low	low fares
16	To get up-to-date training on sports facilities	Get training
17	To monitor the availability of local sports facilities	sf monitor

Source: Adapted from Calvani (2007).

Table 2.5 The positions of CONI Servizi's stakeholders with respect to its objectives

	$cons&trai	$brand exp	linknoc/cs	>qual sf	>Cs brand	$sf	ICT offer	>know	> tr off	Coni image	>netsp	>practice	>netCSsupp	$CSbrand	low fares	Get training	sf monitor	TOTAL
SFC	1	1	1	1	1	o	o	1	1	1	1	1	1	1	-1	o	1	14
OTC	1	1	1	1	1	1	1	o	o	1	o	o	o	1	-1	o	o	11
Coninet	1	o	1	1	1	o	1	1	1	o	o	o	o	o	o	o	o	6
SDS	1	o	o	o	1	o	o	1	1	o	1	1	o	1	-1	o	o	13
PO	o	1	1	1	1	o	o	1	o	o	1	o	o	o	o	o	o	5
OP	o	o	o	1	1	o	o	o	o	1	1	1	o	1	o	o	1	7
T&P	1	1	1	1	o	o	1	1	1	o	o	o	o	o	1	o	1	10
LSFC	1	o	o	1	o	o	o	1	o	1	1	o	o	o	o	1	1	11
PA	o	1	1	1	o	o	1	1	1	o	1	1	1	o	1	1	1	6
NFs	o	1	1	1	o	-1	o	1	o	o	o	o	o	o	o	1	1	10
Private	o	1	1	1	o	-1	1	1	1	1	1	1	o	o	-1	1	1	9
Profess	1	o	1	1	o	o	o	o	o	o	o	o	o	o	o	1	1	5
Customer	o	o	1	1	1	1	1	1	1	1	1	1	o	1	o	1	1	9
Suppl	o	1	1	1	o	o	o	o	o	o	o	o	o	o	-1	o	1	10
CS board	1	1	1	1	1	1	1	1	1	1	1	1	1	1	-1	1	1	16
Number of agreements	7	6	8	14	9	3	7	11	8	9	8	10	4	8	4	6	11	
Number of disagreements	0	0	0	0	0	-3	0	0	0	0	0	0	0	0	-6	0	0	
Number of positions	7	6	8	14	9	6	7	11	8	9	8	10	5	8	10	6	11	

In Table 2.5, the total for each row is the number of objectives on which that stakeholder has a position. The totals for the columns show the number of stakeholders in favour of that objective (positive figure) and the number of stakeholders not in favour of that objective (negative figure). For example, Professionals and Press Office only have positions on five of CONI Servizi's objectives, whereas 'CONI Servizi Board' and Sports Facilities Consulting have positions on nearly all the objectives (16 and 14, respectively). It is logical that CONI Servizi Board should have a position on a large number of objectives; however, it was less foreseeable that this would also be the case for Sports Facilities Consulting. Because it has a position on so many objectives, Sports Facilities Consulting's interests are likely to converge or diverge with those of a large number of stakeholders. For all the stakeholders, the most consensual objective is 'to enhance the quality of sports facilities' (14 favourable positions, 0 non-favourable positions), whereas the most divisive is 'to keep prices low' (4 favourable positions, 6 non-favourable positions).

4. RANK THE IMPORTANCE OF EACH OBJECTIVE TO STAKEHOLDERS

After analysing the number of convergences and divergences between stakeholders, the value stakeholders give to each objective must be ranked. Stakeholders in the CONI Servizi network were asked to evaluate their position on each objective using the following scale:

4: The objective affects the stakeholder's existence
3: The objective affects the stakeholder's mission
2: The objective affects the stakeholder's plans
1: The objective affects the stakeholder's operational processes
0: The objective does not affect the stakeholder.

Stakeholders were also asked to indicate whether the effect was positive or negative. The results are shown in Table 2.6.

Table 2.6 reveals each objective's overall importance to each stakeholder and shows convergences and divergences between stakeholders. For example, 'to enhance the quality of sports facilities' is the objective that concerns the largest number of CONI Servizi's stakeholders and the opinions of these stakeholders are consensual (positive). This can be contrasted with the objective 'to keep prices low', which also concerns a large number of stakeholders but their views are divisive. In general, the position of Sports Facilities Consulting converges with the positions of School of Sport and CONI Servizi Board, and diverges from that of Professionals, Consumers and Public Administration. As well as calculating the matrix of convergences, MACTOR software maps each stakeholder's position with respect to all the objectives (Figure 2.5). The proximity between stakeholders shows the degree of overall convergence with respect to the objectives.

Table 2.6 Matrix showing stakeholders' valued positions with respect to each objective

	$cons&trai	$brand exp	linknoc/cs	>qual sf	>Cs brand	$sf	ICT offer	>know	>troff	Coni image	>netsp	>practice	>netCsupp	$CSbrand	low fares	Get training	sf monitor	CONCERN
SFC	3	3	3	3	3	0	0	2	3	1	2	2	2	1	-3	0	2	27
OTC	1	3	3	3	3	4	2	0	0	1	0	0	2	1	-3	0	0	21
Coninet	4	0	3	1	1	0	4	0	1	0	0	0	0	0	0	0	0	11
SDS	0	3	2	2	3	0	1	3	3	3	2	1	0	1	-1	0	0	27
PO	0	0	0	0	1	0	0	2	0	3	1	0	0	0	0	0	0	11
OP	0	3	0	1	1	0	0	3	3	3	1	0	0	1	0	0	1	11
T&P	0	0	3	3	3	0	2	3	2	2	0	3	0	0	-1	0	3	23
LSFC	2	0	2	3	2	0	0	2	0	3	0	3	2	0	0	2	3	25
PA	0	0	0	3	0	-1	0	2	2	0	2	2	0	0	3	2	3	15
NFs	0	0	0	2	0	-1	0	3	2	3	0	3	0	0	2	2	2	21
Private	3	0	0	3	0	4	0	0	0	0	0	3	0	2	-3	2	2	18
Profess	3	0	0	2	0	0	0	0	0	0	0	0	0	1	0	3	2	11
Customer	0	0	0	3	0	-3	0	2	1	0	0	1	0	0	3	2	2	14
Suppl	0	1	0	2	0	0	0	2	1	0	2	3	3	3	-1	0	2	17
CS board	3	3	3	2	2	3	1	3	3	1	1	3	2	3	-2	0	3	36
Σ importance of agreements	17	16	20	33	19	11	12	24	16	20	12	22	9	13	9	13	25	
Σ importance of disagreements	0	0	0	0	0	-5	0	0	0	0	0	0	0	0	-13	0	0	
Σ importance	17	16	20	33	19	16	12	24	16	20	12	22	9	13	22	13	25	

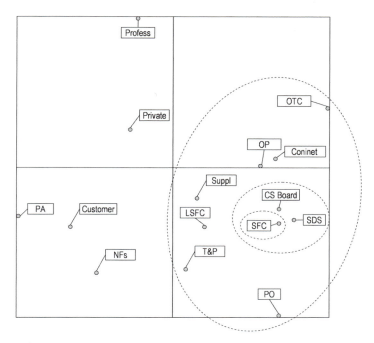

Figure 2.5 Convergences between the stakeholders in the CONI Servizi network.

Sports Facilities Consulting lies in the lower right-hand square, immediately next to CONI Servizi Board and School of Sport, thus confirming the global convergence of their positions with respect to the objectives. Coninet, Olympic Preparation, Suppliers, Local Sports Facilities Consultants, Peripheral Network and Sport Promotion, and Press Office lie in the same sector, indicating that their positions also converge but to a lesser extent than those of Sports Facilities Consulting, CONI Servizi Board and School of Sport. Figure 2.5 also highlights the existence of two groups of divergent stakeholders: Public Administration, Customers and National Federations, which lie in the lower left-hand quadrant, and Professionals and Private Sector, which lie in the upper left-hand quadrant. This analysis can be refined by combing the ranking given to the objectives by each stakeholder with stakeholder ambivalence and stakeholder commitment.

5. IDENTIFY AMBIVALENT STAKEHOLDERS

Two stakeholders that have converging positions on some objectives and diverging positions on others are said to be ambivalent. If they wish to become allies they have to concentrate on their common objectives and put aside their differences. Figure 2.6 shows ambivalence scores for CONI

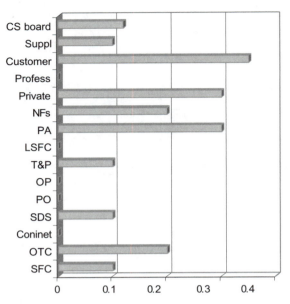

Figure 2.6 Histogram of stakeholder ambivalence.

Servizi's stakeholders. In general, ambivalence is quite low, with scores varying from 0 to 0.3. The least ambivalent, that is to say, the most 'dependable' allies are Coninet, Press Office, Olympic Preparation, Local Consultants and Professionals, whereas the most ambivalent, and therefore the least dependable, are Public Administration, Private Owners and General Public. Sports Facilities Consulting, School of Sport, Peripheral Network, Official Suppliers and CONI Servizi Board all show the same degree of ambivalence.

6. STAKEHOLDER COMMITMENT TOWARDS OBJECTIVES

Figure 2.7 shows the stakeholders' overall degree of commitment to CONI Servizi's objectives. This commitment can be either positive (i.e. in favour of the objectives) or negative (i.e. not in favour of the objectives). The objectives with the highest overall levels of commitment determine the future of the market and are those for which the stakeholders have to establish cooperation strategies. These objectives are:

- to improve the quality of sports facilities
- to monitor the availability of sports facilities
- to develop knowledge and skills
- to increase participation in sport and facilities usage.

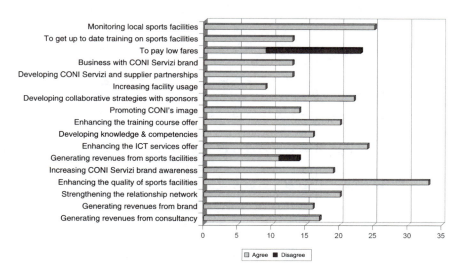

Figure 2.7 Histogram of the commitment of stakeholders to the defined objectives.

Other objectives constitute causes of disagreement in the system, but they concern only a small number of stakeholders. These objectives are:

- to keep prices low
- to generate revenues from managed sports facilities.

This analysis suggests areas in which alliances can be formed based on convergences around objectives. However, recommendations concerning such alliances must also take into account the balances of power between stakeholders.

7. EVALUATE THE BALANCES OF POWER BETWEEN STAKEHOLDERS

The balance of power between the stakeholders in a network is best evaluated using a descriptive approach in which the impact of one stakeholder on another is assessed according to the following scale:

4: 'X' is vital to the existence of 'Y'
3: 'X' is vital to the mission of 'Y'
2: 'X' is vital to the plans of 'Y'
1: 'X' is vital to the management processes of 'Y'
0: 'X' has little influence (is neutral) on 'Y'

Table 2.7 shows the balances of power between the stakeholders in the CONI Servizi network. The most influential stakeholder is National Federations,

Table 2.7 Direct influences of stakeholders

	SFC	OTC	Coninet	SDS	PO	OP	T&P	LSFC	PA	NF	Private	Profess	Customer	Suppl	CS board	Σ direct influence
SFC	0	1	4	2	1	0	2	1	2	0	0	2	1	2	2	20
OTC	0	0	2	0	1	3	0	0	0	2	0	0	1	2	2	13
Coninet	1	0	0	1	1	1	1	0	0	1	0	0	0	0	0	7
SDS	2	2	2	0	0	2	1	2	0	2	0	2	0	0	1	14
PO	0	3	2	3	0	3	1	0	0	1	0	0	0	0	0	11
OP	0	0	1	2	3	0	2	0	2	3	0	0	0	2	0	18
T&P	1	0	0	2	0	0	0	4	2	2	1	0	1	0	0	17
LSFC	2	0	0	2	0	0	0	0	0	0	3	2	0	2	0	14
PA	3	0	3	3	3	0	2	3	0	0	4	3	3	2	0	23
NFs	1	3	0	3	0	3	2	3	2	1	0	1	3	0	1	26
Private	3	0	0	2	0	0	0	3	1	0	0	3	2	2	0	20
Profess	3	0	0	2	0	0	3	3	2	1	2	0	3	3	0	15
Customer	0	4	0	2	0	0	2	0	4	0	4	0	0	2	1	21
Suppl	2	2	2	0	1	0	1	2	2	2	1	2	0	0	0	15
CS board	4	4	2	4	1	2	0	0	0	2	0	0	0	1	0	21
Σ direct dependence	22	20	20	26	11	14	19	20	17	18	15	15	12	19	7	

followed by Public Administration. Conversely, Coninet and Press Office are the least well armed for achieving their objectives and the most subject to pressure from other stakeholders. It is important to remember that balances of power take into account both direct and indirect influences; that is to say, a stakeholder can affect a third party through its influence on an intermediary party.

The direct and indirect influences stakeholders have on each other can be calculated using a diagram such as the one shown in Figure 2.8. Stakeholder status is determined by plotting stakeholder dependence (horizontal axis) against stakeholder influence (vertical axis). Four positions are possible:

- *Dominant stakeholders (upper left quadrant)* can exert strong pressure on other stakeholders without being subject to strong pressures themselves. Dominant stakeholders are mainly external to the system and include Private Owners/Managers and Customers (general facility users). They decide the rules of the game. In addition, CONI Servizi Board occupies an important position as it decides on the actions to be carried out by the organisation's departments.
- *Relay stakeholders (upper right quadrant)* exert influence over some stakeholders and are subject to strong pressures from others. In the CONI Servizi network they form two clusters, one consisting of Public Owners/Managers and National Federations; the other formed by Sports Facilities Consulting, Official Suppliers and Peripheral Network.
- *Dominated stakeholders (lower right quadrant)* have little influence over other stakeholders and are subject to strong pressures. This category includes Professionals, Local Sports Facility Consultants, School of Sport and Coninet. Although the first three members of this group are dominated they occupy a position close to the border with the relay stakeholder segment. In contrast, Coninet occupies a position of strong dependence, isolated at the bottom of the diagram.
- *Autonomous stakeholders (lower right quadrant)* exert little influence but are not subject to much pressure. Press Office and Olympic Preparation are not very interested in sports facility issues; however, Olympic Training Centres should find a more important role in a market that is currently dominated by athletes and National Federations.

When deciding which alliances to strengthen or create, combining descriptive and instrumental analyses allows organisations to take into account influences within the stakeholder system and the degree of convergence around objectives and resources. However, these analyses should be combined with a normative analysis.

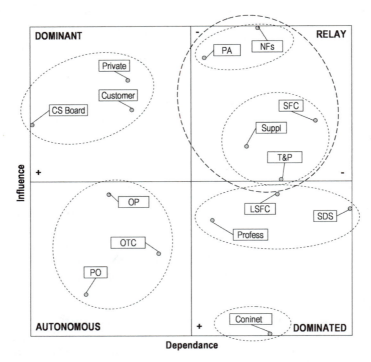

Figure 2.8 Diagram showing the influences and direct and indirect dependences of the stakeholders in the CONI Servizi network.

Normative analysis

Normative analyses enable stakeholders to determine the legitimacy of their stakeholders and their interests. Within sports systems, this legitimacy is mostly derived from an organisation's mission and history. CONI Servizi's mission is to create value for Italian sport:

- via the effective management of the mandate given by CONI
- by enabling CONI to make a financial contribution to national sports federations
- by providing national sports federations with high added value services
- by developing its unique (in Italy) know-how in the sports field and associated disciplines
- by obtaining value from the professional skills of its resources, as well as its facilities.

In order to fulfil its mission, CONI Servizi must concentrate on National Federations and key players in the Italian sports system. As the above analysis showed, National Federations are only relay stakeholders, notably with respect to the private sector and consumers, and their objectives are generally divergent from CONI Servizi's objectives. Despite this, CONI Servizi has to build closer relations with these organisations, as they have a legitimate role to play in fulfilling its mission.

Relationship portfolio analysis

Once an organisation has determined the strategic importance of each of its stakeholders, using the descriptive, instrumental and normative approach described above, it must define the nature and strength of its relationships with its stakeholders so decisions can be made as to whether a relationship should be developed, engaged or terminated.

Assessing the nature and strength of relationships

According to Donaldson and O'Toole (2000: 494), 'both the economic ties and the social bonding of the partners: belief in the spirit of cooperation and trust . . . and actions taken indicate the strength of the relationship'. In practical terms, an organisation must first carry out a quantitative analysis of its relationships with its stakeholders. The simplest way to do this is to draw a diagram showing stakeholder statuses (i.e. end-user, sports organisation internal stakeholder, partner, supplier) and relationships (Figure 2.9).

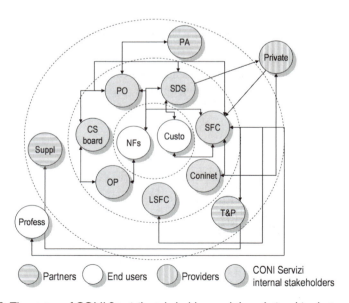

Figure 2.9 The status of CONI Servizi's stakeholders and the relationships between them.

This analysis can be carried out by considering existing relationships to determine the strategic importance and relationship strength of each stakeholder (Figure 2.10).

Next, a qualitative analysis of the relationships between the stakeholders in the network should be carried out based on the variables defined in chapter one. These variables are:

- Stakeholder status
- Loyalty
- Nature of the exchange
- Trust
- Commitment
- Resources provided
- Distance of the exchange
- Benefits linked to the relationship.

The first-order relationships in the CONI Servizi network are summarised in Table 2.8.

It may be useful to also analyse second order relationships (Figure 2.11), in order to consider indirect strategies, that is to say, strategies that will influence one stakeholder and thereby have an indirect effect on another stakeholder.

By combining quantitative and qualitative approaches, it is possible to make strategic recommendations about whether each first order relationship (Table 2.9) should be created, developed or terminated.

Which collaborative programmes and which offer portfolio?

The above-described descriptive, instrumental and normative analyses allow organisations to draw up their relational strategies and to create/modify a stakeholder network. Once this has been done, an organisation must define the programmes and offers needed to activate its network and give the status of each stakeholder. This process falls into the domain of market-oriented

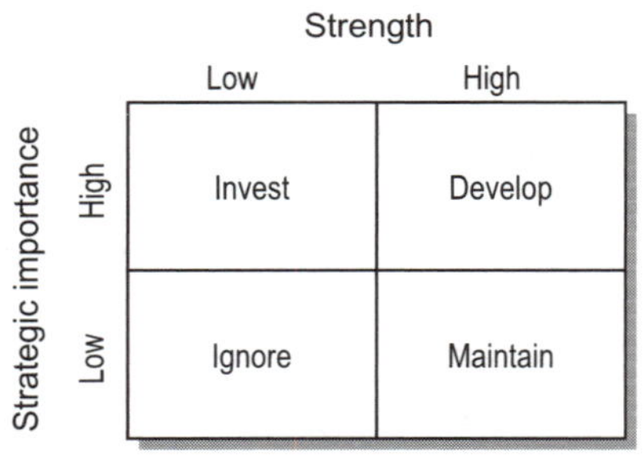

Figure 2.10 Strategic importance and relationship strength

Table 2.8 First order relationships between the stakeholders in the CONI Servizi network (to be filled)

	OTC	Coninet	SDS	PO	OP	T&P	LSFC	PA	NFs	Private	Profess	Customer	Suppl	CS board
Status														
Loyalty														
Nature of the exchange														
Trust														
Commitment														
Resources provided														
Distance of the exchange														
Benefits														

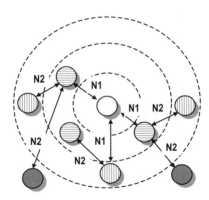

Figure 2.11 Illustration of first (N1) and second (N2) order relationships.

relationship marketing because an offer is always designed to satisfy the expectations of end users and the network. Offers may be devised and delivered with partners who commit resources. It is important to remember that a partner can also be an end user, as in the case of a sponsor who provides services in return for value in kind. For example, Atos Origin, the IOC's worldwide partner for information technology and a sponsor of the IOC's Top Programme, provides computing services for the organisation of the Olympic Games. The company coordinates the contributions made by the IOC's other technology partners and suppliers in order to ensure that the resulting computing service is effective, reliable and capable of providing instantaneous communication for athletes, spectators, organisers, officials, the media, television viewers, and internet users throughout the world. This partnership allows Atos Origin to develop and promote its own skills; therefore, the company is a final beneficiary as well as a partner.

Figure 2.12 illustrates the stages involved in combining network- and market-oriented relationship marketing. A sports organisation must first choose the areas in which it wants to further its marketing actions. For example, a sports club that decides to focus on three strategic areas, athletic performance, education and social change, can choose to combine two complementary pathways. The first takes a market-oriented approach to designing and implementing a programme that will improve the athletic performance of its end users, that is to say, national and international level athletes. The second takes a network-oriented approach to building partnerships with stakeholders (e.g. local authorities, sponsors, schools, etc.) who can provide resources for developing programmes in the domains of education and social change.

In the case of CONI Servizi, the recommendation from Calvani (2007) to SFC would be to introduce a combined market- and network-oriented relational strategy based on the programmes outlined below.

Table 2.9 Recommendations for Sports Facilities Consulting's relationship portfolio

	OTC	Coninet	SDS	PO	OP	T&P	LSFC	PA	NFs	Private	Profess	Customer	Suppl	CSboard
FSC →	Maintain	Develop	Develop	Maintain	Develop	Develop	Develop	Develop	Create and develop	Develop	Develop	Create and develop	Develop	Develop

Source: Adapted from Calvani (2007).

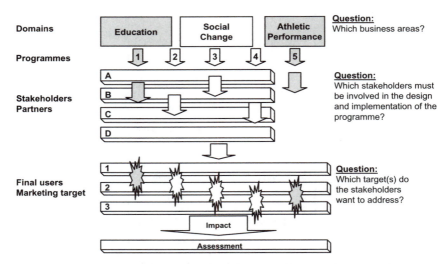

Figure 2.12 Combining market-oriented and network-oriented approaches to a relationship-marketing programme.

PROGRAMME 1: SPORTS FACILITIES CONSULTING + SCHOOL OF SPORT

School of Sport and Sports Facilities Consulting form a tight cluster around the following end goals:

- To generate revenues from consultancy activities and training
- To generate revenues from brand exploitation
- To strengthen the relationship network and strategies between the Italian NOC and CONI Servizi
- To increase CONI Servizi brand awareness
- To enhance the training course offer.

These convergences suggest that Sports Facilities Consulting should merge with School of Sport to create one strong department dedicated to training sports operators.

Common objectives

- To formulate a complete, competitive and up-to-date training-course offer for all parties working in and for sport. The current trend is towards specialization, so it is essential to analyse the market, including from an international perspective, and to evaluate emerging roles and functions
- To enhance the relationships and partnerships with public bodies, universities and research institutes, and to certify the qualifications granted.

Resources

School of Sport: brand name, staff and experience, relationships with national and international organisations involved in education.

Sports Facilities Consulting: staff, technical experience, supplier contacts, sales team.

PROGRAMME 2: SPORTS FACILITIES CONSULTING + PERIPHERAL NETWORK + LOCAL SPORTS FACILITIES + CONSULTANTS + SUPPLIERS

This programme would separate Local Sports Facilities Consulting's non-commercial and commercial advisory services, and create a strong commercial network in a given region (Figure 2.13). Currently, volunteers from CONI's local offices give free basic advice on developing sports facilities. However, they also offer a professional consulting service, which puts them in direct competition with Sports Facilities Consulting. Considering Peripheral Network's opposition to a commercial approach, and in order to avoid misleading customers, the non-commercial and commercial advisory services should be separated.

The non-commercial service would provide free advice on general development plans for local sports facilities, events coordination, general assistance on sports activities and developing a sporting culture. The commercial

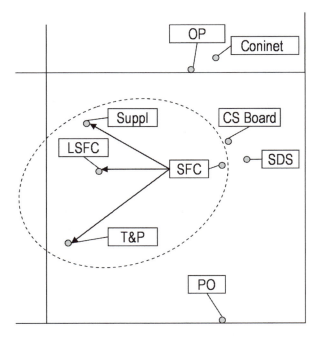

Figure 2.13 Stakeholders involved in programme 2.

advisory service would operate in parallel to give specific technical advice in areas such as the planning and building of new installations and security management. This would require separating Local Sports Facilities Consulting from Peripheral Network and putting it under the supervision of Sports Facilities Consulting. In addition, it is essential to create links between National Federations and Local Consultants to ensure that both parties remain up to date on new sporting rules and regulations governing sports grounds. These links must be maintained and reinforced through regular meetings with suppliers, at which suggestions, new products and development programmes could be shared.

Common objectives
- To generate revenues from consultancy activities
- To strengthen the relationship network and strategies with official sponsors
- To increase CONI Servizi brand awareness
- To monitor the availability of local sports facilities.

Resources
Local Sports Facilities Consulting: global technical experience on sports facilities, detailed knowledge of a region and the availability of facilities.
Official Suppliers: commercial, technical and R&D staff.
Sports Facilities Consulting: tools, training, procedures and supervision.

PROGRAMME 3: SPORTS FACILITIES CONSULTING + SCHOOL OF SPORT + PERIPHERAL NETWORK

The regional Schools of Sport should be unified under the management of the central School. At the moment they come under the auspices of Peripheral Network and Sport Promotion and there is no detailed supervision of their activities (Figure 2.14). If the central School of Sport coordinated all the regional Schools of Sport, it would be possible to develop a generic training offer that avoids overlaps and competition between the centre and the periphery. Italy needs to adopt a single teaching model to ensure a guaranteed level of training for coaches and staff throughout the country. Excellent skills provide a base from which to extend sporting culture, promote healthy lifestyles and obtain good sporting results. Furthermore, School of Sport's capabilities would be enhanced, allowing it to provide tailor-made training 'on demand'.

Common objectives
- To generate revenues from consultancy activities and training
- To develop knowledge and skills
- To enhance the training course offer.

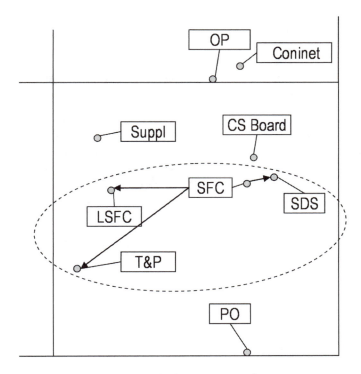

Figure 2.14 Stakeholders involved in programme 3.

Resources
Central School of Sport: expertise and experience, brand name.
Regional Schools: local presence, knowledge of local demand.
Sports Facilities Consulting: coordination and supervision, network capabilities.

PROGRAMME 4: FORMATION OF A COMPANY WITH TEAMS OF PRIVATE CIVIL ENGINEERS AND ARCHITECTS.

To create, in conjunction with other consultancy firms, a company that would be capable of providing worldwide project consulting and of participating in international bids under the CONI Servizi brand. This company could create a network with other international teams in order to expand its sports-facility consultancy services. The network should include the best civil engineers and architects from Italy and abroad, so it becomes a reference in this field throughout the world and especially in the Mediterranean region and Eastern Europe.

Common objectives
- To develop a specific offer
- To generate revenues from consultancy.

Resources
Sports Facilities Consulting: CONI Servizi brand.
Professional: skills.

PROGRAMME 5: ENHANCE 'OFFICIAL SUPPLIER' PRODUCTS THROUGH AN INTEGRATED PROMOTION CAMPAIGN.

CONI Servizi aims to develop co-marketing and cross-selling operations with leading firms in order to create a multiple product/services offer that is tailored to the specific needs of its clients. In addition, an integrated communication plan and joint participation in sector events would help broaden opportunities and increase the range of sponsorship activity targets.

Common objectives
- To generate revenues from consultancy activities
- To strengthen the relationship network and strategies with official sponsors
- To increase CONI Servizi brand awareness.

Resources
Sports Facilities Consulting: technical skills and the brand.
Suppliers: commercial, technical and R&D staff.

PROGRAMME 6: CREATE A SINGLE DEPARTMENT FOR ORGANISING EVENTS.

CONI Servizi's mission is to be the best supplier of services throughout the sports sector; yet, currently, it only provides services in specific areas through its different departments. CONI Servizi could attain its true constellation value by unifying its expertise, experience and network in a single department responsible for organising national and international events. It could then become a world leader in all aspects of event organisation, from technical project studies to project implementation and from facilities improvement to promotional activities. This would send out a strong and very positive signal to National Federations.

Common objective
- To provide a complete consulting service for sports events.

Resources
Sports Facilities Consulting: technical skills.
School of Sport: contacts with NFs and knowledge of their needs.
Olympic Training Centres: sports facilities.

Personalisation of offers

By adopting a network approach, it is possible to develop collaborative programmes that include the design and delivery of services to end-users. Personalisation of the offer is an important factor in building relationships but it is becoming more difficult to achieve, as what were once considered latent expectations of consumers, for example the ability to buy a pre-configured computer or a made-to-measure holiday via internet, have now become standard expectations. In addition, personalisation has a cost in terms of human, technological, logistical and material resources, and this cost may be prohibitive for companies with extremely large consumer bases. For example, some of Europe's largest football clubs have abandoned large-scale personalisation for their millions of spectators and fans throughout the world because of the high cost. This situation is paradoxical in that market-oriented policies require personalised offers but not all sports organisations have sufficient resources to personalise their offers. In some cases, extra resources for this personalisation process may be available within the organisation's network of stakeholders.

As a result, sports organisations must make strategic decisions about which end-users to target with a personalised offer, the form this offer will take and the partners who may be able/willing to contribute resources for creating this offer. The size of the marketing target will determine the extent of the personalisation, which may focus on single people or organisations, or on groups of people or organisations.

Peelen (2005) proposed a classification for the different forms of personalisation based on whether or not the product is modified and on how the personalised offer is presented to the consumer. Peelen's classification describes four types of personalisation: cosmetic, transparent, collaborative and adaptive (Table 2.10). Although this typology was drawn up for products and for

Table 2.10 The different types of personalisation

Type of personalisation	Characteristics
Cosmetic personalisation	The organisation provides a standard service in different ways to consumers who make the same use of the service
Transparent personalisation	The organisation adapts the characteristics of the service, but not its presentation. Thus, each end-user receives a unique product without being aware of its uniqueness
Adaptive personalisation	The organisation provides a standard service that is designed in such a way that users can adapt it according to their needs
Collaborative personalisation	The organisation adapts the product and its presentation. For the offer and its presentation to be valued by consumers, the organisation must keep up to date with its consumers' expectations

Source: Adapted from Peelen (2005).

large-scale personalisation, it focuses on individualised relationships and can therefore be adapted to the services that form the majority of the offers provided by sports organisations.

Sports organisations can map the links between marketing targets (end users), the size of these targets, the forms of personalisation and the partners that provide resources for designing and delivering these offers. Figure 2.15 shows such a map for a professional football club that has adopted different forms of personalisation for different stakeholders. For example, providing its millions of fans with the same information in both computerised and paper forms (with the help of two partners who provide the logistics) is a form of large-scale cosmetic personalisation. Providing its 500 fan clubs with a specially designed service but without explicitly telling them this is a form of transparent personalisation. Each of the 200 companies in its partner club receives a specifically designed package depending on its level of involvement; however, each partner can choose its level of commitment and, if desired, add services (e.g. public relations with a player, company seminars, etc.) if it so wishes. This is a form of adaptive personalisation. Finally, the club offers its three main sponsors a collaborative form of personalisation by developing, in conjunction with the sponsors' marketing departments, unique sponsoring programmes managed by key account managers.

Personalisation requires precise knowledge not only of the client's expectations but also of the history of the relationship; hence, an organisation must develop its listening abilities (empathy) and be capable of acting on what it learns.

What type of relationship to develop with the brand?

A sports organisation usually has one or two brands. In terms of industrial copyright, a brand is a distinctive sign placed on a product or associated with

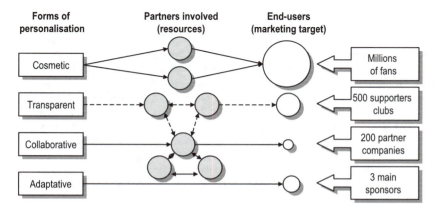

Figure 2.15 Illustration of the different personalisation strategies.

a service in order to differentiate that product or service from its competitors. A brand must have a visual representation – a trademark – that is instantly recognisable, for example, the five rings of the Olympic brand. An organisation must protect its trademark in one or more of the 45 classes[1] of products, in one or more geographical areas and for a definite time. A sports organisation's relational strategy will include the nature of the relationship it wishes to encourage between its brand(s) and its internal and external stakeholders. This may also lead to the creation of relational brands.

What type of relationship with the brand?

Classically, brands are viewed from a market perspective and are seen as a way of developing a relationship between the organisation and its consumers; hence, the brand is a source of value for its consumers. Kapferer (2000) drew up a comprehensive list of the functions of brands for consumers (i.e. personalisation, permanence, hedonism, ethics, etc.). Although these functions are not all equally useful to a sports organisation, the consumer benefits show there is a relation between a brand and the people who use it. The value of a brand is a reflection of the nature and importance of these benefits and of the brand's capacity to satisfy its consumers. When end-users and stakeholders develop a bond with a sport organisation's brand, that brand also becomes a source of value for the sports organisation. According to Kapferer (2000), an organisation can better satisfy the expectations of a segment of its clientele by supplying it in a constant and repeated way with the ideal combination of tangible and intangible, functional and hedonistic attributes, in conditions that are economically viable for it. Thus, a sports organisation can put its stamp on a sector by branding a product. For football fans, FC Barcelona is one of the top ten clubs in Europe. For the club, this means being associated with a product category (i.e. football) and sports events, ensuring that involvement with the club produces benefits (i.e. pleasure, excitement, pride, etc.) and providing competitive advantages in comparison with other clubs.

At the same time, a relationship is built with a club, a relationship is developed with the brand. This relationship concerns all the club's internal and external stakeholders. In fact, sports organisation brands usually reflect the identity of the organisation's network of stakeholders. For example, the Beijing 2008 brand encompasses all the stakeholders connected with the organisation committee for the XXIXth Olympiad and the FC Barcelona brand covers the club's 14 sporting disciplines. Consequently, the brand is also important within the organisation as it can be a unifying force for internal stakeholders, whether they are volunteers, organisation committee staff or part of the club. This is called internal branding. Some organisations create specific brands for internal stakeholders. For example, the organisation committee of the 2006 Winter Olympics in Turin created the 'Noi 2006' brand specifically for its volunteers programme. Figure 2.16 illustrates brand relationships with respect to the three marketing sub-sectors.

Figure 2.16 Brand relationships concern all the sports organisation's stakeholders.

Brand identity, the heart of the brand strategy

A sports organisation must define its foundations (i.e. mission, vision, etc.) and these foundations form the basis for its marketing actions. Where this is the case, it is important to emphasise its relational orientation. After reviewing the work of leading researchers in the branding field (i.e. Aaker, Kapferer, Keller), Lewi (2005) concluded that brand identity is a mental puzzle with three components: associated products or services, the relationship with consumers, and the social role of the brand.

Thus FC Barcelona communicates a specific identity through its slogan 'More than a club', which the club considers to be open-ended in meaning. 'It is perhaps this flexibility that makes it so appropriate for defining the complexities of FC Barcelona's identity, a club that competes in a sporting sense on the field of play, but that also beats, every day, to the rhythm of its people's concerns' (www.fcbarcelona.com).

FC Barcelona is 'more than a club' in Catalonia because it is the sports club that most represents the region and it is one of Catalonia's greatest ambassadors. For different reasons, FC Barcelona is also 'more than a club' for many people living elsewhere in Spain, who see it as a staunch defender of democratic rights and freedom. Today, football has become a global phenomenon and support for Barcelona has spread around the world. The number of club members from outside Catalonia and Spain is increasing daily, and the club wants to respond to that commitment. For 'Barça', this response is essential if it is to meet expectations, and an obligation if it is to fulfil its mission. The club decided that the best way to make this response was to take a step further and become 'more than a club' all over the world; therefore, the idea of FC

Barcelona as a caring and humanitarian organisation needed to be globalised. This strategic decision is in keeping with the club's history and the way that football is continuing to develop worldwide, which is why the club has decided to contribute 0.7 per cent of its ordinary income to the FC Barcelona Foundation, which was set up to develop international development programmes. The FC Barcelona Foundation also supports the UN Millennium Development Goals and has made a commitment to UNICEF's humanitarian aid programmes in the form of an annual donation of €1.5 million for the next five years. In exchange, FC Barcelona has the right to wear the UNICEF logo on its shirts, making it the only club that pays to display a partner's logo.

FC Barcelona's products and services cover the general sporting field and Catalan culture, as well as football. Catalan culture fosters the passionate relationship stakeholders have with the brand, which communicates an image of a club concerned with defending diversity, democracy and liberty. Most importantly, the brand has a powerful social role and that is reflected in the involvement of the club and its stakeholders in the foundation's programmes. This identity shows that FC Barcelona is a relational brand that brings together people who identify with Catalan culture from all over the world.

Brand communities

Muniz and O'Guinn (1996) introduced the concept of brand community to describe 'a specialised, non-geographically bound community, based on a structured set of social relations among admirers of a brand'. Brand communities are based on an affinity linked to a common interest. Modern information and communication technologies have contributed to the rise of these social networks, as they can only form though direct contact between members.

The FC Barcelona brand can be considered a brand community, and community marketing is based on relational strategies. According to Heilbrunn (2003: 491), 'the objective of the tribal (or community) approach is to develop a relationship with the brand based on a shared signification on which the brand's community experience is founded, as well as on the ability to think in terms of significant community, that is to say, the bringing together of individuals around a shared interest, emotion or passion'. Cova and Cova (2001: 71) have described four positions that members of a club can adopt:

1   'Adherents' or devotees of the institution: people who belong to the soccer club: members, volunteers
2   'Participants' in formal and informal gatherings: officials, matches, tours, demonstrations, happenings
3   'Practitioners' or adepts, who have an almost daily involvement in tribal activities: people who play soccer and who have a special bond with the club
4   'Sympathisers' or fellow travellers, who go with the trends: distant fans sharing the same social identity and imagery.

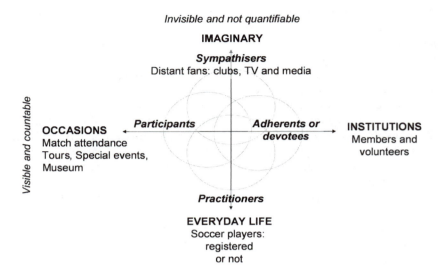

Figure 2.17 Positions adopted by fans of soccer clubs.

In this model (Figure 2.17), physical manifestations of soccer club communities are located on the horizontal or 'visible' axis, which includes actual gatherings, such as tours or away matches, and virtual discussions through the internet. The vertical or 'invisible' axis covers characteristics that come from day-to-day soccer activities, such as playing soccer, as well as from people with similar lifestyles who do not play soccer. These communities/tribes share the values and lifestyles espoused by the club's foundations.

Brand alliances

Network-oriented relationship marketing involves developing strategic alliances between stakeholders. These alliances can take many different forms, including co-branding, licensing contracts or collective brands.

Co-branding consists of two or more brands joining forces to develop or market a product or a service. In marketing terms, the union provides extra benefits for consumers, and the product or service clearly advertises its double paternity. According to Buraud and Boyer (2000), 'co-branding aims to increase the longevity of the brand by enriching its content and image, while enlarging its target consumers and minimising investment in publicity and in research and development'.

Cegarra and Michel (2001) pointed out that co-branding covers various types of brand alliance, for which they have proposed a classification based on the stage in the product's development that the alliance is formed: design, naming or promotion.

Shared development occurs when two organisations combine their expertise to design and/or produce a new product. This type of alliance may result in two different brand strategies: a monolithic strategy where the product is given a different name by each of the two brands, or an endorsement strategy in which a single name is used by both brands. Examples of shared development can be found in high-tech sports, such as Formula 1 car racing.

Co-branding associates a second brand with the sports organisation's brand for one or more products or services and both brands are associated with the product. There are two variants: functional co-branding (Ingredient Branding) and symbolic co-branding. The value created by functional co-branding is linked to the use of the product or service (e.g. the products of official suppliers for sports events), whereas the benefits generated by symbolic co-branding are derived from brand associations (e.g. image sponsoring).

Co-branded products are usually promoted jointly by the two brands, especially in the sports sponsoring field. Partners only pool their resources to develop a publicity or promotional campaign (Samu *et al.*, 1999). This form of cooperation is characterised by both brands being included on all promotional materials (billboards, press adverts, TV commercials, payment cards, etc.), but not on the product itself. Associated advertising (e.g. Visa credit card and the French Olympic and Sports Committee) is distinct from joint promotion (e.g. French railway's strategy for the 2007 Rugby World Cup).

Co-branding strategies require sports organisations to commit resources, which is why they prefer to develop strategic partnerships in the form of licensing contracts. In this form of cooperation, a sports organisation that owns its brand gives another party (the licensee) the right to use the brand, in whole or in part, in exchange for remuneration, which usually consists of a royalty proportional to the use made of the brand.

Licensing, which is very common in the sports sector, is similar to co-branding in that the association between the two brands increases the value for the people the offer is targeted at. In the Olympic movement, which is very active in this field, three entities can accord licenses: Olympic Games organisation committees can give licenses to companies to create souvenirs of the Games; national Olympic committees can sell licenses to produce souvenirs for their own country; and the International Olympic Committee can sell licenses for the whole world in domains such as the cinema, video games and other multimedia products. Licensees pay royalties (usually between 10 and 15 per cent of the product sales revenue) for the right to use Olympic trademarks, imagery or themes.

Collective brands are another type of brand based on cooperation within a network. According to the World Intellectual Property Organisation (WIPO), collective brands are signs indicating the geographical origin, material used, manufacturing method, quality or other aspects of the products or services produced by the companies that use the collective brand. The brand owner can be an organisation to which the producing companies belong, or any other entity, including a public institution or a cooperative. Organisations whose products display a collective brand feel that its recognition and common image provides benefits to its consumers. Sports organisations have developed collective brands in conjunction with their internal stakeholders. For example, the Belgian Football Association (BFA) has introduced the Foot PASS quality assurance system in order to emphasise the importance of having a high-quality youth academy so as to be more efficient in developing home-grown talent. The main goal of professional football clubs' youth academies is to effectively nurture home-grown talent and thereby provide players for the first team. The principles of total quality management espouse continuous improvement of all procedures and a commitment from all stakeholders in order to provide added value. In this context, the BFA aims to guide club and youth academy managers through the process of professionalism. The external stakeholders expect these football academies to adopt a more standardised structure.

How should the marketing system be structured?

Marketing strategy decisions must take into account five key elements: brand foundations, programmes and offers, relationships, stakeholders and brands/ experiences. The implementation of this strategy requires internal organisation, as well as the application of a quality management structure (Figure 2.18). This structure must be managed as a system whose impact depends on the relationships between its constituent elements.

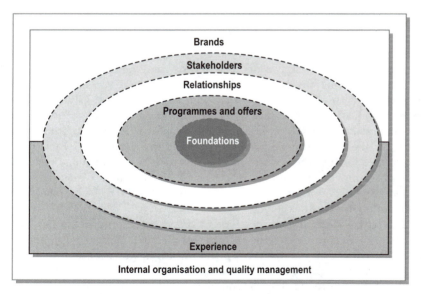

Figure 2.18 Structure of a sports organisation's experiential marketing system.

FC Barcelona's experiential marketing system is outlined in Table 2.11. When brought together, the features and programmes within this system create an experience for FC Barcelona fans. However, for experiential marketing to be most effective, the system must be managed to develop the experiential value given to fans. Despite its history and culture, the club's management has set up a system that is tightly controlled by the marketing

Table 2.11 FC Barcelona's experiential marketing system

Foundations		
	Heritage	• Founded in 1899. Won 24 championship titles in the Copa del Rey • More than a club: the Catalan identity • Tragedy and glory, epic victories and crushing defeats • Catalonia's most difficult years, the flag represented the people's hopes for freedom, and today that flag is the symbolic link which continues to represent the ties between a very special club and its supporters
	Vision and purpose	• To consolidate our place amongst the best and biggest football clubs in the world with our loyal members
	Identity	• Catalan, passion, performance, fair play, non-violence, diversity and tolerance
	Values	• Public spirit, sportsmanship, a sense of accomplishment, solidarity and integrating Catalan nationalism all over the world
Main benefits for club's fans		
		• Forming group identity and a sense of belonging (Catalonia) • Spectacle, emotion and excitement • History and pride
Programmes and offers		
Services related to targeted communities (events and media excluded)	Participants	• Tickets and season tickets • Gent del Barça card • Stadium show entertainment
	Soccer players	• Training • Equipment
	Sympathisers	• FCB Gents Socios Carnet • Fan Club packages
	Members	• Membership card (right to vote)
	For all	• Merchandise products (eight Barça shops in Spain and online) • FC Barcelona Supporter Services Office (Staff 50) • FC Barcelona Premium Zone (e-mail account at @fcbarcelona.com, exclusive videos, etc.) • Barça museum

Table 2.11 Continued

Events	Members	• Festive events in collaboration with fan club association • Fan club annual meeting
	Sympathisers	• Asian Tour 2004
	Soccer players	• Nothing
	Participants	• Stadium show (for UEFA Champions League)
Facilities		• Camp Nou stadium – 98,125 seats, built in 1957 • Ciutat Esportiva (training facilities) • 'La Masia' young players' academy • Palau Blaugrana (Club sports hall) • Miniestadi used by Barca's reserve teams. • Ice Skating Rink • Museum • Eight shops in Spain
People		• Top players, nine countries and four continents • Meeting with fan clubs • Forums on club website
Communi-cation	Website	• In Catalan, Spanish, English, Chinese and Japanese • Mailing list, video gallery, live audio, forum, chat (including player participation) • Milan AC Community (Italian and English)
	TV and radio	*TV Barça* (satellite TV, FCB production)
	SMS	In partnership with Telefónica Movistar
	Magazine	*Barça* (monthly)
	Publicity	Media guides with the best players

Licensing and merchandising

• Both merchandising and licensing
• 25 licensee companies

Co-branding

• FC Barcelona Premium Zone with Terra (web portal)
• With Telefónica Movistar (SMS service)
• With Caxia Bank (buying tickets using cash dispensers)
• With Real Automobile Club Catalonia (travel agency for fans)
• With Sanita Insurance (medical check in Camp Nou)

Social programmes

Fundació Futbol Club Barcelona (created in 1994) is a cultural charity foundation that mainly operates in Catalonia. Its main aim is the non-profit diffusion and promotion of the sporting, cultural and social dimensions of Futbol Club Barcelona as part of the sporting and cultural community of society in general

department, which defines strategy, implements the operational processes related to the marketing action for each segment and manages the brand. In order to meet the expectations of the various communities, the club has appointed project managers to develop offers and control processes. The club focuses on season ticket holders, spectators, sympathisers and players, and runs a worldwide supporters' service.

Conclusion

This chapter described a method and associated tools for making marketing decisions that sports organisations can use in order to draw up and implement a relationship-marketing strategy. To do this, an organisation must answer the following five questions:

1 What are the relational foundations on which the organisations' marketing actions are based?
2 Which relational strategy should be implemented?
3 Which offer portfolio?
4 What type of relationship should be developed with the brand?
5 Which experiential marketing system should be adopted?

The answers to these questions will lead an organisation to combine its network, market and internal marketing strategies in order to create competitive advantages based on its resources and relationships. Morgan (2000) identified three steps in the evolution of an organisation's relationships: creating a relationship, building resource-based competitive advantages and developing and maintaining valuable networks. Sports organisations should follow the process outlined in Figure 2.19.

Internal marketing is vital to the construction of collaborative relationships, as are the resources provided by the organisation and its partners. Morgan (2000) grouped an organisation's resources into seven categories (financial,

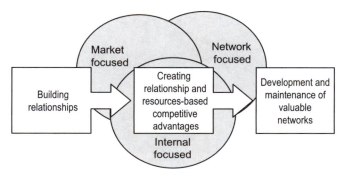

Figure 2.19 The three steps in a relationship-marketing strategy.

physical, legal, human, organisational, relational and informational). He also pointed out that collaborative relationships bring more resources into the network; therefore, the flow of resources in collaborative programmes must be analysed.

Peppers and Rogers (2004) considered collaborative learning relationships to be the crux of managing customer relationships in market-oriented marketing. Organisations build these relationships by obtaining information from their consumers that will enable them to provide offers that will induce loyalty. 'The learning relationship works like this: if you are my customer and I get you to talk to me, I remember what you tell me, and I get smarter and smarter about you. I know something about you that my competitors don't know. So I can do things for you my competitors can't do, because they don't know you as well as I do. Before long, you can get something from me you can't get anywhere else, for any price. At the very best, you'd have to start all over somewhere else, but starting over is more costly than staying with me' (Peppers and Rogers, 2004: 20). This strategy involves the personalisation of the relationship and requires organisations to increase their ability to elicit and manage useful information. This concept can be extended to the relationships between external and internal stakeholders.

Peelen (2005) pointed out that relationship-oriented organisations adopt a more long-term view than transaction-oriented organisations, as the former organisations' marketing strategies are designed to develop special relationships with the end-users of their services and stakeholders. This requires good organisation based on contacts with people and a system for managing internal and external resources that is oriented towards satisfying stakeholder expectations. Such strategies are based on values and require a relational culture.

Chapter 3

Issues in implementing a relationship-marketing strategy

Once an organisation has drawn up a relationship-marketing strategy, the next stage is to implement the decisions and actions contained within that strategy. The implementation methods used will depend on the sub-system (i.e. market, network, or internal) being targeted. This chapter illustrates and explores the processes and tools organisations can use to improve their relationships, constellation and functional values through relationship marketing, and to provide greater experiential value to all the parties involved.

This is a real challenge for most sports organisations. In order to provide a quality service, they must change their culture, allocate human, financial and technological resources, recruit partners, and introduce new processes. Such an evolution can only be achieved in stages and organisations must accept that there may be failures as well as successes along the way. There are many different ways in which relationship strategies can be implemented to improve the probability of success.

Figure 3.1 shows how the orientation of a French professional basketball club's relationship-marketing strategy has evolved. The first step was to set up a consumer database that would allow the club to better target its services by joining forces with sponsors for co-marketing operations. This strategy was reinforced in the second step, in which the club introduced a club card that gave members discounts when purchasing the goods or services of most of the club's sponsors. Internally, the club carried out actions to promote the

Figure 3.1 Evolution of a French professional basketball club's relationship-marketing orientation.

project and improve quality. The third and final step was the introduction of a CRM system and the launch of electronic ticketing. The club extended its collaborative programmes with its partners in order to carry out joint operations with social (e.g. introductory courses for schools and local associations) and commercial (e.g. promotional events with sponsors) end goals. Internally, staff and volunteers were involved in the setting up of quality assurance processes.

Organisations that apply this approach will encounter obstacles and setbacks, so change will not be linear. However, the value of this approach has been demonstrated by organisations, such as USA Taekwondo, which used relationship marketing to re-launch the development of the Association.

Case study: Innovative marketing – USA Taekwondo

David Stotlar, Director, School of Sport and Exercise Science, University of Northern Colorado
Bob Gambardella (former CEO, USA Taekwondo) Director, Sport Partnerships, United States Olympic Committee
Monica Paul (formerly with USA Taekwondo) USA Volleyball

Case focus:

The focus of the case is the marketing tactics and strategies of USA Taekwondo, the National Governing Body (NGB) for the sport of taekwondo in the USA. Due to financial concerns and the mismanagement of the United States Taekwondo Union, the United States Olympic Committee decided to restructure the NGB. A new Board of Directors, with a new CEO, was appointed to take over the management of the newly formed USA Taekwondo. The challenge was to integrate marketing and management to increase membership and attain financial sustainability. The new CEO took over the management of USA Taekwondo and developed new marketing strategies and secured new marketing partners. The focus of the strategy was to develop relationship-marketing elements integrating members and marketing partners.

Case diagnosis:

In 2004, USA Taekwondo embarked on an innovative marketing strategy in an effort to revitalise the organisation after years of mismanagement. Membership numbers were low and the revenues from marketing partners (sponsors) were minimal. The important aspect of this case is that multiple relationship-marketing elements were implemented simultaneously to achieve success.

Pitts and Stotlar (2007: 69) defined sports marketing as 'the process of designing and implementing activities for the production, pricing, promotion and distribution of a sport product to satisfy the needs and desires of consumers and to achieve the company's goals'. Because USA Taekwondo is a 'business', it needs to survive. The survival of any business relies on meeting the needs of consumers. For USA Taekwondo consumers exist in two distinct areas – members and corporate partners. The result was a marketing focus where the organisation needed to market itself to potential members (individuals and affiliated clubs) and to marketing partners (sponsors). The strategy of choice was relationship marketing.

Ultimately, priority was given to meeting member needs so that USA Taekwondo could attract and maintain members. Second, if the membership figures increased, the organisation would have greater power to attract marketing partners through sponsorship.

To accomplish these goals, USA Taekwondo needed a well-defined marketing plan. This case study demonstrates how USA Taekwondo developed specific marketing tactics to meet their objectives. Through the techniques of relationship marketing, the organisation became more athlete-centred, focusing on the interactions between members and the organisation.

Case development:

Because the old NGB (United States Taekwondo Union) was restructured by the USOC, USA Taekwondo's first challenge was identity and brand development. As a result, a new logo was developed (see Figure 3.2) where the five coloured points of the star represent both the colours of the Olympic rings and the five tenets of taekwondo (courtesy, integrity, self-control, perseverance and indomitable spirit). USA Taekwondo CEO Bob Gambardella commented to the media, 'As we continue to increase our marketing efforts on behalf of taekwondo athletes in the U.S., we felt that it was necessary to modernize our image as an organisation. An organisation's name and logo are its most visible images. We also feel that our new logo has a very modern look while adhering to the ideals that make the sport of taekwondo unique'. This re-branding of

Figure 3.2 USA Taekwondo logo.

the organisation was essential for all stakeholders, as it represented the new organisation and the new direction. The USA Taekwondo logo was unveiled on a variety of merchandise for organisation members. Not only did the re-designed logo provide publicity for the new direction of the organisation, the sale of merchandise provided significant revenues as well.

In order to attract and maintain members, in 2005 and 2007 USA Taekwondo instituted data-driven research through the Sports Marketing Research Institute at the University of Northern Colorado to secure member data and determine member service shortfalls. The data revealed that the membership of USA Taekwondo is predominantly male (66 per cent of respondents), Caucasian/white (61.1 per cent of respondents), affluent (35.2 per cent of respondents have an annual household income of over US$100,000), and highly educated (49.6 per cent of respondents have at least a college degree). Further, they are likely to be married (57 per cent of respondents) with two or fewer children living at home (45.4 per cent of respondents). They are typically homeowners (64 per cent of respondents) and frequent internet users (89 per cent of respondents make purchases via the internet).

This data was essential in helping USA Taekwondo attract sponsors because many corporations would like to develop relationships with this consumer segment. Other data in the report showed that members are very loyal to the organisation, with 84 per cent of respondents indicating that they are at least 'likely' to purchase a product from a USA Taekwondo sponsor. This is significant because 73 per cent of respondents spend an average of between US$50 and US$500 per month on taekwondo-related goods and services. Of particular importance, the data showed that the membership values travel discounts most highly and many indicated that they want to travel to Korea on a taekwondo-related trip. This would be quite valuable information for the organisation in attempting to acquire an airline sponsor. Another highly rated member benefit was 'discounts on taekwondo apparel'. Thus the organisation could gain revenues through its own merchandising programme and could extend the opportunity for profits to its apparel and equipment sponsors.

USA Taekwondo affiliated clubs ranked 'liability insurance' as the most valued benefit for joining USA Taekwondo. By joining together many previously unaffiliated clubs, USA Taekwondo could bundle customers for an insurance broker and reduce costs to member clubs. Clubs also valued the marketing assistance provided in the USA Taekwondo Success Kit. The Success Kit was developed through a partnership with the Martial Arts Industry Association (MAIA). MAIA is an organisation of companies and clubs focused on growing the martial arts industry. In partnership with USA Taekwondo, the Success Kit provided professionally created advertisements and marketing materials for use in a variety of media. Thus, small taekwondo clubs had access to high quality ads to increase their membership. USA Taekwondo benefited by attracting more new members, and MAIA benefited because its business partners had a broader market for taekwondo products and services (win-win-win).

Another innovative marketing strategy was the USA Taekwondo Awards. This programme was intended to recognise the efforts of USA Taekwondo members and to bring additional publicity to the organisation. Awards include: USA Taekwondo Award for Excellence, Athlete of the Year (Senior and Junior levels for both males and females), Referee of the Year, Coach of the Year, Volunteer of the Year, Lifetime Service Award and the Directors Leadership Award. When the awards were announced, taekwondo received considerable publicity through the media. This process got the membership more involved in the organisation and also generated positive attachments.

With member service as a significant marketing goal, USA Taekwondo developed and enhanced its website. The timing of the website development was perfect. In the early 2000s, more people began to use the World Wide Web for personal information management. Thus, the organisational member benefits matched well with increased web usage. USA Taekwondo was therefore able to make member registration, tournament information, team and organisational publicity, and sponsor recognition more accessible.

The final element was a restructuring of USA Taekwondo events. Six new events were added to the national schedule. This allowed more members to participate in qualification events, allowed sponsors better access to organisation members and added revenues to the organisation. Again, USA Taekwondo research assisted in this process. The Sports Marketing Research Institute at the University of Northern Colorado conducted an economic impact study at one of the major events and found that the event had a US$6 million impact in the community via hotel bookings and community spending. These data were used to entice other cities to bid for championship events. In this market condition, USA Taekwondo could leverage the impact to reduce expenses. One very creative element that was added was the creation of an event equipment truck (Figure 3.3) displaying event schedules and sponsor graphics to deliver equipment to all major events. Again, this provided a service to the organisation, event managers, members and sponsors.

Case results:

By 2007, USA Taekwondo's relationships with its members had improved significantly and revenues from sponsorship had increased by more than 100 per

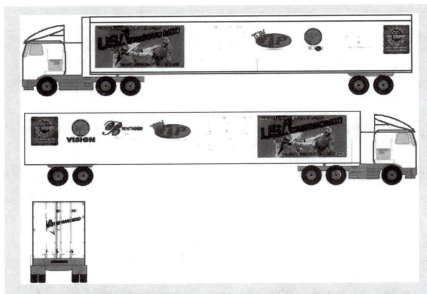

Figure 3.3 USA Taekwondo graphic truck.

cent. All of the key stakeholders were targeted through relationship-marketing efforts. Most critical were members of the organisation. Relationships were built through communications via the website and newsletters. Member services were improved through events and merchandising. Member clubs received add-itional marketing assistance through cooperation with MAIA. Advances in membership also allowed the organisation to increase sponsorships. Sponsor relations also improved because the organisation served as the connecting point between sponsors and their target markets. Collectively, these results provided a sustainable financial base for the organisation. Overall, the organisa-tion went from a deficit of US$1.3 million to a situation of financial stability.

The improved website offered new consumers an opportunity to enrol as members, as well as affording existing members access to their membership information. News, highlights and special offers were also posted to the web. Organisational research indicated that 90.3 per cent of the athletes, coaches, officials and parents surveyed replied that they would like to have advance schedules for upcoming competitions. As a result, tournament competition schedules were uploaded to the website as soon as possible prior to events, providing a better service to members. Another popular service of the enhanced website was the posting of tournament results. The website also helped increase the sale of USA Taekwondo and event-specific merchandise.

Because the research showed that 56 per cent of USA Taekwondo members spend an average of 1–2 hours per week reading taekwondo-related publications, a newly developed sponsor-supported newsletter was extremely successful. Not only did sponsor advertising underwrite the cost of the newsletter, but the newsletter also served as a benefit for members and also helped sponsors sell more of their product to USA Taekwondo members and clubs.

The improved relationships with its membership allowed USA Taekwondo to seek and secure more marketing partners through an invigorated sponsorship programme. Previously the US Taekwondo Union had few sponsors. Through the new marketing structure, USA Taekwondo was able to increase the number of sponsors and to double revenues.

Sponsor recognition research revealed that event participants were very successful in recalling event sponsors. The recognition rates ranged from 43 per cent to a high of 78 per cent. These results compare very favourably to other sporting events and proved quite valuable in sponsorship renewal.

USA Taekwondo's approach is very business-oriented. The success of its relationship strategy is based on six lines of action: corporate identity, data driven research, success kit for clubs, liability insurance (joint marketing), USA Taekwondo awards and website. These lines of actions and their effects are summarised in Figure 3.4.

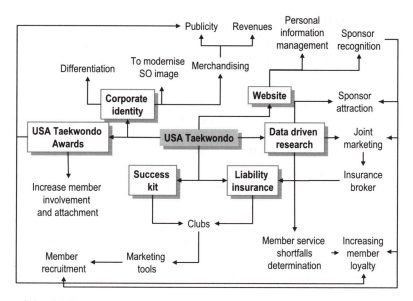

Figure 3.4 USA Taekwondo marketing actions.

USA Taekwondo's actions had an impact on all three sub-systems:

- In the market sub-system, the re-definition of the corporate identity allowed the organisation to stand out from its competitors and the data-driven research enabled it to identify its consumers.
- In the network sub-system, increasing the number of members, and gaining detailed knowledge of their socio-demographic characteristics and their consumer universes allowed the organisation to introduce joint-focus marketing operations with its partners. This had a positive effect on loyalty and the recruitment of new members.
- In the internal sub-system, the values associated with the corporate identity and the USA Taekwondo Awards, allowed the organisation to strengthen members' involvement and attachment. In addition, the Success Kit enabled clubs to improve the effectiveness of their marketing actions.

This example shows that individual lines of marketing action are part of a global system formed by the three relationship-marketing sub-systems. Methods and tools for implementing relationship-marketing strategies in each of these sub-systems are described below. In order to provide an easy-to-follow introduction to this system, the methods applicable to each sub-system are presented in turn. These methods and tools are illustrated by examples from a wide range of organisations operating in different countries.

Market-based relationship strategies

Relationship marketing involves adapting the offer to the characteristics of the people for whom it is destined. Analytical relationship marketing allows an organisation to improve its knowledge of the people with whom it comes into contact (e.g. use of the service, information requests, participation in promotional operations, etc.) and to evaluate this information in order to develop its relationship with the people targeted. Operational marketing is designed to strengthen relationships in order to encourage loyalty (defensive objective) and increase recruitment (offensive objective).

Analytical relationship marketing

Information as a strategic resource

In order to personalise its relationships, an organisation must have accurate information about the expectations of the people concerned. In this context, information becomes a strategic resource. Sources of information (Figure 3.5) can be classified into three categories:

- Information from clients and prospects
- Information produced by market research
- Information from loyalty-building actions.

INFORMATION FROM CLIENTS AND PROSPECTS

This consists of relationship data based on records of a sports organisation's interactions with its clients. The CRM systems required to obtain this information require specific technological resources. Most sports organisations have a deficit in this domain and this is a weakness because this type of information can be used to design defensive actions that will reduce the number of people leaving the organisation.

Clients can also tell a sports organisation what they want or need, thereby giving information that is needed to build loyalty. Peppers and Rogers (2004) believe that 'collaborative learning relationships' constitute a competitive advantage. This advantage is obtained by creating a personalised relationship of trust and by increasing the ability of staff to elicit information and to identify and manage useful information. It is important to take into account complaints and to consider dissatisfied consumers as important collaborators because they provide precious information that an organisation can use to increase its knowledge about its 'end users' and thereby improve the quality of its service and adapt its relationships.

INFORMATION FROM MARKET RESEARCH

Market research is an essential source of information because it can be used to resolve specific problems and to monitor the results of actions taken. It is also

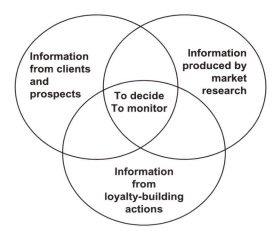

Figure 3.5 Sources of information for sports organisations.

an important decision-making tool, as it provides valuable information on which decisions can be based, as well as feedback on the impact of marketing actions. However, before carrying out a market survey, it is important to collect and study existing data in order to pinpoint the problem to be resolved and to focus objectives.

INFORMATION FROM LOYALTY-BUILDING ACTIONS

Reactions to actions designed to strengthen relationships and build loyalty must be carefully evaluated. Sports organisations can achieve this in a number of different ways, such as invitations to an event, competitions, direct marketing operations or loyalty programmes. The reactions of the people concerned (e.g. participation, request for information, registration, purchase, etc.) should be added to the database in order to build a profile of each person that can be used to personalise the relationship.

Retention actions, which are designed to keep a consumer in the organisation as long as possible, must de separated from development actions, which aim to increase a consumer's total expenditure, most notably through the use of cross sales. Peelen (2005) stressed that, from a relationship point of view, these objectives can only be achieved by answering two questions.

Who are the people likely to leave a sports organisation and who may be persuaded to remain by a personalised contract?

In order to answer this question it is necessary to define the criteria that can be used to determine whether or not a person has ended his/her relationship with the organisation. This may seem simple when a membership is not renewed, but it is more difficult to judge in the case of spectators that come to two or three matches per year and who decide to no longer come to the stadium because they prefer to watch on television.

If no data is available, an organisation should carry out an exploratory study of consumers who leave, in order to identify the explanatory variables and incorporate them into a predictive model. This requires data (i.e. members, registered players, etc.) that can be used to study profiles and draw up a typology that will allow an organisation to take anticipatory action for people with the same characteristics. This work is easier when consumers have numerous interactions with the organisation and these interactions are recorded in a database. It is also possible to carry out telephone interviews with consumers who leave in order to determine why they left.

Who are the people who the organisation should offer an associated product or service in order to strengthen the relationship with the organisation and its partners?

The relationship between a consumer and a sports organisation can be strengthened by offering other products or services. Crié (2002) uses the term 'loyalty-inducing' products and services. This requires knowledge of the consumption universe of the people concerned so offers that provide extra value can be identified. USA Taekwondo adopted such a strategy in the form of cross selling, that is to say, selling services to consumers who already buy at least one other service. When this is done as part of a network approach, it should include joint marketing operations.

Develop an information system

A sports organisation has numerous ways of obtaining information, the difficulties lie in recording, processing and selecting the information needed for marketing actions and in combining information from different sources. The organisation must build a 'data model' that defines the structure of the database and that provides a template for how information will be organised and analysed. Figure 3.6 shows an information system that can be used

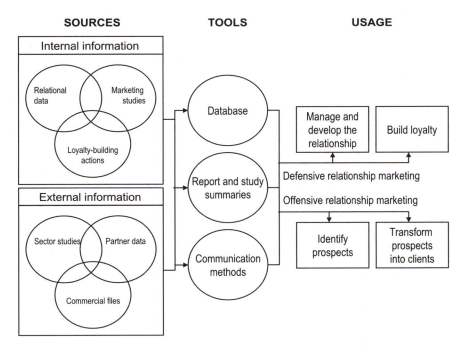

Figure 3.6 Information system for marketing.

to reproduce and manage the interactions between a sports organisation and its consumers and users. This system has three fields: information sources, information processing tools and information use with respect to the marketing action.

SOURCES OF INFORMATION

Internal sources of information consist of relationship data (e.g. history of interactions between consumers and the sports organisation), data from loyalty-building actions (e.g. membership of a loyalty programme, type of response to co-marketing actions) and market research data (e.g. market, competition). Table 3.1 presents a French professional basketball club's internal and external sources of information.

INFORMATION STORAGE AND PROCESSING TOOLS

Information must be recorded in a single database, with information about each person arranged in rows and columns that correspond to the different categories of data (e.g. socio-demographic characteristics, expectations, responses to marketing actions, history of transactions, etc.). Analyses of columns of data can then be used to reveal similarities and differences in expectations and in responses to marketing actions. They indicate what people want and allow the organisation to meet these expectations. Analyses of rows of data can be used to design the most appropriate actions to optimise the quantity and quality of the interactions and transactions with each person. This relates to

Table 3.1 Internal and external sources of information of a French professional basketball club

Internal sources of information	External sources of information
• Supporters list with socio-demographic data, status (member or not), segment to which each supporter belongs, membership of the loyalty-building programme and the mailing list, list of transactions with the club, communication methods used and events (e.g. birthday)	• Surveys of the sports and basketball markets published in the specialist press
• Prospects list, including promotional operations, publicity with couponing, participation in events, etc.	• Files of the club's partners (e.g. travel agency, temp agency, chain of sports shops, fast food chain)
• Survey data: match attendance, satisfaction, perceived quality, etc.	• The telephone directory can be used to target a geographical area for direct marketing campaigns
• Market research data (e.g. characteristics of competitors, offers, prices, communication, distribution, name recognition, image and strong and weak points)	• Purchase of commercial data files for certain promotional operations

'lifetime value'; therefore, it is important to accurately identify the expectations and behaviour of the targeted person in order to provide the most appropriate marketing responses.

Some of the information provided by market research and sector surveys cannot be included in the database. This information should be summarised in the form of computerised reports or files (Word, PowerPoint, etc.). Sports organisations also dispose of a certain number of marketing action tools, which will be presented in the section on operational aspects.

USE OF INFORMATION

Technology can also be used to reduce the time between information processing and decision-making. Data must be used for both offensive and defensive actions. Offensive actions include identifying prospects in order to turn them into consumers, whereas defensive actions involve strengthening relationships with consumers in order to build loyalty. The London Marathon and Rugby Football Union cases studies illustrate these strategies.

From a one-to-one relationship to strategic segmentation

In an ideal world, sports organisations would be able to manage relationships on a one-to-one basis. However, this type of interactive marketing requires substantial human and technological resources, as well as changes to the whole marketing process (Peppers and Rogers, 2004). For example, when a football club creates a system for communicating with its consumers by e-mail, not only does it have to employ enough staff to be able to reply within 24 hours, it also has to introduce systems for processing this information and implementing the resulting actions. As McKenna (1998: 66) pointed out, 'consumers look for a product that suits their needs, but they also want the company to show them that it takes into account their individuality in all its contacts with them.'

These conditions can be met when managing a small number of contacts, such as sponsors, for whom a key account manager can be appointed. It is much more difficult, or even impossible, to individualise relationships with large numbers of people. Sports organisations that want their marketing actions to stand out without having to provide every person with an individualised offer divide the market into segments. Segmentation involves using a number of criteria to divide the market into sub-groups of similar consumers. Hence, an organisation can choose to target certain segments and adopt its marketing actions to suit the characteristics of the people in those segments. In addition, some sports organisations have adopted a niche-marketing approach by focusing their actions on a small target group with very specific characteristics. This was done by the International Federation of Basque Pelota (FIPB), which was founded in Buenos Aires (Argentina) on

19 May 1929 and that now consists of 26 national federations, mostly from Spanish-speaking countries.

The segmentation procedure has three main phases:

- A survey phase, which is divided into stages. The first stage consists of individual or focus group interviews to evaluate behaviour, motivations, expectations, etc. The second stage involves the analysis of this data in order to draw up a questionnaire for use in the second phase.
- An analysis phase, in which typological analyses are performed in order to divide consumers into different segments on the basis of one or more segmentation variables. The characteristics of the people in each segment should be as similar as possible and the differences between segments should be as great as possible.
- A description phase, in which the characteristics of each segment are defined using descriptive variables. In general, each segment is given a name that reflects its essential and differentiating characteristics.

The pertinence of the segmentation depends on the segmentation variables chosen during the analysis phase. Generally, these variables are divided into two categories: intrinsic characteristics of the people concerned (i.e. socio-demographic, geographic, psychographic, etc.) and their responses (i.e. purchases, advantages sought, usage mode, etc.). The most commonly used segmentation variables are socio-demographic and geographic characteristics, lifestyle and desired advantages.

For a segmentation to be fully operational it must allow specific actions to be taken for each strategic segment. Many different segmentation variables are available, each of which has its advantages and disadvantages. The most important variables that can be used in a relationship-marketing approach to define segments or describe the resulting segments are listed below. These are the variables that characterise the relationship with the sports organisation and its brand. Variables that should be considered for the market sub-system include:

- Status (i.e. buyer or non-buyer), purchase circumstances (i.e. ordinary, special)
- Loyalty, which can be both functional and emotional
- Benefits sought (i.e. functional, social, emotional, psychological)
- Distance of the exchange (i.e. intimate, face to face, distant, no contact)
- Trust and involvement
- Type of relationship with the organisation and the vectors used (wheel).

Olympique Lyonnais football club has divided its supporters into six segments on the basis of behavioural loyalty (number of matches watched at the ground) and emotional loyalty (attachment to the club). These six segments are listed below and illustrated in Figure 3.7.

- Season ticket holders
- Regular spectators, who attend more than half the club's league games
- Opportunists, who only go to important matches
- Distant supporters, who watch matches on television and who follow the club through the media and the club's website
- TV switchers, who are only interested in clubs that are doing well and who watch Olympique Lyonnais matches when the club is at, or near, the top of the league
- The disillusioned, who have been disappointed by the club and reject it.

Operational market-based relationship marketing

The data provided by the analytical phase can be used to determine which type of action should be taken to create or strengthen relationships with the target population. However, before the operational phase is launched, the foundations of the marketing action must be defined.

Defining the foundations of the marketing action

Relationship-oriented marketing actions are based on three elements.

Marketing targets and communication targets

Targeting is directly linked to the strategic segmentation. Marketing targets are those people to whom it is wished to sell a product or a service (i.e. season-ticket, membership of a club, etc.), or to those who it is wished to actively

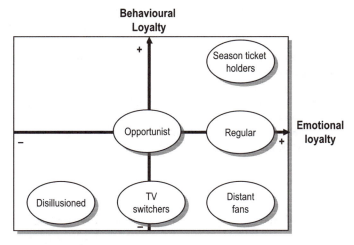

Figure 3.7 Segmentation of OL fans.

involve in a programme (i.e. volunteer, co-marketing, etc.). Communication targets are the people to whom communication actions or programmes are directed. A communication target may have an impact on a marketing target. For example, the Olympic Health Foundation wanted to involve children and parents (marketing target) in its action programme. To do this, the Belgian Interfederal Olympic Committee carried out a press-relations action to encourage journalists (communication target) to promote the initiative, and an information action for doctors (communication target) to encourage them to discuss sport and health with parents and children.

Type of relationship with the target

A relationship can be one-to-one (i.e. involving personalised treatment), distant (i.e. providing information to a large number of people at the same time), or collective (i.e. social bonding). These three categories highlight two important dimensions of a relationship: distance and the number of people involved. Different tools are suited to developing different types of relationship (e.g. direct marketing for one-to-one relationships, television for communicating with large numbers of people, and public relations for social bonding). The most suitable media mix can be determined using Peppers and Rogers' (2004) Preferred Media Package because each person uses several media channels for contacting and obtaining information from sports organisations.

Push or pull tactics

Sports and brands do not all have the same degree of attractiveness for the people targeted. For example, football is the most attractive sport for young boys living in Europe. Consequently, professional football clubs often use 'pull' tactics to attract members of their marketing target to the organisation and its offers. Football clubs rely in particular on widely broadcast events. However, most sports do not have the same degree of attractiveness as football; therefore, they tend to employ 'push' tactics to recruit members. Push tactics require an aggressive approach in which events, direct marketing and sales promotions are used to create contacts with targets. They allow organisations to increase their social impact at a local level, while creating and developing a strong relationship with their members. Strategies can also use a combination of push and pull tactics.

The choice of marketing tools and the implementation process: Links with CRM

A wide variety of marketing tools are available. In each case, the most appropriate tools will depend on the type of relationship an organisation wishes to create with its targets, with different tools being particularly appropriate for each of the three types of relationship. For example, the most suitable tools for creating and developing a one-to-one relationship are personal selling, counter sales, direct marketing, direct sales, telemarketing, consumer contact management and e-mail. When the aim is to provide information to as many people as possible, printed material, advertising, press relations, product placement and sales promotion are more suitable tools. Finally, the most effective tools for social bonding between groups of people are sports events and public relations (Figure 3.8).

However, other tools may be more appropriate in situations where these three types of relationship interact:

• Point of sale (POS), internet, promotions, merchandising and coupons can be used to address a large number of people prior to establishing a personalised relationship. For instance, a well-referenced and multi-lingual website can be used to contact people all over the world (e.g. AC Milan's site has been translated into six languages, Italian, English, Portuguese, Japanese, Chinese and Spanish). Websites enable clubs to identify supporters and to collect personal data through registration for direct e-mail contact with the club or to chat with players.

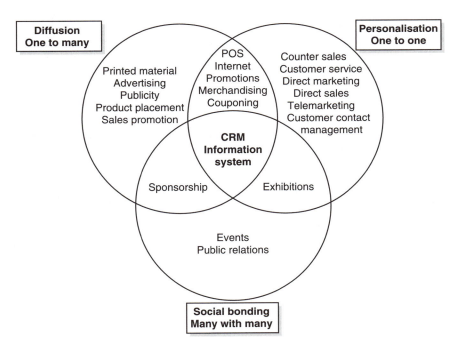

Figure 3.8 Typology of marketing tools with respect to the type of relationship with the target.

- Exhibitions lie at the intersection of one-to-one relationships and social bonding because they allow organisations to contact individual targets and these contacts can be used to create or strengthen personal ties or to promote social bonding. When a sports club takes part in an exhibition aimed at developing a sport in a city, it will have direct contact with people interested in that sport. This contact can then be activated by a personalised e-mail to invite contacts to a competition organised by the club.

- Sponsoring lies at the intersection of diffusion and social bonding. Sponsors increase their name recognition and improve their image by placing their names and brands on products and promotional materials. At sports arenas, sponsors are in direct contact with the participants and spectators and they can therefore develop relationships with them.

CRM and, more generally, marketing information systems are at the intersection of the three types of relationship. These tools allow organisations to collect and analyse information from different sources, thereby contributing to the construction of 'learning relationships'. They also help improve the efficiency of the service, allowing sports organisations to do more with fewer resources.

Peppers and Rogers (2004) suggest that success is linked to the good management of 'touchpoints' between the organisation and the people concerned. This involves introducing a series of actions that form a process that will produce the desired result. Each targeted person has a preferred type of interaction. For example, some season-ticket holders prefer communicating with the club via e-mail, rather than face-to-face. Others prefer to have direct contact with the club's staff. It is important for organisations to identify what Peppers and Rogers (2004) termed the 'Preferred Media Package', which allows an organisation to understand the behaviour and expectations of each target by establishing a dialogue. 'Each interaction is not only a chance to build a deeper Learning Relationship with each consumer, but also a chance to gain important information from a consumer that is unavailable to competitors. Such information falls into two general categories: consumer needs and potential value' (Peppers and Rogers, 2004: 179).

It should be remembered that an organisation's objective is to develop its relationship with the people targeted. The permission marketing method, popularised by Seth Godin (1999), is highly appropriate in this context. In permission marketing, relationship-marketing programmes are used to encourage consumers to join a community, and then to progress through increasing levels of consent with respect to a product. First, contact is made with potential consumers to encourage them to agree to receive information. This is achieved by offering consumers something of value that will arouse their interest, for example, a club newsletter containing exclusive information. Next, the relationship is strengthened by informing consumers about the products and services provided by the club. The relationship is then developed into a relationship of 'proximity' and 'trust'. Incentives may lead consumers to extend the permission given at the beginning and it is only at this moment that a consumer's buying behaviour can be modified to produce benefits for the club. A permission-marketing strategy based on e-mail is considered to be one of the internet's 'killer applications', as it is a very powerful, cheap, fast and flexible direct marketing tool that also allows organisations to accurately measure the impact and profitability of their campaigns. However, it has become a victim of its own success, as many people reject e-mail communication due to the volume of e-mails they receive.

Given the characteristics of their targets and the constraints imposed by their situation, objectives and resources, sports organisations tend to design and implement processes that combine different types of action in order to create and develop a relationship with each person targeted. The actions needed to create a relationship and those needed to develop it are shown in Figure 3.9.

For example, an Italian tennis club that wanted to introduce a programme of actions to recruit young adults living in its 'catchment area' first aroused the interest of people belonging to this marketing target, and then created and developed the relationship in order to recruit these people. To do this, the club adopted the following process (Figure 3.10):

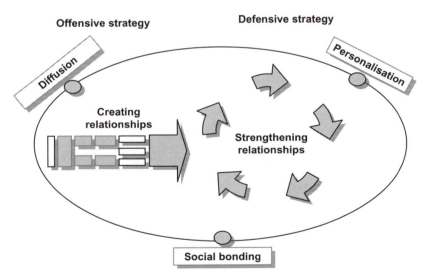

Figure 3.9 Creating and developing relationships.

PHASE 1: PROVIDE INFORMATION TO AROUSE INTEREST

- Post the club's campaign 'Live better, live tennis' on the homepage of its website. Ask people who wish to be informed about the dates of events to join a mailing list
- Distribute flyers in letterboxes in the catchment area
- Advertise on the local, partner radio station
- Press relations, especially targeting journalists at the local daily newspaper and the free press (communication target).

PHASE 2: CREATE A SOCIO-EMOTIONAL LINK

- Organisation of a 'Live better, live tennis' event over three Saturdays to allow targets to test facilities, measure their fitness under the supervision of a sports doctor and to receive advice from a coach. People who are interested can sign up by telephone, e-mail or at the club.

PHASE 3: INDIVIDUALISATION OF THE RELATIONSHIP TO CONVINCE TARGETS OF THE WORTH OF JOINING THE CLUB

- Direct marketing campaign using the list of people who took part at the event and of those who signed up for the mailing list and who agreed that the club could contact them to invite them to a Saturday afternoon public-relations operation they could attend with a friend or relative.
- Telephone and e-mail contact to make appointments to join the club and to have a free lesson with the coach.

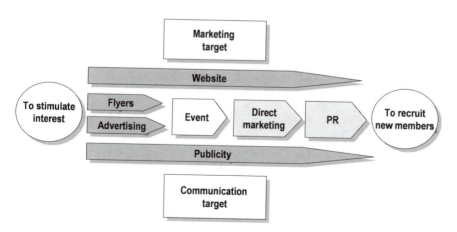

Figure 3.10 Example of an operational process designed to encourage targets to join a club.

This process includes marketing actions that combine the three types of relationship. First, information is sent out (internet, flyers, advertising, press relations) to encourage people who are interested to come forward and register for the event (direct contact, telephone, e-mail), which is designed to create a socio-emotional link and to individualise the relationship (direct and personal relationship with the doctor, the coaches and the staff) that will lead to membership (direct marketing).

This succession of actions forms an operational process that directly contributes to the creation and strengthening of the relationship. Given the diversity of their situations and objectives, sports organisations must implement a number of operational processes that require the use of two other types of processes (Figure 3.11):

- The support process includes the marketing information system (including the action evaluation method) and the resources to be committed by the organisation and its partners
- The management process includes the choice of targets, the type of relationship and the tactic to adopt.

The management of these processes is the result of the work carried out by the organisation and some of its partners to determine, share, implement and improve the practices that create value for the organisation's internal and external stakeholders.

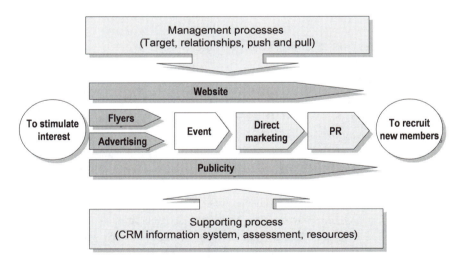

Figure 3.11 Relationships between operational, support and management processes.

Case studies showing best practices of market-based relationship marketing

This field covers a wide range of marketing actions:

- Managing the personal relationship with fans through a defensive and offensive strategy (CRM, identification and loyalty programmes)
- Offering personalisation and increasing the perceived quality of existing offers
- Developing e-relationships through the internet and mobile phones
- Managing relationships with dissatisfied stakeholders
- Offering innovation in current and new markets
- Assessing and monitoring the market-based relationship strategy.

The case studies presented below illustrate these aspects. The Ruby Football Union's (RFU) marketing action involved creating a membership scheme, called the England Rugby Supporters Club, to build relationships with England rugby followers. However, as the RFU does not have sufficient in-house resources, it appointed a specialist sports membership company 'Goodform' to run the scheme. A similar approach has been taken by the London Marathon. Its 'How to Engage Participants and Spectators for the Long term' strategy is part of a defensive and offensive approach based on a CRM system. These two case studies are followed by an example of a loyalty-building programme run by professional clubs; the San Diego Padres, a Major League Baseball team based in San Diego, California.

MOVING MEMBERSHIP SCHEMES FROM TRANSACTIONAL TO RELATIONSHIP MARKETING

Case Study: Goodform and the RFU

Stuart Dalrymple, Managing Director – Goodform Ltd

For many years, the Rugby Football Union (RFU) had the enviable position of selling out all of its England matches at its stadium in Twickenham, London. The demand for tickets by far outstretched supply as the tickets were distributed and sold via its 800 clubs and their members. There were no public sales to these major games. In 2002, the RFU realised they had little or no data on the many thousands of individuals who attended these games each year, so they decided to create a membership scheme to build relationships with England Rugby followers, which they called the England Rugby Supporters Club (ERSC). The RFU did not have the in-house experience or resources to launch such a scheme, so they appointed specialist sports-membership company 'Goodform' to provide the resource.

In launching the scheme the RFU had a number of objectives:

1   To create a consumer database
2   To create a new revenue stream
3   To sell secondary products beyond match tickets
4   To communicate directly with their consumers
5   To provide individuals who weren't members of rugby clubs the opportunity to get tickets for major matches at Twickenham
6   To bring rugby followers closer to the sport's governing body.

It was decided that a genuine 'Product' had to be created to provide members with both tangible and intangible benefits and to bring the membership to life. An annual fee of £39 was set and the RFU and Goodform set about marketing the ERSC (Figures 3.12 and 3.13).

The ERSC was launched in February 2003 and in its first 12 months, just over 23,000 people joined. A junior scheme and product was launched in 2004 with a different price point and different benefits designed for 8–12 year olds.

The internet played a significant role in the marketing and sign up of new

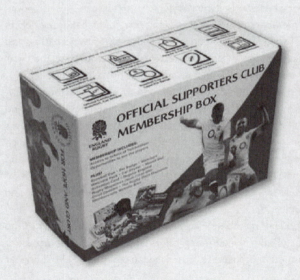

Figure 3.12 Product design and content.

Figure 3.13 Product design and content.

members, as over 75 per cent of members joined via the internet and the RFU's website. A good presence on the homepage and easy to follow instructions on how to join in the members part of the site ensured rapid take up. The phones were also hot at Goodform's offices, where up to 100 people a day were joining pre- and post- the 2003 Rugby World Cup in Australia, which England won. A significant number of people also joined by buying the 'product' through WH Smith, Tesco and other online and offline retailers.

The key benefit of membership was, and still is, access to the ballot for tickets for England games at Twickenham. Members of the club have always had a good chance of getting tickets in the twice-yearly ballots but it soon became clear that this was not the only reason for joining and renewing each year.

A fortnightly 'e-zine' was found to be the second most popular benefit following regular research of the members. As well as containing interesting and unique rugby editorial content, the e-zine includes information on members events and special benefits, and it provides members with 'breaking news', such as England team selections, before the information is available to the media and subsequently the general public. The e-zine has also ensured that the RFU has over 95 per cent of members' e-mail addresses, which ensures quick and cost-effective communication.

There are also a series of members-only events, a members-only part of the website and a variety of affinity marketing offers and schemes for members, as well as a discount on merchandise purchased from the RFU's 'Shop at Twickenham'.

So, what was initially a transactional relationship, with the RFU selling their 'products' to unknown consumers, has now turned into a real 'ongoing' relationship that provides the RFU with the following:

1   The ability to communicate with their 'consumers' on a regular basis
2   The opportunity to 'up sell' further products to their consumers, e.g. merchandise, tickets for non-international matches
3   The chance to distribute tickets for England international matches further than just the traditional routes
4   The chance to provide the whole membership with various, 'urgent' information quickly and cost-effectively by e-mail
5   The opportunity to 'profile' its members and ultimately all England Rugby supporters.

Goodform's initial contract with the RFU was renewed and they now provide the following for the ERSC:

- Management and operation of the 'membership services' office, including processing of all new applications, providing information and dealing with all members' queries by phone, e-mail and post
- Advice on the production of the Sales and Marketing Plan, and involvement in all initial, current and future sales and marketing activity
- Research on membership trends, reporting back to the RFU with all statistics and feedback from members
- Ad hoc projects when needed, such as direct promotions, surveys and international ticket ballots
- Outbound telesales to 'lapsed' members
- Coordination of monthly mailings and reminders
- Collection of manual payments
- Event management at members-only events.

Stuart Dalrymple, the managing director of Goodform says,

'The England Rugby Supporters Club has been a great success for the RFU and for Goodform. The sports industry is terribly guilty of not treating its consumers like consumers and so, by creating a club that people feel part of and have an influence on, the ERSC has ensured that they feel that they are being treated like consumers. We experience this every day and have now been able to share the success of the scheme with many other sports clients.

I believe that a key factor in all good CRM and in particular sports consumer relationships is that the consumer can pick up the phone and speak to someone at their 'club'. These consumers are usually very passionate about their club or their sport and they want a human element to the relationship. There is a much greater likelihood that these consumers will spend more money with you if they like you!'

Since its inception, the ERSC has gone from strength to strength. It has attracted over 40,000 members and met the challenges of retention and renewals. It has also generated well in excess of £1 million per year in membership revenue and in excess of £2 million per year in secondary income. The club has certainly achieved all the objectives the RFU initially set out.

SUCCESSFUL RELATIONSHIP-MARKETING STRATEGIES FOR MEGA-EVENTS: HOW TO ENGAGE PARTICIPANTS AND SPECTATORS FOR THE LONG TERM

Case Study: London Marathon

Nick Bitel, CEO London Marathon

Overview and background

The London Marathon is a relatively young brand in sport, having been first run in 1981. At first sight it is not an immediately obvious candidate for the use of relationship-marketing strategies, since it has no paying spectators and has been oversubscribed for entries since its first year. In 2007, the event turned away over 80,000 applications to run in it.

However, the London Marathon has recognised the relationship-marketing approach as being important in a number of traditionally identified areas, such as consumer retention, developing strong ties with sponsors and partners (Grönroos, 1994), securing a loyal consumer base, fostering legitimacy, and improving quality and interdependency between the event and its partners (Shani, 1997).

Leonard Berry is generally credited with introducing the term relationship marketing in 1983 in the context of services marketing. He described it as a 'strategy to attract, maintain, and enhance consumer relationships' (Berry, 1983). However, consumer relationship marketing (CRM) is not just about putting out a corporate message to a semi-targeted list.

Of course, the London Marathon has a massive advantage in that it is seen as being aspirational and a service that is much desired. People are much more likely to want to have a relationship with it than, say, a manufacturer of disinfectants.

The problem with much of what is called 'relationship marketing' is that, in far too many cases, there really is not a relationship. In these cases, CRM is just a fancy phrase for personalized direct marketing, with no real meaning behind it.

Development of CRM aims:

In 1995, a new management team took over the running of the London Marathon. At this stage, the organisation had an annual profit of £310,000 and organised just two events a year. The company was heavily dependant upon sponsorship income and a new title sponsor was being sought in what was perceived as being a difficult economic climate.

The London Marathon had developed a premium entry product called 'Golden Bonds' aimed at the charity market but take up on these had been slow.

According to Gordon (1999), the traditional four Ps of the marketing mix — Pricing, Product management, Promotion, and Placement — are too limited to provide a usable framework for assessing and developing consumer relationships in many industries and should be replaced by an alternative model where the focus is on consumers and relationships rather than on markets and products. The London Marathon believes this is especially so in sport.

At the same time it was considered important to avoid the pitfalls of CRM. Surveys have shown that consumers 'don't see themselves as having ongoing relationships with a company and don't want one'.[1] Furthermore, increasingly people are becoming concerned about consumer privacy invasions.[2]

The management team quickly identified a number of key objectives that CRM could help deliver:

* To drive up demand for entries to help increase perceived value of, and demand for, Golden Bonds
* To build brand equity and help cross sell new events and sponsorships
* To enhance the charitable reputation of the London Marathon.

CRM practices

Creating a database

At the time, the only way in which to enter the race was to obtain an application for an entry form from one of a number of outlets in Britain. The potential runner would then have to send this to the London Marathon, together with a modest payment, in return for which they would be sent an entry form. Since this was seen as revenue generating, there was no desire to create a database and just send an entry form out to those who had previously expressed an interest in running the event.

The decision was taken to sweep away this practice and to create a database of interested people to whom entry forms could be mailed free of charge. The database consists of people who have run or who have applied to run the London Marathon in the previous 5 years. It contains over 330,000 names and is updated every year.

Very few of the 330,000 people a year who receive communications from the London Marathon request to be taken off the database (perhaps 20 a year), which is evidence that a relationship is built between runners and the London Marathon.

Magazines

In conjunction with the creation of a database, a series of magazines (*Marathon News*) was launched and sent to sectors of the database each year. The magazine with the largest print run (550,000), sent in August, includes the entry form and is also available free of charge in sports shops. It is profitable through advertising and is highly prized by people on the database. The magazines have even been seen for sale on eBay.

Runners who apply to take part then receive one of two other magazines in December depending on whether or not their application has been successful.

E-mail communications

The use of e-mail communications in CRM can be difficult as generic blasts of e-mail newsletters, too often the online relationship-marketing silver bullet, are frequently not dialogue-building tools. Further, given the opportunity to opt out, a sizeable percentage of people (50 per cent) are said to want their names removed from e-mail lists.

For these reasons, the London Marathon took the initial view that it would run an 'opt in' system for collecting e-mail information and use that information to first build a relationship with runners, rather than to merely sell products. At the end of the first year, over 90 per cent of runners had voluntarily signed up with their e-mail details, giving them:

- Regular electronic newsletters
- Special offers on race-day photographs

- Access to an online training route planning tool
- The possibility to purchase personalised running programmes
- Access to post runners blogs and online runners' forums
- Access to online fundraising tools.

Training sessions

The best way to build a relationship with consumers is often face-to-face. The London Marathon and its sponsors wanted to be able to do this outside of just race day. Therefore, runners competing on a Golden Bond entry were given the opportunity to take part in a free, one-day training seminar. On average, over 20 per cent of runners take up this opportunity each year.

Case results:

The foray into CRM has had dramatic results for the London Marathon.

Golden Bond

From struggling to sell these premium entries, the London Marathon has been able to increase capacity and sell out. The waiting list is currently closed to new applicants, as current projections indicate that it will take over 20 years to be able to fulfil the requests of those already on the waiting list.

New races

By creating a relationship with runners and enhancing the perception of the brand, a number of new races have been launched successfully. In 2008, seven events will be staged in Britain and the latest event, the BUPA London 10,000, sold out within three weeks, entirely from responses to e-mail marketing and electronic newsletters.

Charity

As a result of increasing Golden Bond sales to charities, the use of online fundraising tools and getting the charity message over to runners through the more effective CRM methodology described above, the sum raised by runners has risen substantially (from £10 million in 1996 to £46.5 million in 2007), making the London Marathon the world's largest annual fundraising event.[3]

RELATIONSHIP MARKETING THROUGH CONSUMER LOYALTY
PROGRAMMES

Case Study: San Diego Padres Baseball

David Stotlar, Director, School of Sport and Exercise Science, University of Northern Colorado

Case focus:

The focus of this case is the relationship-marketing strategy implemented through a consumer loyalty programme by the San Diego Padres Major League Baseball Team. Founded in 1896, Major League Baseball oversees the operation of 30 privately owned professional teams in North America. The San Diego Padres are located in San Diego, California, a city of 1.3 million people. The team name 'Padres' was chosen to honour the history of the city, which was founded in 1602 by Catholic priests (Padres) as a mission. The city was named by Spanish explorers for the Catholic Saint Diego. Since it was founded in 1969, the team has had periods of success and disappointment. In the 1990s, with changes in ownership, the team's strategy became to establish a loyal consumer base on which to build revenues and a competitive team.

Relationship marketing has been shown to provide two very important benefits to an organisation. First, it allows managers and marketers to become more knowledgeable about consumers through the collection of essential data. These data are subsequently developed into a database that is used to better communicate with consumers. The second benefit is purely economic. Estimates vary, but it is generally accepted that it costs at least five times as much to recruit a new consumer as it does to maintain an existing one (Levine, 1993). Pride and Ferrell (1997: 275) noted that in service marketing, 'relationship marketing becomes critical'. Principally, loyal consumers buy more products over a longer period of time than do occasional purchasers. In professional sports, as in any business, the best consumers are those who make repeat purchases and recommend the business to their friends. Based on these marketing principles, the San Diego Padres implemented a consumer loyalty programme called the 'Compadres Club' (compadre is a Spanish word originally meaning 'co-father' but has developed to mean close friend).

Key concepts:

- Relationship Marketing
- Consumer Loyalty.

Case diagnosis:

Patterned after the airline industry's frequent flier programmes, consumer loyalty programmes in sport typically offer fans membership of the fan club, special incentives for repeated purchases and exclusive offers on merchandise and other team services. Following the best practices established by the San Diego Padres, many other US professional sports teams have adopted similar programmes. The details of the San Diego Padres' programme are presented below.

Compadres Club Rewards registration is available online and inside the stadium at specially designed stations (kiosks) where consumers can register and immediately receive a Compadres membership card. Whenever fans attend a game, they can earn 10 points by simply scanning their Compadres card and Padres game ticket at any Compadres kiosk location. By scanning their Compadres card at every game attended, fans can take advantage of special savings and other benefits specified by accumulated point values each season. As a member of the Compadres Club, fans also receive Compadres coupons at every game they scan their card. These daily coupons include exclusive savings throughout the season for use in the stadium, online or with team sponsors. Discounts on in-stadium concessions and merchandise are 10 per cent, with many sponsors offering similar discounts for purchases when consumers show their Compadres membership card. The details of the 2007 reward structure are outlined below.

2007 Compadres rewards

10 point reward

Half-price Padres tickets. Receive up to two $12 tickets for half price or take $6 off two tickets priced $12 or more for selected Padres home games

30 point reward

Star Player Poster. Compadres Club Limited Edition presented by Golden State Graphics (a Padres sponsor)

50 point reward

Free Movie Pass to UltraStar Cinemas (a Padres sponsor)

70 point reward

Compadres Padres Championship Collectors Pin. Compadres Club Limited Edition

100 point reward

Star Player model baseball cap. Compadres Club Limited Edition

150 point reward

Free Padres Game Ticket

200 point reward

Star Player Mesh Jersey T-shirt, provided by Hornblower Cruises & Events (a Padres sponsor)

300 point reward

Invitation for two people to attend the Compadres Club Season Ticket Holder Field Day, on 22 September, 2007

400 point reward

Compadres Club Season Ticket Holder Towel, plus a Silver Star Member Pin

500 point reward

$50 Gift Certificate for the Cohn Restaurant Group (a Padres sponsor)

600 point reward

Compadres Season Ticket Holder Batting Practice Event

700 point reward

Star Player Commemorative Photo

800 point reward

2007 Gold Star Member Baseball Bat, autographed by a Padres player, plus a Gold Star Member Pin.

Case development:

The programme outlined above presents several points of interest. First, because most US baseball stadiums are only about 50 per cent occupied, giving away free tickets has no real cost to the team. This clearly would not be a good strategy where capacity crowds are likely. From a marketing perspective, the baseball game as a product looks better with a fuller stadium, and this also presents a better image for television. In addition, if more fans attend each game, additional revenue streams are realised through parking fees and merchandise sales. Data on average consumer purchases of parking, souvenirs and concessions food for baseball show that each consumer spends an average of $35.00.

All US major professional teams have websites where fans can access team statistics and stories, but can they interact and develop meaningful relationships with fans? In addition to the rewards and prizes, the Padres programme offers online forums and chat sessions that have been found quite effective in building positive relationships with fans. They create the 'buzz' and 'community' that McConnell and Huba (2004) propose as key elements in creating loyal fans. This has resulted in more loyal fans that consume at higher rates and that have become repeat consumers. Furthermore, these fans are less price-sensitive if the team increases the price of tickets or merchandise. Through relationship building, consumers can become involved with a sports organisation as a partner, not just a consumer. In many ways, these new marketing methods are similar to those of long ago. Get to know your consumer, visit your consumer, and design products and services to meet their individual needs. Insisting on traditional techniques and interruption marketing will produce former consumers. Regardless of the label or designation assigned to the marketing programme, in relationship marketing it is essential for an organisation to carefully evaluate the market and consumers to design programmes that meet their needs.

Case results:

The programme was started in 1995 and by 1998 the Padres had enlisted 90,000 members. Data indicate that 46 per cent of members increased their attendance by 6.67 games over the previous season, and 2002 data showed that club members had increased the number of games attended by 10.7 games. Financially, the programme was a success. With an average ticket price of $27.00, the 90,000 consumers were spending an extra $289 per year on tickets, thereby generating an additional $26 million in revenue for the team. As noted above, data show that the average consumer spends $35.00 on parking, souvenirs and concessions food, thus adding another $33.7 million. The exact cost of the incentives was not known, but many of the rewards are paid for (self-liquidated) by Padre sponsors. Others, such as free or half-price tickets, do not cost the organisation anything because the seats were going unused. However, some of the items do have a cost (hats, photos, pins, etc.). The key marketing ingredient is that these items are exclusive to Compadres Club members and cannot be purchased by the general public. The team also makes available products that cannot be purchased, such as on-field experiences or stadium functions. Ultimately the return on investment is substantial, creating positive relations and increased revenues.

Resources

Levine (1993)
McConnell and Huba (2004)
Pride and Ferrell (1997)

Website

San Diego Padres Fan Club, http://sandiego.padres.mlb.com/sd/fan_forum/compadres.jsp

Network-based relationship strategies

Network-based relationships provide a platform for market relationships. They focus on stakeholder alliances, competition and institutional regulations in the sports organisation environment. Marketing programmes are designed to engage strategic stakeholders and their resources. This section describes a model for implementing network-based relationship-marketing strategies, and then presents a number of programmes that illustrate best practices in this field.

Implementation of a network-based relationship-marketing strategy

Figure 3.14 shows a four-phase model for the implementation of a network-based relationship-marketing strategy. The four phases are: strategic choices, construction of relationships between stakeholder partners, implementation of relationship-marketing programmes, and enhancement of the value constellation.

Strategic choices

The strategic diagnosis (described in the previous chapter) allows sports organisations to take strategic decisions in relation to:

- The foundations of the marketing action (i.e. mission, values, vision and functional strategies)

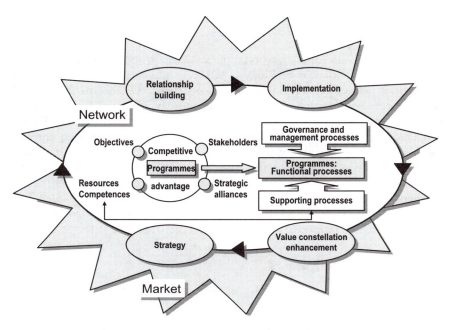

Figure 3.14 Model for implementing network-based relationship-marketing strategies.

- The relationship strategy to implement, which involves specifying marketing targets, the stakeholders with whom it is desirable to collaborate, and the internal stakeholders that need to be involved
- The offer portfolio, taking into consideration the marketing targets and the stakeholders that contribute to the offer
- The nature of the relationship with the sports organisation's brand
- The structure of the marketing system.

Putting these strategic decisions into operation involves implementing a number of actions.

Construction of relationships between partners

The first operational phase involves the construction of relationships between partners through the introduction of collaborative programmes that will satisfy the expectations of the marketing targets and create a competitive advantage. The following dimensions must be made to converge:

- The stakeholders who the organisation would like to involve
- The objectives of the different parties

- The skills and resources of the different parties
- The type of strategic alliance desired.

Alliances can develop along two axes: the value chain and the value constellation. Figure 3.15 shows a typology of strategic alliances based on these two dimensions. The collaboration between two structures (1) forms the basis of all alliances. For example, the collaboration may take the form of a co-marketing action between a sports equipment manufacturer, such as Puma, and a national team, such as the Cameroon soccer team. If a sports equipment distributor is added to the system (2), strategic alliances can be built within the distribution chain. Collaborative systems can also form constellations (3), for example, if a television channel is added to the system it will promote the partnership through advertising (value in kind). Much more complex collaborative systems are also possible (4, 5, 6); however, the more complex the system, the more complex its governance and management.

Implementation of programmes

The second operational phase is the use of process management techniques to implement the programmes. According to Mongillon and Verdoux (2003), this is the result of collaborative work that will allow an organisation to identify, share, clarify and improve value-creation practices for its stakeholders. These operational processes are related to the organisation of the different actions that must be implemented to deliver a service to its end-users. The operational processes of the Slovenian Olympic Committee's (SOC) sponsoring programme for the Athens Olympics are presented in Table 3.2.

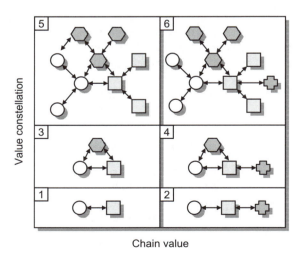

Figure 3.15 Typology of strategic alliances.

Table 3.2 The operational processes of the Slovenian Olympic Committee's sponsoring programme for the Athens Olympics

Process units	Stakeholders engaging competences and resources
From marketing and commercial action to sponsorship agreement	
1. Match analysis	SOC Marketing department
2. Customised proposal	SOC Marketing department
3. Negotiation and adaptation	SOC Marketing department + Secretary General + Sponsor
4. Contract validation	SOC Marketing department + Partner company EOS BDO + Secretary General + Sponsor
Before the Athens 2004 Olympic Games	
5. Activation strategy	SOC Marketing department
6. Media agreement	SOC Marketing department + Media partner
7. Ambush protection	SOC Marketing department + MERIDIAN
8. Personalised follow-up	SOC Marketing department + Sponsor Marketing department
During the Olympic Games	
9. Logistic implementation	SOC Marketing department + Sponsor Marketing department
10. Detailed information	SOC Marketing department + Media partner
11. Hospitality	SOC Marketing department + Slovenian Tourist Board + Slovenian Embassy in Athens
12. Brand exposure	SOC Marketing department + Media partner
After the Olympic Games	
13. Debriefing	Management of SOC + SOC Marketing department + Sponsor
14. Impact analysis	SOC Marketing department + Partner company + Sponsor
15. Project prospect	SOC Marketing department + Sponsor
16. Action plan enhancement	SOC Marketing department + Sponsor + Partner company

Implementation of the operational processes identified in the preceding phase requires a number of support processes. These support processes are essential to ensure that the operational processes are executed correctly. They call upon the resources of the organisation and its partners (i.e. information system, logistics, administrative management, computer systems management, etc.). In the case of event sponsoring, this involves managing information, legal aspects, infrastructure and resources, as well as events experience (Table 3.3).

It is also necessary to implement processes to ensure the programme is well governed and well managed. Governance covers the programme's power structure, and decision-making and control processes. Management involves determining priorities and objectives, and choosing communication, information processing and operation monitoring methods (Table 3.4).

Table 3.3 Illustration of the support processes needed to implement the operational processes involved in events

Stages	Tasks	Partners providing resources and skills
Manage information	Analyse the impact Understand the companies' strategies Inform	Marketing agency Sports organisation's marketing department
Manage rights and contracts	Manage commercial rights on a worldwide basis	Legal departments of the sports organisation and of sponsors
	Manage contracts Prepare to fend off ambush marketing	Legal department of the international federation
Manage the infrastructure	Competition site Hospitality arrangements	Sports organisation's events department
		Regional authority that owns the infrastructure
		Sponsor partners
Manage resources	Human resources management Financial management	Project leader for events Project leader of the organisations involved in this collaboration

Thus, delivering a quality service to sponsors depends on the implementation and coordination of these three types of process.

Enhancement of the value constellation

Every programme aims to create value for its end-users and for all the partners involved in designing and producing the programme (value constellation). A programme's impact cannot be evaluated solely in terms of end-user satisfaction and perceived quality; it must take into account all the stakeholders

Table 3.4 The governance and management processes involved in events sponsoring

Stages	Tasks	Partners providing resources and skills
Steering	Adjust and implement the strategy Communicate the strategy	Steering committee
Communicate	Internally Externally	Each partner's communication department
Quality management	Design a system for evaluating perceived quality	Steering committee
	Modify the programme as a function of the results	Specialist partner

involved. Thus Slovenia's Olympic Committee, through its key account managers, has regular discussions with each partner and organises marketing seminars with all the stakeholders involved. The evaluation of the marketing programme is carried out in conjunction with the partner companies BDO EOS, which is a partner for media monitoring, and Genion Clipping, which is a public opinion and market research partner. The contributions of both these partners are in the form of value in kind. This enables the SOC to strengthen ties, identify areas that can be improved and design new programmes involving other organisations.

Network-based relationship-marketing programmes

The combination of the structural dimensions (i.e. marketing targets, stakeholders, objectives, skills and resources, type of alliances) can be used to design and implement a large variety of programmes. The following sections describe how programmes of this type can be categorised and then provides some examples illustrating best practices in this domain.

Categorisation of network-based relationship-marketing programmes

Classically, sports organisations work with their partners to implement six types of programme.

1. MARKETING STRATEGIES FOR SPORTS EVENTS

Organising a sports event requires collaboration between different types of stakeholders from the sporting field (i.e. national and international federations, clubs, athletes, etc.) and the events field (i.e. marketing agencies, media, sponsors), as well as from regional (i.e. local authorities, public opinion, members of the local business, cultural and educational communities, etc.) and extra-regional (i.e. European Union, State, competing regional authorities, etc.) bodies. Event organisation is the domain in which most sports organisations implement relationship-marketing strategies, starting at the bidding phase for international sports events (e.g. Olympic Games).

2. IMPLEMENTING SPONSORSHIP PROGRAMMES

Sponsoring is another sector in which a sports organisation can gain advantages by implementing relational strategies with respect to stakeholders such as sponsors and the media. Moreover, according to Ferrand et al. (2006) the activation strategies that allow value to be obtained from sponsoring programmes are designed to build relationships between the sports organisation, its sponsors and a wide range of marketing and/or communication targets (e.g. participants, public, clubs, schools, etc.).

3. MANAGING MEDIA RELATIONSHIPS

The media form an increasingly complex system with which sports organisations must build long-term links based on trust and mutual understanding. This can go as far as a strategic partnership as part of a sponsoring operation, or societal programmes (e.g. Olympic Health Foundation). The Finnish National Olympic Committee has divided its media relationships into two categories (Table 3.5).

4. DESIGNING AND RUNNING SOCIAL MARKETING PROGRAMMES

The convergence between the stakeholders that make up a sports system is becoming stronger and stronger in terms of social end goals. Sport is a vector of integration and social development that is increasingly in phase with the end goals of political, economic, educational and social actors. This favourable context has led to the introduction of a large number of social programmes based on relationship marketing.

Table 3.5 Categorisation of the Finnish Olympic Committee's media relationships

Categories	Media	Actions
1st category Personal relations One-to-one meetings Unofficial discussions	1. Yle 2. MTV3 3. Helsingin Sanomat 4. IltaSanomat 5. Iltalehti 6. Urheilukanava 7. Nelonen 8. Urheilulehti	Proactive interpersonal relationship, including press conferences, press releases and story promotion. Story promotion means tipping story angles or checking whether some media are running a story concerning, for example, a NOC press release. This is not scooping, this is more a way of promoting one's own agenda
2nd category Media level relations Unofficial discussions	9. Etelä-Suomen Sanomat 10. Aamulehti 11. Turun Sanomat 12. Kaleva 13. Ilkka 14. Kaleva 15. Satakunnan Kansa 16. Lapin Kansa 17. Länsi -Savo	Basic communication includes: an online newsletter, which NOC sends four times per year, official and unofficial meetings with media representatives and information given to the media in collaboration with sports federations. In this way, a proactive relationship is formed

Source: Adapted from Elo (2007).

5. BRANDING STRATEGIES AND OFFERING EXTENDED SERVICES

Co-marketing strategies provide the basis for a large number of collaborative programmes. The most classic concern merchandising and licensing operations, in which a club allies itself with its equipment supplier to develop a specific line of products (e.g. Arsenal FC http://onlinestore.arsenal.com). An organisation may also provide specific services, such as insurance (e.g. USA Taekwondo). The rewards provided by loyalty-building programmes often involve a sports organisation's partners (e.g. San Diego Padres).

6. INTEGRATING MULTI-CHANNEL INFORMATION AND COMMUNICATION PLATFORMS

Information management is a strategic resource for designing and implementing relationship-marketing strategies. Certain stakeholders belonging to sports systems possess information that may be useful to a sports organisation. In such cases, collaboration strategies lead to the sharing of that information, thereby allowing the creation of value for end users and partners. USA Swimming (www.usaswimming.org), which is the US national governing body for the sport of swimming, implemented a data integration project to manage information so it would be able to serve its members better. This project was designed and implemented in collaboration with Statera, an information technology consultancy firm based in Denver. The resulting system is based on a 'niche web portal', which provides a gateway to all the internet-based services the organisation offers its members, as well as a 'centralised data base' that contains all the member information collected by USA Swimming's 2800 clubs and 59 local committees across the country. McCubbrey *et al.* (2005) found that this technology-based system has allowed USA swimming to develop innovative services for its members.

Illustration of best practice for network-based relationship-marketing programmes

The following case studies illustrate the different types of strategy and show the diversity that is found across the globe. The first case study, the 62nd FIM Rally: Bikers in Cesenatico (Italy) is a good example of a sport-, leisure- and tourism-oriented national sporting event. The second case study concerns UK Athletics' (UKA) Norwich Union sponsorship agreement (a six-year £50 million contract), which was signed and is managed by Fasttrack, and is the biggest commercial sponsorship deal in British sport outside football. This is followed by studies of two very different sports on two continents: Yachting New Zealand's 'Sailing . . . Have a Go' programme and Canada Athletics' 'Run Jump Throw' Programme. Sponsorship programmes are also very important, as illustrated by the success of the UK Athletics–Norwich Union

Sponsorship Relationship which was set up in order to develop the sport at grassroots level.

Case Study: 62nd FIM Rally: Bikers in Cesenatico. Five days of sport, leisure and tourism

Patrizia Marchesini, CONI Servizi, Scuolla dello Sport, Rome (Italy), Communication & Marketing Department

Case focus:

The FIM Rally is an international meeting for motorcyclists with about 2,000 participants from approximately 30 nations. It is held once a year in different countries in order to make the culture of the organising country known to the participants through local folklore performances, regional food, guided tours, etc.

Fifty per cent a competition between countries and 50 per cent a tourist and leisure event: this is the spirit of the FIM Rally format, and this is what the International Motorcycle Federation looks for when a NMF bids for the event. In 2007, the Italian Motorcycling Federation (FMI) was assigned to organise the event and the 62nd FIM Rally was held in June 2007 in Cesenatico, a seaside town in northern Italy (25,000 inhabitants), a well-known tourist destination for summer holidays.

Case diagnosis:

For this event, there were almost 1,800 participants from 29 different European and extra-European countries; 20,000 meals served during the event period; 1,300 bikes in the Parade of Nations; 20 km of advertising banners; 1,000 sq. m of covered surface (Rally Centre) close to the beach; one title sponsor, two official partners, five commercial supporters and one media partner; 50 vehicles hired for the bus excursion; almost 3,000 badges printed; 300 Rally-related road signs displayed; 15,000 event booklets printed and distributed; 600 people camping in a dedicated area and more than 500 hotel rooms booked.

These few figures represent the effort that the Organizing Committee faced in order to achieve the pre-established goals: the success of the event was assured by establishing a network-oriented relationship among the event's key-stakeholders. These stakeholders were chosen according to the nature of the event, which is both sport and tourist oriented. After winning the bid, one and a half years before the event, the FMI Marketing Director and the Federal Motor-Tourism Councillor were appointed to establish the Organising

Committee and start planning the event; one more resource was hired in the specific role of Event Project Manager.

The choice of the host-city – Cesenatico – was a strategic one, both for logistic and practical reasons: it is a tourist destination; it is easy to reach and well served by motorways; it has a strong sporting tradition and culture. Furthermore, local people are friendly and festive – a characteristic that provides the right environment for the event.

Last but not least, an appropriate building was quickly identified to become the Rally Centre (nerve centre of the event), and most of all, from the very beginning the Municipality proved to be fully committed to offer its support for the event, in particular through its Tourist Board 'Gesturist'.

The Organising Committee was aware that delivering a high quality event to match the participants' expectations was the most critical factor; in fact, most of the bikers take part in the FIM Rally every year, therefore they have experience of many Rallies and comparisons between one edition and the previous are definitely candid. That is why the key stakeholders were deeply involved from the beginning, to enhance the possibility of providing a top class event; on the other hand, a value constellation was established within the network to make it become a win-win situation.

Case development:

The basic programme for the event is provided by the International Motorcycling Federation. A contract is signed between FIM and the hosting NMF, and the programme offered during the event must match the required standards.

The FIM Rally is a three-day event. Nowadays, organised tours are arranged before the official opening so early arrival is acceptable and even encouraged. Very often, for practical reasons, participants from the same country arrive together, which makes it a festive part of the whole meeting. There are 17 different ways of winning a FIM Rally trophy[4] but there are no official individual prizes: only an affiliated country with its team or club can be declared winner. Each participant applies to take part through his National Federation. The registration fee varies from year to year but normally includes two packed-lunches, three dinners, one excursion by bus, boat or train and souvenirs. The registration fee is usually around 180 Euros.[5] The participants pay their fees at the time of application. As far as accommodation is concerned, approximately one-third of the participants choose to stay in hotels and two-thirds opt for camping.

62nd FIM Rally Stakeholders

Table 3.6 shows the event's main stakeholders, the objectives that must be fulfilled according to the Rally official programme, the resources available and the expectations of the parties involved.

The result of putting actors and objectives in a system is the involvement of each stakeholder in the related programmes. Some of the programmes activated are compulsory (they are listed in the official procedures, e.g. parc-fermé, parade of nations, official protocol); others are run specifically according to the Organising Committee's needs (e.g. merchandising or leisure programme).

For the first time in the history of the FIM Rally, the 62nd edition had a full sponsoring programme and a media partner, the Sky channel 'MotoTV', followed and broadcast the event. Merchandising products dedicated to the event were produced and sold, together with official FMI merchandise. In general, as a result of the FMI's overall marketing strategy, the event was intended to produce valuable income for the federations.

Furthermore, an effort was made to create a strong connection between the

Table 3.6 62nd FIM rally stakeholders objectives

List of stakeholders	List of objectives
Federazione Motociclistica Ita (FMI)	Enhance the movement (Movement)
FMI operative Staff (Staff)	Event income (Income)
Fédératione Intern.Motocyclisme (FIM)	Logistics (Logistics)
Italian Olympic Committee (CONI)	Media exposure (Visibility)
Main sponsor (DriveBeer/Sponsor)	Merchandising (Merchandise)
Local authorities (Loc.Aut)	Accreditation (Accreditation)
Local Police (Police)	Accommodation Staff (Staff accom.)
Security service (Security)	Hotel accommodation (Hotel accom.)
Local Tourism Board (Gesturist)	Official protocol (Protocol)
Venues Owner (AGIP)	Parc-fermé (Parc-fermé)
Campsite Owner (Campsite)	Bus Excursion (Bus Excursion)
Logistic service supplier (DBO)	Parade of Nations (Parade of Nat.)
Volunteers (Volunteers)	Leisure programme (Leisure progr.)
Other Motorcycle Fed. (NMF)	Optional excursions (Opt. excurs.)
Foreign Participants (Participants)	Security & health (Sec. Health)
Media (MotoTV)	Catering, food & beverage (Catering)
Spectators/tourists (Spectators)	Environmental impact (Environment) Tourism and promotion (Tourism)

Rally venues and the host-city. Usually, a FIM Rally is organised far from the town centre, in a large, empty dedicated area. This time, the Italian Federation chose to hold the Rally within the host town – in this case a seaside town. The Rally Centre was set up in a big building (former holiday camp) on the beach. This obliged the Organising Committee to embrace an unusual solution: separating the Rally Centre and the campsite. As almost two-thirds of the participants choose to camp, the two venues are usually close to each other. In fact, after the evening entertainment programme at the Rally Centre, the festivities continue at the campsite. But this was not possible in Cesenatico: the campsite area (a fully equipped one) was 3 km from the Rally Centre. For this reason, logistics was one of the main concerns of the Organising Committee (shuttle buses from/to the campsite and the Rally Centre, traffic control in the town centre, dedicated parking areas) and the support of both the local police department and the municipal authorities was essential (Figure 3.16).

These additional efforts made it necessary for the Organising Committee to rely upon the network of stakeholders, and each stakeholder found additional value within the network itself.

Accommodation is recognised to be one of the most challenging Rally issues, and for this reason, the partnership with Gesturist proved to be fundamental. In fact, Gesturist holds the relation with most of the hotels in town, and the Organising Committee entrusted the Tourist Board with booking all the rooms and establishing the connection between the staff and the hotel owners.

Results:

The network-based relationship-marketing approach adopted to run the event allowed value to be shared among all the actors involved. Figure 3.17 summarises the relationships between the main actors and the related benefits obtained (the efficient cooperation brought either financial benefits or advantages related to making the procedures smooth and easy, and sometimes cheaper).

Resource websites

62nd FIM Rally, www.rallyfim2007.eu

Federazione Motociclistica Italiana, www.federmoto.it

Fédératione Internationale de Motocyclisme, www.fim.ch (Area: Leisure Motorcycling) 'FIM Rally: Economic impact survey' (pdf in English)

Municipality of Cesenatico, www.cesenatico.it

Gesturist (Touristic Agency in Cesenatico), www.gesturist.com

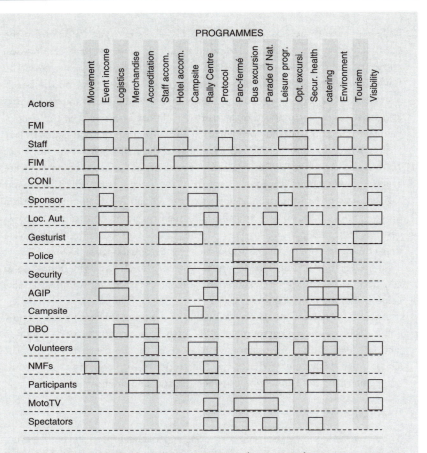

Figure 3.16 Actors involved in the programmes (squares indicate important objectives for the stakeholders).

Case Study: Relationship Marketing; Sailing . . . Have a Go – Yachting New Zealand

Denis Mowbray: MEMOS graduate, Past Chair and Board Member of Yachting New Zealand

Strategic issue

The Yachting New Zealand (YNZ) bi-annual survey identified declining membership as a key issue for the future of yachting clubs. Sailing is often seen as

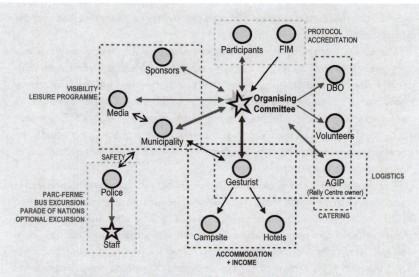

Figure 3.17 The stakeholder network for the 2007 FIM Rally.

difficult to undertake, and this reluctance to try is a barrier to early participation. This has resulted in declining numbers of young sailors joining clubs. The Sailing . . . Have a Go programme is offered to schools throughout New Zealand. It is designed to give students in Years 6, 7 and 8, the opportunity to experience the pleasure of sailing in a safe and well-managed environment and, most importantly, to have fun!

The programme has two aims. The first is to allow children within the target age group to experience the thrill of sailing; the second is to encourage those that participate to continue their involvement in the sport by joining the club where they had their Sailing . . . Have a Go experience.

Project development:

YNZ is New Zealand's national body for competitive and recreational sailing, with around 30,000 members, represented by some 160 member clubs and class associations. It is estimated to have 150,000 participants. Yachting is a sport with considerable connection with New Zealanders.

The YNZ 2005 bi-annual club survey highlighted that club membership has dropped gradually in at least the last 6 years at around 2 per cent per annum. This is typical of most sports as the 24/7 working week takes its toll on volunteers, and the seductiveness of the couch, with increasingly addictive computer games, tightens its hold on those who might otherwise be physically active. These factors ultimately threaten the existence of many clubs and the active, healthy kiwi lifestyle.

The survey identified that the major concern of clubs, by far, was participation levels, identified by 56 per cent of respondents. With environmental matters 11 per cent and coaching 8 per cent polling the next highest. The survey confirmed a continuing low level of female participation (29 per cent of club members). Consistent comments from clubs suggested that YNZ was too focused on high performance sailing and was neglecting the grass roots. The survey also expressed strongly that there was a need to pay more attention to regions outside Auckland.

The downward trend in club membership which yachting was experiencing, combined with its partnership with SPARC to promote a more active and healthier nation encouraged dramatic action. The 24/7 economy, risk management concerns and other pressures were all making the task of running clubs and gaining members increasingly difficult. Schools, a source of young members for clubs, have their own pressures and generally resist new programmes advanced by sports.

With the above in mind, the 'Sailing . . . Have a Go' programme was designed to involve schools, yacht clubs and young people, to create interest in sailing and a desire to pursue that interest.

As a 'not for profit' organisation the initial aim was to secure sufficient funding (circa NZ$500k) to launch the programme and then to deliver the following goals:

- More young people (9–13 years), all decile (socioeconomic categories) schools, to be given the experience of sailing – up to 2,000 each year (particularly those with no previous connection to sailing)
- More young people keen/enabled to join yacht clubs
- More schools with active sailing programmes
- More young people to be given the opportunity to consider the marine environment – Sir Peter's final mission (Blake Expeditions) was creating awareness of risks to the marine environment.

YNZ was aware of possible sources of funding – principally the Team New Zealand 2000 Trust – which had funds to be applied for charitable purposes from its successful America's Cup challenge in 1995 and its successful defence in 2000. The opportunity that presented was to convince the Trust that YNZ had a concept that would fulfil the late Sir Peter Blake's vision that the Trust's funds be invested 'to provide an opportunity for young people to experience the pleasure of sailing'.

The decline identified in yacht club membership, the need to offer an attractive option to children – encouraging a more active and healthy lifestyle – and our need to grow sailing to ensure its continued success and contribution. Sir Peter's wish for children to be given an opportunity to experience the pleasure and thrill of sailing while creating awareness about the marine environment provided drive, direction and a way to assist clubs and schools. A successful programme would also demonstrate perfect alignment with YNZ's major funder Sport and Recreation New Zealand (SPARC). One of SPARC's three major goals is a 'more active nation'.

Sailing . . . Have a Go Programme

There are four constituent groups involved in the successful delivery of the Sailing . . . Have a Go programme. YNZ, which manages the financial and core logistical needs (staff, transport, pods etc), schools (sports/outdoor activities teacher), local yacht clubs (required to provide facilities, chase-boat and support instructor) and young people (9–13 years). The decision was made to pilot the programme within our Northern region (Auckland/Northland). If successful, the programme would then be rolled out in the Lower North Island region and in the South Island.

Market size initially (pilot phase) was all Auckland/Northland primary and intermediate schools. There was no direct competitor apart from the clutter of other sports wanting growth through schools, and teachers too busy to deal with increasing complexity and stress. The major message was that sailing was a very exciting sport and that 'Sailing . . . Have a Go' made trying it out very safe and really easy – within anyone's reach and capability – the 'Have a Go' phrase embodied the thinking. The programme's educational focus on the marine environment was also important in attracting schools. The dual deliverables of a sailing experience that embodies education outside the classroom (EOTC) objectives have been key in the programme's success.

A modest charge of NZ$20 per day per child, less than 20 per cent of the fully costed programme was set. This would be and has been waived for lowest decile schools to encourage those who might be least connected to sailing. Emphasis was to be on a safe and fun programme.

To facilitate the highest potential participation rate, the communications plan involved a number of elements (posters, newsletter inserts, website, e-mail and personal visits/presentations). This marketing and communications plan was targeted at schools, children, parents and yacht clubs.

In addition, the programme launch was designed to attract television news coverage – advertising the budget could not pay for! Television New Zealand (TVNZ) and TV3 not only covered the launch of the first pod, but TVNZ did a follow-up news story on the pod – highlighting its operation and effectiveness. Total coverage equated to 5:00 minutes.

Results:

The Sailing . . . Have a Go programme has been a huge success. There are now three mobile sailing units or 'pods' covering the whole of NZ with a fourth planned. Each pod includes × 1 Toyata Prado, × 1 enclosed trailer, × 1 chase boat, × 6 Optimist dinghies, × 3 Topper Taz two-handed dinghies and all safety clothing and equipment for children. A fully qualified instructor manages each pod.

From schools we typically hear: 'This programme would rate as the best I have been involved with' (Teacher); and from children: 'Thank you. It was awesome to have you. I have more confidence now' (Gabrielle). Children who might never have sailed are sailing – 'It was the best day I have had since a long time, thank you' (Tim).

Over 60 per cent of children want to further their sailing. This is providing new members for yacht clubs. 'Sailing . . . Have a Go' is booked out 12 months in advance, which proves its value to schools – encouraging school sailing programmes. 'Sailing . . . Have a Go' also educates children about the marine environment.

Based on completed courses, and on 100 per cent forward bookings made, our target of 2,000 young people will be achieved this year. Our feedback research – compiled by 1975 students and 83 schools – indicates that over 60 per cent of students wish to do more sailing (55 per cent without any prior experience) – just over three times the 20 per cent KPI set for 'Sailing . . . Have a Go'.

The average decile of participating schools – range 1–10, was 6. The desire for further sailing experience was independent of school decile and so the programme has embraced all young people equally. This programme has been made available to Home Schooled Students in Marlborough and recently hosted a Ministry of Education Special Needs Workshop for students with disabilities in Northland.

Male and female students are fairly evenly represented (52 per cent : 48 per cent) in 'Sailing . . . Have a Go'. This is significantly higher than sailing club female membership at 29 per cent. Yacht clubs now realise the great potential for new members for their learn-to-sail programmes, and there is anecdotal evidence already of membership gains.

'Sailing . . . Have a Go' was recognised by the International Sailing Associations' Federation (ISAF) at its annual convention in Singapore. It was one of only two great examples recognised for contributing to its 'Connect to Sailing' initiative for children. 'Sailing . . . Have a Go' was presented to all sailing nations.

Resource websites

ISAF: Connect to Sailing, www.sailing.org
YNZ: Sailing . . . Have a Go, www.yachtingnz.org.nz

Network-based relationships

Designing and running a social marketing programme

Case Study: Run Jump Throw Program – CANADA

Donna Kaye, Manager coach development, Joanne Mortimore, CEO – Athletics Canada

Athletics Canada is the national governing body for the sport of track and field, including cross-country running, road running and road racing. Its purpose is the pursuit of leadership, development and competition that ensures world-level performance in athletics. The association believes in physical health and fitness, individual excellence and personal growth, individual development beyond sport, as well as inclusiveness and integrity. Track and field is a sport for people of all ages and abilities.

Run, Jump, Throw – Project Description and Objectives

Programme description

The Athletics Canada 'Run, Jump, Throw' (RJT) Programme can make a significant contribution to a child's ability to acquire fundamental movement skills. RJT develops the basic motor skills of running, jumping and throwing; it is designed to give children a strong background in sports skills that will not only serve them well in the sport of track and field, but also build an effective skill set that will serve them well in other sports. No matter what sport or physical endeavour children attempt in their lifetime, the mechanics of running, jumping and/or throwing will inevitably come into play.

Children aged 7–12 have been selected as the target group for the first phase of RJT programming because peak motor skill development occurs between 8 and 12 years of age. If children are not exposed to opportunities that enable them to develop the capacity to move during this critical window of opportunity, it is likely that incomplete motor skill development will result. A child that has not developed their fundamental motor skills by age 12 will likely not reach their genetic athletic potential. A second phase targeting ages 12–16 is in design and will be delivered at the National Legion Camp.

Project description

Run, Jump, Throw (RJT) is Athletics Canada's official grassroots programme. Throughout the past 2 years the programme has been tested and piloted. It is now ready for national implementation. The focus of the RJT programme for the next 4 years will be to achieve nationwide implementation through partnerships that enable Athletics Canada to build capacity. Partnerships essential to capacity building include those with provincial branches, other National Sports Organisation's (NSOs), and the private sector.

The RJT National Coaching Certification Program (NCCP) Instructor programme will serve as the primary vehicle for capacity building.

Programme objectives:

The purpose of Athletics Canada's Run, Jump, and Throw Programme is multifaceted:

- To increase awareness of and participation in Track and Field Athletics in Canada
- To supply a programme of physical activity that will serve as a strong foundation for all other sports
- To assist children in learning to move 'efficiently' so that they grow into adults who are active, productive and healthy citizens

The long-term vision for Athletics Canada's Run, Jump, and Throw Programme includes:

- The implementation of Run, Jump, Throw across Canada so that every child in Canada has the chance to participate in a Run, Jump, Throw Programme and develop a positive athletic identity as well as the capacity to move well
- The development of effective relationships with Special Olympics Canada,

The Aboriginal Sport Circle and Cerebral Palsy Sport so that people with disabilities and those living in remote communities have the opportunity to develop fundamental motor skills and be physically active

- The adoption of Run, Jump, Throw as an official grassroots programme of the IAAF or the national athletics federations of individual countries.

Provincial/Territorial Sports Organisation (P/TSO) Partnerships

Each provincial branch will be responsible for contributing to building capacity of the RJT programme through the training of Master Learning Facilitators, the implementation of RJT NCCP Courses and the development of RJT programmes in schools, clubs or through community initiatives.

The branches, along with Athletics Canada, will also contribute to RJT development through the funding of a RJT staff position in each province. The costs of the employee will be shared between HRSDC, Athletics Canada and each branch office.

Multi Sport Organisation (MSO): Coaching Association of Canada (CAC)

Explanation of partnership: CAC is a partner in the development of Athletics Canada's RJT NCCP Instructor course. Funding was provided to offset the cost of consulting fees as well as developing and piloting the course material.

Multi Sport Organisation: Canadian Athletics Coaching Centre (CACC)

Explanation of partnership: The Canadian Athletics Coaching Centre will contribute to the development of the Athletics Canada RJT programme through the provision of human resources to manage the delivery of RJT nationally.

MSO: Special Olympics Canada (SOC)

Explanation of partnership: SOC will adapt and use the technical progressions for Athletics Canada's RJT NCCP Instructor Course in the Special Olympics Community Coach Course. The partnership between AC and SOC enables SOC to ensure their athletes develop fundamental motor skills while allowing Athletics Canada to increase the reach of RJT programmes and reach athletes with a disability.

MSO: Canadian Association of Health, Physical Education, Recreation and Dance (CAHPERD)

Explanation of partnership: Athletics Canada and CAHPERD are currently negotiating a distribution agreement. If struck, CAHPERD will promote the Athletics Canada RJT programme across Canada and serve as the official distributor of RJT equipment to Canadian Schools. The partnership will increase the reach of RJT by potentially linking Athletics Canada RJT with every school in Canada.

MSO: Cerebral Palsy Sport (Sport Ability Alberta) (CP Sport)

Explanation of partnership: Sport Ability Alberta has received a grant to adapt the RJT progressions for use in CP sports programmes. The partnership increases the reach of RJT to an additional group of athletes with a disability.

Others

Royal Canadian Legion

Support or donation in kind: The Royal Canadian Legion contributes substantially to a national camp and competition for athletes 17 and under. The Run, Jump, Throw Programme forms the basis of the 14- and 15-year-old camp programme.

Human Resources and Skills Development Canada (HRSDC)

Support or donation in kind: Athletics Canada is pursuing a grant that would provide a salary subsidy for a RJT employee in each provincial branch. A full time salary would be supported through contributions from the provincial branch and Athletics Canada.

Marketplace response to RJT:

Athletics Canada has been very active in pursuing corporate partnerships for Run, Jump and Throw. The promotion of this grassroots, community based programme, with a focus on physical fitness and a promotion of healthy living for children and youth, has been met with enthusiasm, but no financial commitment to date.

Athletics Canada will continue to present this unique opportunity to companies in hopes that a marketing partnership can be finalised to support the expansion and growth strategies in the programme's 2005–2008 aggressive business plan.

Results:

The focus of the Run, Jump, and Throw programme has been on building a foundation upon which a successful national grassroots programme could be sustained.

Three specific areas were targeted for development in phase 1:

1   Alignment with the NCCP and the creation of materials to support RJT NCCP course development
2   The creation of partnerships that have the potential to build capacity and increase the overall reach of Run, Jump, Throw
3   Build and strengthen capacity for delivery through Athletics Canada's provincial branches.

A brief summary of the accomplishments in each of the target areas follows.

NCCP alignment and material development

- RJT included in the Athletics Canada Coach Development Model (CDM) and Participant Development Model (PDM)
- Development and piloting of the RJT NCCP Instructor course materials
- Development and piloting of the RJT NCCP Instructor Course for Educators
- Development of Learning Facilitator materials
- Training of Master Learning Facilitators from every province.

Partnerships

- **Special Olympics Canada** has adopted a portion of the Run, Jump and Throw NCCP course for use within their NCCP Community Sport Coach programme. Special Olympics Canada reaches *over 5000 coaches and 28,000 athletes annually*.
- **Sport Ability Alberta** (Cerebral Palsy Sport) is adapting the Run, Jump and Throw technical progressions for use with programmes targeted at athletes with a disability. Once completed the adapted progressions will become part of the course material for the RJT NCCP Instructor course and the RJT Instructor course for educators.
- A partnership between CAHPERD and Athletics Canada has been proposed whereby CAHPERD would serve as the official distributor of RJT equipment as well as assist Athletics Canada in marketing and promoting

the programme to schools across Canada. In addition to the marketing and distribution network, Athletics Canada will be applying to have the RJT material officially endorsed by CAHPERD.

- Discussions have been initiated with the Aboriginal Sport Circle; however no agreements have been struck at this time. Reaching aboriginal communities was a focus of RJT development throughout 2005–2006 and will be in the future. Saskatchewan and NWT had clinics in 2005.
- Athletics Canada is awaiting the HRSDC call for national proposals for the Career Focus programme. If successful, Athletics Canada (through a HRSDC grant) would be able to place a RJT employee in every branch.

Capacity building

Each province has committed to training at least one Master Learning Facilitator (MLF) who will return to their home province to train other Learning Facilitators and RJT Instructors/coaches. The training of MLFs is the first step in creating a national foundation for RJT. Following MLF training each province will be able to train their own Learning Facilitators and RJT Instructors whenever there is a need to do so.

Resource website

http://www.bcathletics.org/main/rjt.htm

To illustrate an example of a true long-term relationship between a rights holder and a sponsor we have chosen an example from the world of athletics. UK Athletics (UKA), the governing body for the sport, originally established a relationship with Norwich Union in 1999, as the headline sponsor for a wide range of key athletic events on the yearly calendar. Norwich Union also sponsored GB & NI elite teams at all levels and contributed a significant amount of money to develop the sport at grassroots level. This partnership was highly successful and Norwich Union was recognised as the principle sponsor of UKA. Norwich Union is the UK's biggest insurer and part of Aviva, the world's sixth-largest insurance group.

Case Study: UK Athletics – Norwich Union Sponsorship Relationship

In mid-2006, Norwich Union and UKA announced that the Norwich Union would extend and broaden its commitment to athletics until the end of 2012 in what was the largest UK sports sponsorship deal outside of football, worth nearly £50 million to the sport over a six year period.

The new agreement commenced on 1 January 2007 and it placed more emphasis on the preparation of future champions as the sport targets the Olympic Games in London in 2012, and at the same time widening the appeal and reach of athletics to encourage increased participation amongst all children. The level of investment in grassroots athletics was trebled. It is estimated that as a result of this increased investment by Norwich Union, over 10 million children and 1.5 million families will be involved in the various grassroots schemes by 2012. Training for over 100,000 teachers in over 5,000 secondary and 20,000 primary schools will also be provided through 'Elevating Athletics', revolutionising the way athletics is delivered in schools. As such, it is the most comprehensive sport sponsorship deal in the UK, influencing and helping all levels of the sport.

In addition to the current deal of seven live televised events, the Norwich Union Great Britain and Northern Ireland athletics team at all levels, and the expansion of the current grassroots schemes, the additional funding of the new agreement will allow the sport to widen its reach into communities to engage even more children and families in sporting activity.

New highlights include:

Junior Mentoring

Following the on-going success of the Norwich Union funded 'On Camp with Kelly', which sees Dame Kelly Holmes continue to mentor a group of up and coming middle distance runners, the renewed cash injection will allow UK Athletics to develop similar mentoring schemes with Norwich Union in other athletics disciplines and with other mentors.

Athletics festivals

Following the success of the Norwich Union Sportsparks in 2004, free event festivals will run in the host cities of five of the seven Norwich Union televised events. Focused on engaging the local communities, the aim is to generate excitement in the lead up to the events and provide a platform to showcase Norwich Union's commitment to grassroots athletics. Schools and families will be targeted to ensure they are well attended and lead to an increase in sporting participation and interest in athletics.

Get Britain's kids active

With Britain facing rising levels of obesity, it is vital that a healthy, active lifestyle is promoted and facilitated among children. Since athletics is the basis of all sport, a new joint initiative between Norwich Union and UK Athletics will be launched to encourage teachers and parents to work together to help youngsters get more active.

Schools curriculum and teacher training

To capitalise on the renewed enthusiasm for athletics, and focus on the preparations for 2012, a new resource – Elevating Athletics – will be made available to schools across the country, allied with an extensive teacher training programme. In this way, UK Athletics and Norwich Union will be further contributing to the Government's vision of delivering more high quality sporting activity for schoolchildren.

The partnership truly extends from grassroots development to the highest level – with a wide range of initiatives. These are:

Elite athletics

- Title sponsorship of seven live televised events in the UK
- Title sponsorship of the Norwich Union GB & NI Team
- Coaching support for current and future elite coaches.

Junior athletics

- Title sponsorship of age group Norwich Union GB & NI Teams
- Title sponsorship of age group national championships
- Mentoring support from retired athletes.

Grassroots athletics

- Norwich Union shine:awards

    - The core platform from which athletics is introduced to children at school. The nationwide awards scheme for 3–18 year-olds measures their athletics progress in a variety of skills and disciplines.

- Norwich Union star:track

    - 8–15 year olds of all abilities receive expert athletics coaching from trained coaches and can try events that they would not normally have a chance to, e.g. pole-vaulting, discus and javelin

- This will be enhanced to maximise participants and events.

- Norwich Union sports:hall

  - The pinnacle of the Grassroots schemes that allows for competitive indoor team athletics for U11s, U13s and U15s. Festivals take place from November, Regional Finals from January to March, and the National Final is held at the National Indoor Arena in Birmingham.

- Elevating Athletics with Norwich Union

  - National curriculum resource for schools aimed to increase interest in the sport of athletics as well as encourage literacy and numeracy
  - Extensive teacher training programme to engage over 100,000 teachers from 20,000 primary schools and 5,000 secondary schools to ensure quality and uniform coaching of athletics in schools.

Athletics in the community

- Norwich Union Athletics Festivals

  - Free athletics festivals to be run in the host cities of five of the seven Norwich Union televised events to engage local schools and the community in athletics.

- Get Britain's kids active

  - An initiative to encourage teachers and parents to work together to help their children and pupils get more active.

This is an example of a sponsorship that has become a true partnership – with the sponsor adopting a position of responding to the needs of the Association, in partnership, and putting valuable resources in the key areas required to assist in the overall development of the sport. This situation is not common. Sponsors are often reluctant to dedicate resources to lower profile areas. UKA has committed significant resources to develop this partnership, with a dedicated project manager and a large staff in the Communications section to support the activity.

This is a fantastic partnership and the NGB, and many thousands of coaches and players will benefit from the opportunities it will create. UKA has done a great job of working in partnership with a commercial entity to ensure the agreement delivers to the key objectives of the NGB – and Norwich Union has established a real impact relationship with an emerging body and will benefit from this strong association with growing success at all levels. A real win-win situation.

Resource websites
www.ukathletics.net
www.norwichunion.com

Internal relationship strategies

In order to put into operation its marketing strategy, a sports organisation must commit, organise and coordinate the necessary resources and skills. The way this is done depends on the structure of the organisation; hence there is a strong link between strategy and structure.

The relationship approach is based on networks, which, according to Gummeson (2006: 181), form nano-relationships and 'provide the antecedents for implementation of marketing actions'. Successful market- and network-based relationships can only be achieved if internal relationships are well managed. Dunmore (2002) has termed this 'inside-out marketing'. The following section shows the benefits an organisation can obtain by applying relationship management techniques to its internal sub-system. These benefits mostly result from the fact that relationship management techniques enable organisations to increase the loyalty and efficiency of their staff and to recruit the best staff and volunteers.

From a structural approach to a relationship approach within sports organisations

The structural approach involves defining a sports organisation's different components, their hierarchical and functional relations and the way in which they are coordinated.

Figure 3.18 shows the organisation chart for the Belgian Interfederal Olympic Committee (COIB). The COIB's marketing department is part of the Committee for the Development of Sport in Belgium (CDSB), which occupies the top left-hand corner of the organisation chart. The CDSB provides marketing resources to the COIB, which is responsible for their deployment. The marketing department has a transversal action that concerns top-level sport, services to sports federations and Olympic promotion, and this accounts for more than 70 per cent of the department's income (Figure 3.18). The CDSB, like the Olympic Health Foundation (OHF), is a complementary association of the COIB.

From a functional point of view, the marketing department has relations

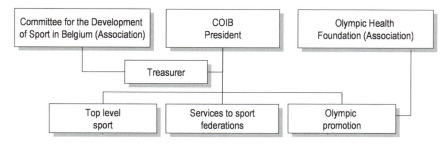

Figure 3.18 Structure of the Belgian Interfederal Olympic Committee.

with all the components of the COIB, that is to say, top-level sport, services to federations and Olympic promotion. These three components come under the auspices of the COIB, which coordinates their actions. Hence, marketing is an element in a network that comes under the authority of the organisation's General Secretariat (Figure 3.19). Primacy is given to the relations between the different components.

Sports organisations must not be seen uniquely in terms of formal structures; they should also be viewed as networks. Two types of network, functional and strategic, coexist within sports organisations. Functional networks are composed of the units that provide resources and skills for carrying out programmes. For example, OHF develops its action programmes (i.e. 'Olympic Schools', 'Sport à l'école', 'Fou de Santé', 'Olympicnic', 'Olympisme & Jeunesse', and the 'OHF Science Prize') in synergy with other components, including the marketing department (Figure 3.20). Strategic networks consist of the stakeholders responsible for decision-making processes. The COIB's strategic network consists of the CDSB and the OHF, which are integration structures that were set up to deal with the main issues facing the sports organisation (Figure 3.21).

Detrie *et al.* (2005) pointed out that operational systems are based on the principle of the self-organisation of the base units and the relations between these units. This self-organisation relies on the ability of each unit to integrate the new demands determined by integration structures (entities composed of parties from the different departments involved in a project) and to

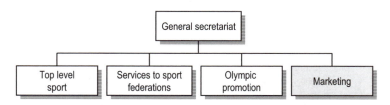

Figure 3.19 Functional structure of the Belgian Interfederal Olympic Committee.

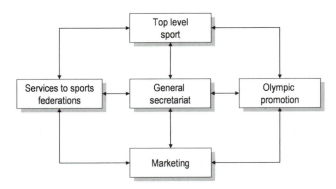

Figure 3.20 Network structure of the Belgian Interfederal Olympic Committee.

modify their behaviour as a consequence. For this approach to be effective, the parties that make up an integration structure must be chosen for their skills, rather than for their position in a hierarchy.

As Figure 3.22 shows, a sports organisation's network is formed by the interactions between parties from the network's components, whose skills are brought together to define and implement strategies. The orientations and dynamics of the relationships within the network depend on the activation of the system's components, which is based on the resources and skills they contribute to actions. This type of organisation provides the flexibility needed to improve adaptation. Hence, when it is necessary to adapt to change, it is easier to reconfigure the network than to modify the structure.

A network-based approach makes permeable the boundary between the internal organisation and the external sub-systems with which it establishes relationships. This border is not a strict division defining the communication boundary between two entities; it is a nebulous interface across which networks interconnect. As shown above, the impact and effectiveness of an action depend on the skills and resources committed by the different components of the system, as well as on quality of the relationships between these components.

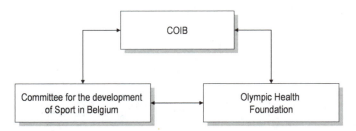

Figure 3.21 The three components of the COIB's strategic network.

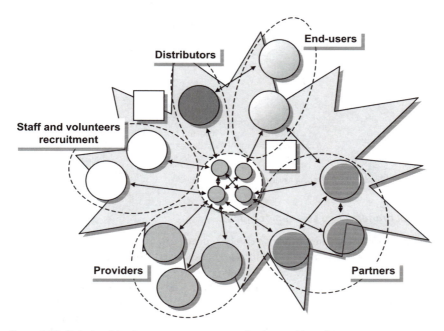

Figure 3.22 Relationships between a sports organisation and its sub-systems.

The first part of this chapter looked at the development of relationships in the market and network sub-systems. The following section investigates operational aspects of the construction, activation and development of internal networks, taking into consideration the different statuses of the people who make up these networks.

Construction and development of relationships within a sports organisation

As in the market and network sub-systems, a sports organisation must set up marketing actions that will develop the commitment and loyalty of the people who work within the organisation. These people belong to two main categories: paid staff and volunteers.

Internal relationship-marketing programmes

The different types of internal marketing action have been classified into four categories (Figure 3.23). These four types of action can be combined.

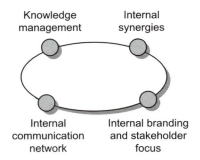

Knowledge
management

Internal
synergies

Internal
communication
network

Internal branding
and stakeholder
focus

Figure 3.23 Internal marketing actions.

Internal branding and stakeholder focus

A sports organisation must actively communicate, both externally and internally, its vision, mission, values and end goals. This requires introducing an internal branding strategy that will create an internal identity for the organisation. Such strategies are part of the wider concept of employer branding. According to Crozier (2006: 271), 'this process has to take into account and manage the synergistic relationship between the values, systems, policies, and behaviours deployed by the company or organisation in pursuit of its objectives through its people'.

For a sports organisation, branding consists of creating a brand that is rooted in the organisation's values, and then developing recognition for that brand outside the organisation. In order to achieve this, the organisation's external communication must be consistent with the values of its brand. For example, in 2000, the Italian Motorcycling Federation (FMI) decided to improve its communication and to adopt a relationship-marketing approach. In order to do this, it was necessary to modify the actions of the people and organisations concerned so they would contribute to the commitment and satisfaction of all parties. Table 3.7 presents the FMI's vision, mission, values, end goals and positioning statement. They demonstrate a stakeholder focus and a relationship-based outlook.

This brand identity must be actively communicated to all the FMI's staff, volunteers and regional committees so it can be turned into action. This involves going through the following stages: inform → understand → accept → commit → act → assess.

Internal communication and network structure

Internal communication is a vital tool in implementing relationship-oriented internal marketing. It enables a sports organisation to specify its identity and to take actions that will ensure everyone understands their role in ensuring

Table 3.7 The FMI's vision, mission, values, end goals and positioning statement

Dimension	Italian Motorcycling Federation
Vision	A dynamic Federation with great traditions and prestige that professionally and skilfully addresses and resolves issues in the world of motorcycling
Mission	Sports results, quality services for members and partners, social marketing, improving economic impact and communication
Values	Courage, freedom, passion, tradition
End goal	Develop a sporting culture within Italy through a powerful relational network in order to generate economic, cultural and social benefits
Positioning statement	The FMI works for all responsible motorcyclists (For whom?) Covers motorcycling in all its forms (What?) Join an organisation that combines tradition, skills and social responsibility (Why?)

end-users' needs are satisfied. In addition, it allows interested parties to suggest changes that may improve this satisfaction. A large variety of channels can be used. The FMI mostly uses face-to-face communication – a very effective method – associated with team meetings, intranet and news bulletins, newsletters, a magazine and notice boards.

It is also essential to take into account the structure of the internal information system. Information is a strategic resource that must be managed in a way that suits the structure of the network. This requires defining end goals, circuits, types and times for internal communication.

Knowledge management

Skills form another strategic resource that can be difficult to capitalise on due to the loss of individual skills (e.g. staff turnover, retirement of experts), the loss of collective skills (e.g. breaking up of project teams, reorganisations), forgotten knowledge (e.g. previous experience, rejected solutions, failures) and undiscovered skills (e.g. insufficient knowledge of skills profiles, poor sharing of skills, ignorance of new solutions). In order to create value from its intellectual capital, a sports organisation must set up a knowledge management system. Bukowiz and Williams (2000: 2) defined intellectual capital or knowledge as 'anything valued by the organisation that is embedded in people or derived from processes, systems, and the organisational culture – individual knowledge and skills, norms and values, databases, methodologies, software, know-how, licences, brands and trade secrets, to name a few'.

Knowledge and skills may be shared by people who do not necessarily belong to the same unit and who may be widely separated geographically. Relationship-based internal marketing creates a multi-directional dialogue between management, staff and other interested parties, thereby providing an environment in which training, discussion and knowledge-transfer needs can be met through the development of learning communities. A learning community is a group of people who share common values and beliefs, and who are actively engaged in learning from each other. In dynamic communities, all members share control and everyone learns, including the teacher or group leader (Wilson and Cole, 1997; Scardamalia and Bereiter, 1994). For example, the aim of Olympic Solidarity 'is to organise assistance to NOCs, in particular those which have the greatest need of it. This assistance takes the form of programmes elaborated jointly by the IOC and the NOCs, with the technical assistance of the IFs, if necessary' (Article 5 of the Olympic Charter). It supports NOC management programmes that reinforce the NOC's knowledge and skills, and that encourage and support exchanges of experiences and information. This takes the form of:

- NOC-organised courses for sports administrators, which are aimed at improving sports administrators' knowledge and at strengthening the management of Olympic sports organisations
- The Executive Masters in Sports Organisation Management (MEMOS), which is an international training programme organised in partnership with universities and the Olympic world
- Dialogue between NOCs and regional forums, which are designed to facilitate the exchange of knowledge and experience on a national or continental basis.

These programmes were designed to enable NOCs to train sports administrators and to permit these administrators to exchange information and experiences in order to improve the management of their organisations (Figure 3.24). This is facilitated by the use of intranet, which allows the sharing of best practices, most notably in terms of marketing and through the

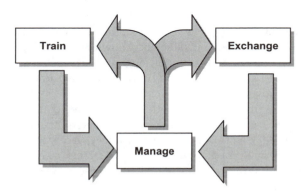

Figure 3.24 Relationships between the three objectives of NOC management training programmes.

creation of an internal market in knowledge exchange between departments, organisations, countries and continents.

Internal development and collaboration

Network-based marketing is based on cooperation between an organisation and its stakeholders; however, many organisations do not apply this principle internally. This is the case of some departments of CONI Servizi, such as Sports Facilities Consulting and School of Sport/Sports Science Institute. Each department has set up its own marketing office and offers a catalogue of services. The only example of synergy in this system is School of Sport including in its catalogue the sports facilities management service provided by Sports Facilities Consulting.

These four types of marketing action are linked and are affected by three other aspects of management. Human resources management allows organisations to motivate their personnel and to increase their skills in order to improve their effectiveness and efficiency in implementing the organisation's strategy. Quality management aims to ensure the expectations of stakeholders are satisfied and at the lowest cost. Implementing the processes required to meet this objective, for example, the definition of standards for services and the introduction of methods for evaluating satisfaction and perceived quality, requires the support and commitment of the entire organisation. Finally, an organisation's structure must be adapted to meet the needs of its strategy. The structure 'is all the functions and relations that formally determine the missions each unit of the organisation must accomplish, and the modes of collaboration between these units' (Détrie et al., 2005: 253). These relationships are presented in Figure 3.25.

Recruiting personnel

An organisation's personnel are a vital resource in the provision of sports services; however, it will not always be easy to recruit the best people, as there will be competition for this resource from other organisations. Personnel can be divided into a number of different categories:

- Salaried personnel who are linked to the organisation by an employment contract
- Volunteers who take part in the functioning of the sports organisation without any financial reward or compensation and without any obligations
- Personnel provided by a partner organisation. These contract workers remain employees of the partner organisation, which is responsible for their remuneration, social security cover, insurance and promotion

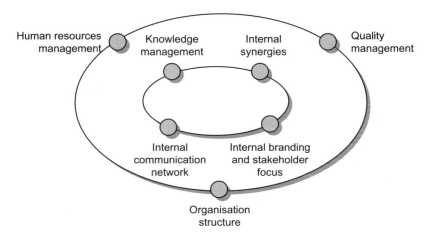

Figure 3.25 Relationships between internal marketing actions and other management fields.

- Personnel seconded to the organisation (e.g. civil servants working for the state or the local authorities).

Table 3.8 presents data from the Athletissima international athletics meeting in Lausanne, where 88 per cent of the people employed are volunteers and only 12 per cent are paid staff.

The recruitment market covers all the categories of people who may be employed, as well as the stakeholders that serve as access channels. Organisations have to activate networks that will allow them to create a relationship with potential employees, and then market themselves to these people in order to recruit them. An organisation that adopts a relationship-based marketing approach will strive to attain the following three objectives:

BE THE PREFERRED ORGANISATION OF PROFESSIONALS AND VOLUNTEERS

In order to recruit the best professionals and volunteers, these people must be persuaded to apply for available positions, and then to accept the employment offer they are given. Most sports organisations do not offer competitive salaries compared with the private sector, so it is essential to use the organisation's brand capital, in particular its foundations (i.e. vision, mission, values on which the internal branding is based) to attract personnel who share the organisation's values and with whom it is possible to create a socio-emotional link. An organisation's name recognition and image play a vital role in this; therefore, it is unsurprising that organisation committees for major inter-

Table 3.8 Status of the personnel under the authority of the Athletissima organisation committee

Status	%	Number of people
Salaried staff	<1	2
Contracted personnel	11.73	107
Seconded personnel	<1	3
Volunteers	87.71	800
TOTAL	100	912

national sports events are very attractive (e.g. more than 40,000 candidates for the volunteers programme for the 2006 Turin Winter Olympics).

UNDERSTAND THE EXPECTATIONS OF TARGET GROUPS SO THEY CAN BE OFFERED THE BENEFITS THEY SEEK

This is a difficult objective to attain given the wide range of profiles, statuses and cultures of an organisation's targets. An accurate idea of the expectations of professionals and volunteers can be obtained through interviews in which potential candidates can be asked to express their expectations and perception of the organisation. The information provided by these interviews must then be collated and processed. Some organisations have carried out studies to determine the motivations of potential staff or volunteers. For example, the results of a survey carried out by the organisation committee for the 2006 Turin Olympics to identify the main motivations of its volunteers are presented in Table 3.9.

Volunteers' key expectations must be met; however, this is facilitated by the fact that these people share the same values and that they will work in a positive socio-emotional climate. In addition, an organisation must provide opportunities for their volunteers' professional development and training, both within their job-skill area and in areas such as cultural sensitivity and personal development. It must also respect its volunteers' abilities and time commitment, and be able to offer a wide range of job opportunities that will meet their needs.

BUILD NETWORKS OF STAKEHOLDERS FOR RECRUITMENT

By adopting a network approach to relationship management, an organisation can manage the relations between several sub-systems. Relationships must be identified and built with stakeholders that can contribute to recruitment, some of which may provide staff as part of a partnership agreement. This is very important for sports organisations that need to recruit large numbers of people, such as the organisation committees for major international sports events.

Table 3.9 Motivations of the volunteers for the 2006 Turin Olympics

Motivation	%
Participate and be part of a unique event	90
Have new experiences and learn new things	87
Meet other people and make new friends	86
Promote Italy's image and the values of sport	80
Be part of an extraordinary sports event	60
Develop self esteem and demonstrate one's knowledge and capabilities	55

Illustration of best practices in internal relationship-marketing programmes

The cases presented below illustrate the interactions between the different dimensions of relationship-based internal marketing. The first study looks at the volunteers programme for the 2006 Winter Olympic Games in Turin (Italy), in which recruitment and loyalty-building strategies were built up around a specific brand strategy: the 'Noi 2006' brand. The second case illustrates the practical development of an Olympic Academy in the United States, showing the value for large sports organisations of creating a common identity that will unite programmes managed by different departments. The final case study presents the communication audit approach adopted by a French professional ice-hockey club. This approach enabled the club to identify ways of improving its information management – an important strategic resource for a sports organisation.

Case Study: The Volunteers Programme for the 20th Winter Olympic Games in Turin: Noi 2006

Case focus:

Organising the Olympic Games requires setting up a volunteers programme that will allow the organisation committee to recruit thousands of people, and then to motivate these people and build their loyalty. The Noi 2006 volunteers programme for the 20th Winter Olympic Games in Turin was built on a relationship-marketing strategy based on cooperation between key stakeholders, the creation and development of a one-to-one relationship with each volunteer and the creation of a specific brand, called Noi 2006. By building a one-to-one relationship with its volunteers, the organisation committee was able to recruit the best people and build their loyalty. The Noi 2006 brand was used to create a collective identity based on the values of a shared objective.

Case diagnosis:

Volunteer management programmes for sports events encompass the programming of all the volunteer human resources management actions (before, during and after the event). Its main objective is to have the right people in the right place at the right time, and to do this at a much lower cost than if the required number of people had to be paid. However, saving money is not the only managerial objective. For many participants, the volunteers personify the event, and volunteers play an essential role in promoting the event during the competition phase. On an operational level, volunteers programmes can be structured into six phases. The first three phases are aimed at acquiring the necessary volunteer human resources (i.e. scheduling, needs analysis, recruitment and assignment). The objective of the final three phases (i.e. integration and training, operational management, evaluation, follow up and conservation) is to maintain and cultivate these human resources.

The volunteers programme as a collective project

A volunteers programme is capable of creating value and of providing a link between the event's stakeholders. In the case of the Turin Winter Olympic Games, the involvement of primary stakeholders, such as the IOC, TOROC, the Italian government and the local authorities, was essential to the success of the event. The Olympic Games volunteers programme was defined mainly by the TOROC, the IOC and the local authorities. Those stakeholders were sensitive to the issue of volunteers, as well as to corporate social responsibility (CSR), and the programme combined organisational and societal objectives. Actions were carried out to ensure volunteers were trained to perform their allotted tasks 'well' (individually and collectively) so the operational implementation of the event ran smoothly. However, training was also oriented towards ensuring social development (notion of legacy) by valorising the skills acquired by the volunteers and thereby facilitating their professional and/or social integration. In this type of context, one objective cannot be dissociated from the other.

There were five phases in the development of this process:

1   Achieving stakeholder agreement on the programme's objectives
2   Choosing the stakeholders needed for the programme and gaining their commitment
3   Designing the volunteers programme
4   Programme implementation
5   Legacy and activation of valuable networks

Four main stakeholders engaged financial, technical and human resources for the Noi 2006 volunteer programme. Table 3.10 shows the contribution of each of these parties.

Programme development

The Noi 2006 volunteers programme lasted approximately two years, starting from the recruitment phase. During the recruitment, selection and general training phases it was run entirely by the volunteers department. During the assignment, specialist training and scheduling phases, the volunteers department took on a steering role, with the direct management of the volunteers being delegated to the different departments. The complete programme management process (i.e. beginning and end of each task) is outlined in Table 3.11.

Case development:

The volunteers department was part of the organising committee (TOROC) and under the direct responsibility of the general management. It was completely separate from the human resources department, which was responsible

Table 3.10 The contributions of the four main stakeholders in the Noi 2006 volunteers programme

The city of Turin	Adecco employment agency	Asics	TNT
Turin City Council worked with the organising committee on drawing up and producing local publicity for the recruitment campaign	In its role as official supplier for selecting volunteers, general training and team leader training, Adecco was responsible for: • the selection and training project, following the strategy defined by the volunteers department • convening applicants and carrying out interviews • convening the volunteers and carrying out general training • producing the teaching materials for the general and team leader training	Also an official supplier, the sporting goods manufacturer Asics equipped all the personnel for the Olympic Games and for the Paralympics (uniform, etc.)	Official sponsor for the transport of uniforms and equipment for the personnel for the Olympic Games and for the Paralympics

Table 3.11 The stages of the Noi 2006 volunteers programme

Stage	Length (months)	Beginning	End	Tasks
1	18	01/2004	05/2005	Collecting application forms
2	5	05/2004	09/2004	Face-to-face interviews
3	12	10/2004	10/2005	General training
4	9	05/2005	01/2006	Specialist training
5	4	09/2005	12/2005	Functional and geographic assignment
6	3	12/2005	02/2006	Definition of the work programme
7	3	12/2005	02/2006	Accreditation and distribution of uniforms
8	0.5	02/2006	02/2006	Olympic Games
9	4	03/2006	07/2006	Assessment and legacy

for managing the salaried staff on the organising committee. The process of managing the volunteer programme was divided into three phases:

1   Create relationships with recruitment targets and recruit them
2   Develop the relationship in order to establish loyalty
3   Legacy and activation of efficient networks.

In order to fulfil these objectives the volunteers department implemented three action lines.

Branding

A specific brand, Noi 2006, was created for the volunteers programme in order to create a feeling of belonging to the team. The branding strategy was based on the following values: passion, sense of belonging, pride, solidarity and achievement. The brand's communication materials used the present tense to give the idea that the team already exists, simple and direct language, and the colour red to symbolise the volunteers' passion for the event. Olympic champions Alberto Tomba and Piero Gros were chosen as ambassadors for Noi 2006. They played a fundamental role in expressing brand values and in attracting volunteers.

An integrated communication strategy

The communication plan aimed to:

•   encourage applications from volunteers who already had accommodation at one of the Olympic venues, especially in the mountain resorts

- promote applications from inhabitants of the Olympic valleys
- encourage hospitality amongst the volunteers (so local volunteers would house others from further afield)
- motivate the volunteers and ensure they take responsibility for their actions
- ensure maximum commitment to the Games from the volunteers by guaranteeing each volunteer at least ten days' work.

The communication conveyed the message that the Olympic Games is an exceptional event: for most volunteers this was a unique opportunity to participate in a global event with definite sporting and social values. It was important to find a 'happy medium' between a volunteer being an 'ordinary person' (so as not to frighten potential applicants) and, at the same time, a 'special person' (in order to stimulate the creation of a team spirit).

Frequency

- Communicate regularly throughout the programme (internet site, newsletters, mailing, text messages, etc.)
- Organise special events to mark determining moments in the campaign, for example:
  - Launch of the programme: January 2004
  - Recruitment of the first ten volunteers: big party on 15th February 2005 (a year before the event)
  - Test events for the competition venues (sports events): January–March 2005
  - Official presentation of uniforms: September 2005.

Communication actions

Pre-event

- Internet site: with access to a reserved area for downloading training materials and broadcasting information
- Newsletters
- General training manual
- Specialist training manual: using the same design, list of themes and general information for all functions
- Training rooms decorated with the Noi 2006 programme design
- Venue guide: pocket guide with practical advice to follow during the Games

- Text message and e-mail countdown, invitations to special events
- Job offers: official confirmation of the volunteer's recruitment and assignment (role, tasks, venue, etc.)
- Invitation to collect official uniforms
- Exclusive New Year's greetings cards
- Virtual venue tour: interactive training on the Olympic venues.

During the event

- Volunteers bulletin: daily newsletter written by the volunteers for the volunteers and coordinated by the volunteers manager for each venue
- Televideo (teletext): pages dedicated to operational information
- Radio programme: dedicated to volunteers' stories.

After the event

- Parties, where feedback was collected
- Internet site
- Newsletters.

Collaborative programmes with 'sourcing' organisations

The volunteers department developed collaborative programmes with various organisations in order to promote the volunteers programme and to gain the loyalty of volunteers. Young people and people who already belonged to associations were targeted.

Young people

Young people represented about 63 per cent of applicants. Many special projects and initiatives were launched to obtain this result, including:

'Ragazzi del 2006'

- Initiative promoting civic voluntary work introduced by the City of Turin and the Province of Turin in 1999
- A specific agreement was signed with TOROC in March 2004 (G-2).

'Città delle Alpi'

- Association of 25 cities belonging to 5 countries (Italy, France, Austria, Switzerland, Slovenia)

- A specific project for Olympic voluntary work was created ('Young Volunteers from the Alps').

Universities

- Special initiative cancelling lessons and exams during the Games (high school and university)
- Credits granted (1–10) to all students who served as volunteers for at least 10 days
- Specific training sessions in conjunction with the Politecnico di Torino (topics: infrastructure, transport and logistics, technology).

Erasmus students

- Special project to encourage foreign students present in Turin during the Olympic period to volunteer
- The project's objective was to integrate the Olympic experience into a traditional training programme.

Associations and organisations

- Seven thousand candidates for the Noi 2006 Programme, corresponding to about 17 per cent of all applicants, belonged to partner associations, including:

'Coordinamento no profit'

- Network of associations for voluntary work, cooperation and social promotion that was created to support and promote Olympic and Paralympic events among their members
- The association continues to work with the Olympic Foundation in an initiative to develop the Olympic legacy of volunteers.

Firms

- A significant number of candidates were employees or former employees of local companies, most notably FIAT and the San Paolo Group.

Alpini (army)

- Specific cooperation project with former soldiers from the 'Alpini' corps to manage critical areas in logistics and transport.

Sports associations

- A large number of candidates were members of sports associations and groups
- In December 2004, an agreement was signed with high schools offering courses in mountain-sports and ski clubs.

Results:

Out of 42,500 applicants, more than 30,000 candidates were contacted and 29,950 interviews were performed: 24,349 volunteers were selected and about 18,000 trained. Table 3.12 presents the profiles of the volunteers.

The results in terms of attendance widely exceeded expectations, with an average attendance of 93.8 per cent during the Olympic Games period (varied between 100 per cent and a minimum of 68.5 per cent). After the event, 89.2 per cent of volunteers declared they were very satisfied or satisfied with their experience. This can be considered a good satisfaction rate.

Two years after the event, volunteers from the Noi 2006 programme still regularly participate in the organisation of other events. In addition, the cooperative networks of organisations created during the Olympic Games are still in place and promote the development of new projects, particularly as part of the Olympic Foundation.

Resources

Ferrand A., Chanavat, N. (2006a)

Table 3.12 Profiles of the volunteers at the 20th Winter Olympic Games, Turin 2006 by age group

18–35 years old	*36–54 years old*	*Over 55 years old*
• Mostly women (52%)	• Mostly men (64%)	• Mostly men (79%)
• Mostly students (69%) or employees (27%)	• Mostly employees (82%)	• Mostly retired (81%).
• Well qualified (18% university and 58% secondary school).	• Well qualified (22% university and 54% secondary school).	• 11% had a university degree and 48% had a secondary school diploma
• Excellent linguistic skills: 83% spoke at least one foreign language and 44% spoke two or more languages	• Good linguistic skills: 57% spoke at least one foreign language and 32% spoke two or more languages	• 34% spoke French or another foreign language

Resource websites

www.sentedalps.org
www.olympic.org

Case Study: The Practical Development of an Olympic Academy in the United States

Jeffrey Howard: United States Olympic Committee

Case focus:

As with all Olympic terminology, the word 'Olympic' resonates with individuals throughout the world. At its core, the Olympic brand can be considered the most recognised sports brand in the world. Therefore, the United States Olympic Committee's non-use of the strong Olympic Academy brand since the dissolution of the US Olympic Academy in 1991 has been seen as a significant missed opportunity in the eyes of some within the Olympic Movement.

The re-engagement of this important Olympic brand is important to the United States Olympic Committee. However, the reinstitution of the US Olympic Academy must be practical; meaning, costs, significant reach and inclusion of key stakeholders are key components to the ultimate success of its re-establishment.

Case diagnosis:

It seems that in the eyes of some, the ability for a National Olympic Committee to say that it is living up to the expectation that it has a viable Olympic education programme is directly related to it having an Olympic Academy. For that reason, the United States Olympic Committee needs to re-establish an Olympic Academy. However, current trends within the organisation to reinstitute programmes that have failed in the past require a change in strategy and programme format for ultimate acceptance. Therefore, the new Olympic Academy needs to be constituted in such a way that it reaches the masses in American society versus a select few.

The previous United States Olympic Academy came into existence on 19th June, 1977. The Academy started as a three-day programme with the University of Illinois – Chicago Circle serving as the event's host institution. The coordinator for the inaugural Olympic Academy was Dr Nina Pappas, a participant in the International Olympic Academy programme in 1972. Through the subsequent 15 years of existence, the attendance for the programme varied, but never exceeded 400 participants.

US Olympic academy participation

Figure 3.26 details some statistical information on each of the previous US Olympic Academies.

Case development:

As our history indicates, the United States Olympic Committee has always taken a great deal of pride in its programmes that go to promote the Olympic Ideals and Values. Though many of these programmes have changed through the years, and in some cases ceased to be viable initiatives, the organisation has always supported some measure of activity that could be considered Academy programming.

Currently, the United States Olympic Committee has a diverse group of activities that are making positive inroads in American society. The programmes consist of both education- and group-based activities (Table 3.13).

The United States Olympic Committee is also making a concerted effort to engage its most viable resource, Olympians and Paralympians, as key contributors to the promotion of its Academy-based programmes.

Based upon the current climate at the United States Olympic Committee in combination with the varied stakeholders that a US Olympic Academy is

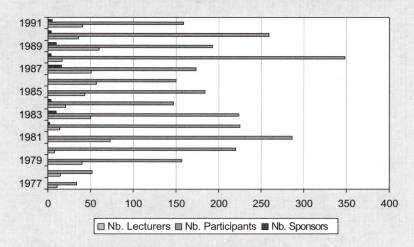

Figure 3.26 Previous US Olympic Academies participation.

Table 3.13 Education and group-based activities programmes

Programme	Year established	Description	Impact
F.L.A.M.E. (Finding Leaders Among Minorities Everywhere)	1994	The F.L.A.M.E. programme was developed to help educate, encourage and demonstrate to minority youth that any goal is attainable through commitment and perseverance. The young men and women selected to participate have already demonstrated the pursuit of excellence within their own communities through achievements in academics, sport, leadership and community service. Once in the F.L.A.M.E. programme, they are exposed to the ideals and values of the Olympic Movement, thereby furthering their personal and professional development	More than 30 college students per year
Regional F.L.A.M.E	2007	Because the original F.L.A.M.E. programme reaches a minimal number of participants, the United States Olympic Committee is seeking to impact a larger number of minority youth through an outreach effort focused on impacting athletes at earlier stages in their careers. The Regional F.L.A.M.E. programme is targeted toward high school minority student-athletes (freshmen, sophomores, juniors and seniors) across the country. The United States Olympic Committee's goal is to expose student-athletes to the unique opportunity to be mentored by Olympians and Paralympians, while instilling the understanding that each participant is also a role model to younger fans	More than 500 student-athletes
Olympic Week in America	2007	The United States Olympic Committee identified 30 April–4 May for the first Olympic Week in America. The new, week-long initiative is a comprehensive, interdisciplinary programme on Olympic Ideals and Values for grades kindergarten through five (ages 5–11). The Olympic Week in America programme was created for educators' use in expanding student awareness and appreciation of the Olympic and Paralympic Games and the Olympic Movement. Its lessons and activities enhance core curricula taught in the classroom. Through a focus on the Olympic Games, students reinforce their skills in language arts, social studies, maths, science, and physical education	More than 1,000 teachers and 200,000 students

Olympians in Life	2007	The United States Olympic Committee has developed 'Olympians in Life' – educational lesson plans for grades kindergarten through 12 (ages 5–17). The comprehensive effort focuses on Beijing as it promotes Olympic Ideals and Values to each of the four major educational strands: K–2, 3–5, 6–8, and 9–12. All materials for 'Olympians in Life' are distributed free to educators through www.usolympicteam.com	Expected impact, 1 million
Red Ribbon Week Programme	2006	Fair play and drug prevention are the messages promoted by United States Olympians and Paralympians to America's youth during Red Ribbon Week. The United States Olympic Committee coordinates appearances of Olympians and Paralympians during Red Ribbon Week in conjunction with its multi-year National Olympic Education Programme, which promotes Olympic Ideals and Values. Olympians and Paralympians visit schools and community centres in cities across the country as ambassadors for the ideals and values associated with the Olympic Movement. National Red Ribbon Week serves as a tribute to DEA Special Agent Enrique Camarena, who was murdered by drug traffickers in Mexico in 1985	Approx. 2,000 students in 12 US cities
'Real Athletes ...'	2005	The United States Olympic Committee announced in 2005 the creation of a National Olympic Education Programme with Olympic Values serving as the platform for the initiative. Through a multi-year campaign, the United States Olympic Committee seeks to positively impact Americans by showcasing and championing the principles associated with the Olympic Movement. Olympic Ideals and Values include: inspiration, friendship, fair play, perseverance, mutual respect, sacrifice, hope, dreams, patriotism, unity and joy in effort	Public Service Announcements have reach more than 10 million

(Continued overleaf)

Table 3.13 Continued

Programme	Year established	Description	Impact
Athlete Speaker's Referral Network	2007	The United States Olympic Committee is in the process of creating an Athlete Speaker's Referral Network to allow the general public to contact US Olympians, Paralympians, and hopefuls to schedule speaking appearances for corporate events, civic organization meetings, school visits, etc. Athletes interested in becoming an athlete speaker in the network will complete biographical information involving their sport and speaking experiences. The general public will then be able to access the speaker bios by going to the Athlete Speaker's Referral Network located on www.usolympicteam.com and select an athlete speaker by utilizing several search filters to fulfil the parameters of the request. The Athlete Speaker's Referral Network was launched to the public in August 2007	More than 175 Olympians and Paralympians registered
Project Rebound	2007	On 20 April 2007, more than 2,000 students at 10 New Orleans schools received an unexpected surprise as Olympians, Paralympians and elite athletes attended school assemblies and physical education classes to spread a message of hope and donate much needed sports equipment lost during the Hurricane Katrina disaster. United States Olympic Committee corporate sponsor, Nike, donated more than 2,000 pairs of shoes to students in grades 5–8 (ages 11–14) at each participating school. The Major League Baseball Players Trust also supported the initiative by donating $5,000 toward the purchase of baseball equipment. USA Badminton, USA Basketball, USA Diving, USA Swimming, USA Table Tennis, USA Tennis, USA Triathlon and USA Team Handball donated a wide assortment of equipment and apparel and Olympian Julie Foudy donated over 200 soccer balls	More than 2,000 students

Olympic Gold Exhibition	2007	Together the United States Olympic Committee and the National Jewelry Institute amassed the largest collection ever assembled of medals won by US Olympic and Paralympic competitors for display at the Forbes Galleries in downtown New York. The Forbes Gallery, located on Fifth Avenue, offers an unprecedented opportunity for the American public and an international audience to view medals and other collectibles from America's greatest Olympians and Paralympians. The exhibit traces the history of American athleticism and offer spectators a special view of the unique journey an athlete takes while representing their country at the Olympic and Paralympic Games	More than 50 Olympic Gold Medals on display for the public in New York City
Olympic Opportunity Fund	2007	The Olympic Opportunity Fund was adopted by the United States Olympic Committee in 2007. With goals to increase multicultural urban youth participation and membership in Olympic and Paralympic sports, this programme ties directly to a USOC objective to increase the relevance of the Olympic and Paralympic Movement in American society through grassroots programmes	More than 5,000 youth
Community Olympic Day	1997	Expanded support of International Olympic Day at the headquarters of the United States Olympic Committee	More than 3,000 visitors in 2007

expected to reach, it is recommended that the United States Olympic Committee position its Olympic Academy as an initiative that reaches a significant audience number. For this positioning to occur, the United States Olympic Committee must establish a common portal for the dissemination of Olympic Academy information. It is recommended that this occur through a dedicated website that lists all Olympic Academy programmes and initiatives.

This means that the United States Olympic Committee should not return to the previous format of its Olympic Academy, but embrace a format that will allow the US Olympic Academy to sustain its viability and evolve to positively impact the new challenges that may face the worldwide Olympic Movement. The final product should seek to reach all of the stakeholders with a concerted interest in Olympic Academy programmes (Figure 3.27).

Preliminary model

This new direction would have a structure that consists of the United States Olympic Academy serving as the umbrella under which all Olympic Education and Outreach Programmes would reside. By placing the Olympic Academy in the position of being an overarching theme, programmes and initiatives will be added and dropped in the future to ensure the Olympic Academy concept is both timely and relevant to its constituents. A preliminary model for the Olympic Academy could be displayed as in Figure 3.28.

The goal for the US Olympic Academy should at its very core embody the notion of 'Olympism for All'; meaning, it is the responsibility of the US Olympic Academy to maintain programmes and initiatives that reach the masses.

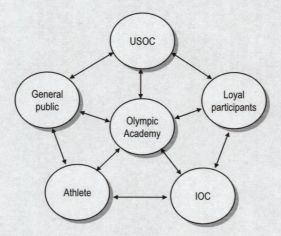

Figure 3.27 USOC Olympic academy main stakeholders.

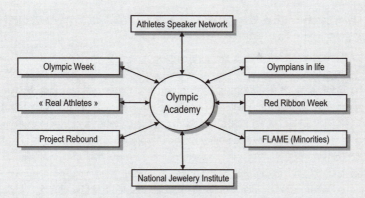

Figure 3.28 USOC programmes under the Olympic academy umbrella.

Results:

Accepting what is currently being proposed as the US Olympic Academy, the diversity of programmes and the potential of significant reach, make it much more viable in today's times.

Based on the current leadership of the United States Olympic Committee, the SWOT analysis conducted on some of the National Olympic Academies throughout the world, the results of a survey of Olympic Academies and the success of the Olympic education and outreach programmes that currently exist within the USA, the new model/direction should be embraced and supported by the many constituent groups that support the US Olympic Movement, because there is clearly more opportunity to be involved in more diverse programmes.

With this new model, the United States Olympic Committee can legitimately state that its Olympic Academy programmes touch millions of Americans either directly as a part of in-person programmes or indirectly as a result of posters and public service announcements espousing the Olympic Ideals and Values.

Resource websites

http://www.usolympicteam.com
http://www.ioa.org.gr
http://usocpressbox.org

Case Study: The diagnosis of internal communication as a support for action marketing

Sylvie Montagnon – Hommes & Développement

Sports organisations are complex, living entities. What makes them what they are, are the people within them. Whether or not a sports organisation is run as a business, it can only carry out its actions if it is suitably and efficiently organised, and this is affected by the ability of the people working within the organisation to communicate.

This case study presents a procedure for auditing internal communication, illustrated with reference to a French professional ice hockey club, the Hockey Club Mont Blanc (HCMB). The results of the HCMB audit were used to build an internal communication plan for the club. This audit was carried out by combining a number of existing tools with tools that were specifically created for this purpose.

Internal communication diagnosis method:

The diagnosis method follows the classic stages of a 'SPRIT' analysis: situation evaluation, problem identification, resolution of problems, information, techniques). The SPR section is carried out sequentially, the IT section is transversal.

S . . . situation

The first step is to evaluate the current situation and to identify the parties involved in internal communication and their working environment. This also involves identifying hierarchical and functional sub-groups within the structure, inter-dependencies, internal stakeholders, the organisation's culture and values, the mentality of the parties, and the sub-culture of departments.

It must be remembered that internal communication also involves parties outside the 'marketing' department. The 'situation' stage assesses what already exists and what is missing, and differentiates between what is satisfactory and what is unsatisfactory. Findings must be presented in a purely factual way, leaving any discussion of the results or proposals for changes and improvements to a later stage.

The tools used:

1   The W8H2, in its 'internal communication' version (Montagnon, 2005). The W8H2 questionnaire is based on the classic and comprehensive

W5H2 questions: Why? Who? What? Where? When? How? How much? It is used to collect the 'building blocks' that will form the basis of the audit and the search for solutions. It is a 'clear out' tool that gives an overall view of internal communication, distinguishing between the strategic level and the operational level.

2 For extra finesse, the W8H2 was crossed with two strategic analysis tools, PESTEL (Political, Economic, Social, Technical, Environmental and Legal) and SWOT (Strengths, Weaknesses, Opportunities, Threats). Although PESTEL is a macro-economic analysis tool, it can provide satisfactory input at the micro, or internal level. SWOT mostly focuses on the internal dimension of the communication system (SW); however, the external dimension (OT) also provides information about factors that influence a sports organisation's communication system.

This stage of the audit reveals 'primary problems', defined as the parties' feelings about the current situation. These feelings tend to be expressed spontaneously and categorically, and although they can be highly subjective, they provide strong clues to the actual situation. In this type of analysis, feelings about 'a thing' are as important as 'the thing' itself.

These clues are reinforced, validated or invalidated by a subsequent survey in which parties are given the opportunity to evoke malfunctions and weaknesses in the system and in the circulation of information. In general, people tend not to recognise and/or indicate a system's virtues; nevertheless, care must be taken to identify these virtues so they can be preserved.

Similarly, 'primary responses' are often evoked, for example, '. . . we have to take minutes at every meeting' and '. . . we should make everyone communicate by e-mail'. It would be detrimental to suppress this mode of expression, as any comments providing information are welcome. This information must be recorded so it can be analysed and validated (or invalidated) during the functional analysis.

3 In order to follow information flows, it is first necessary to identify the people who transmit information and those who receive it, that is to say, the *actors* of the communication. This data is used to draw up an *information organisation chart*, which is often different from an organisation's hierarchical or functional organisation chart.

4 The constituent elements of the communication are then identified by describing the communication parameters for each category of the FiNi-ViT (Flow, Type, Vector, Time/place) tool (Montagnon, 2006):

- Information flows show who 'transmits' to which 'receivers' and at what frequency or intensity (shown by an arrow linking two parties of the communication)
- Information type indicates the content at a macroscopic level, in terms of Economics, Human Resources, Organisations and Strategy – EROS method (Montagnon, 2007)
- Information Vectors, both formal and informal, e.g. e-mail, meetings, non-organised, direct verbal communication, etc.
- Time (time and place) the information is transmitted, e.g. meeting room, coffee machine, one's office, etc.

P . . . problems

It is as important to identify aspects that do not work as aspects that do work. In general, problems emerge more easily than virtues, and these problems are evoked in terms of their *effects*. Therefore, the input is in the form of the consequences of dysfunctional systems. These consequences must be noted, as they indicate the nature of the problem. Once the *effects* have been identified, the next step is to find their cause(s), so problems can be treated at their source.

Finally, both the causes and their effects are listed and ranked. Strategic choices must then be made in order to define the field of action. This can be done using Pareto's law to restrict the number of points to treat.

The tools used:

1   Causes can be identified using ISHIKAWA diagrams to link each of the effects of a dysfunction to its cause(s). FiNiViT provides input (communication parameters) for each 'category'. This involves answering the questions: 'What is at the origin of . . .?' 'What produces such effects?'

2   Identification of needs: 'a need is generated by an identified dysfunction that produces a dissatisfaction that is important enough to merit finding a solution'. This involves listing all the causes of the dysfunction of the environment that justify taking corrective action and answering the question: 'Why do (why set the process in motion), create or improve?'

3   Similarly, the analysis is completed by identifying aspects that work and are satisfactory, and that merit preserving. This involves answering the question: 'Why keep?' Paradoxically, systems that work are more difficult to identify than dysfunctional systems, as things that work appear normal and therefore remain invisible. This has been termed 'unidentified internal communication'!

Specifying the need for change at this stage restricts the field of application of the action that has to be carried out (requires defining what the field includes and excludes). Pareto's law shows that eliminating 20 per cent of the negative effects will improve 80 per cent of the functioning. This provides answers to the questions: 'What won't we improve (immediately) and why?

R. . . resolution

Once the organisation's needs have been determined, the next stage is to translate them into functions that must be satisfied by possible solutions. In other words, 'goals' must be set, answering the question 'why (do)?', in order to identify all the functions and services expected of the new system.

Tools:

1   The functional analysis is used to draw up the specifications to be met by potential solutions. Thus, the need will be expressed as follows: 'the solution (improvement) should . . . (verbal group describing the effect to correct)'. In this way, all the functions involved will be listed.
2   Value analysis can be used to ensure the analysis is comprehensive and that none of the functions or services to be provided is overlooked. In addition, the choice of which solutions to retain must take into account the environment in which the organisation operates. The elements that will be made to interact by the function are listed using key words. These elements are put in a circle and possible links between them are explored systematically.

Conclusion

The analysis process provides a clear view of the sports organisation's internal communication system. Now, it must be brought to life! This requires considering the information as a resource to be assigned to a task, just like a financial, human, temporal or material resource. This system is most effective when it is used in a project-management framework, but it is also applicable to hierarchical systems (Figure 3.29).

For each action, the input and output information to be brought together must be identified.

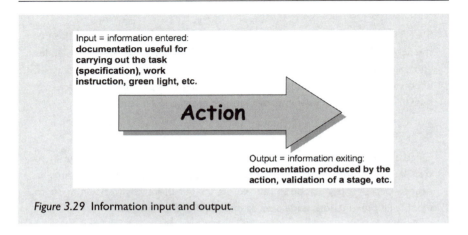

Figure 3.29 Information input and output.

Diagnosis of internal communication: a practical illustration

The following case study provides a practical illustration of the internal communication diagnosis method. The Hockey Club Mont Blanc (HCMB) runs seven ice hockey teams, one of which, the senior elite team, is a first division side. The club's sporting objective is to remain in the top part of the Magnus League and to have the best ice-hockey training centre in France.

Case Study: The Hockey Club Mont Blanc

Sylvie Montagnon – Hommes & Développement

Situation

This example focuses on the management of complaints. It uses the FiNiViT and EROS methods.

The club's personnel appear to believe that the club does not listen to, or take into account their remarks, complaints and requests. In terms of mobilising the club's human resources and the company culture, this perception is harmful. Once internal marketing had identified these difficulties and validated the value of working to overcome them, it was necessary to look for solutions.

This required analysing information flows within HCMB. The Fi (Figure 3.30) and Ni parts of the FiNiViT analysis provided an overview of internal communication that could be used to focus the audit on the issue of the Board's response to complaints and suggestions (bottom-up aspect only).

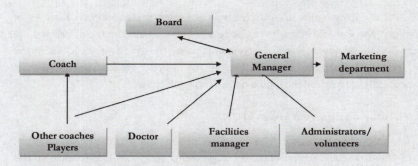

Figure 3.30 Information flows within HCMB.

Ni: information type

E(ros) = Economic

The General Manager centralises information relating to means or material resources: resources that the Board provides and that the personnel request. The General Manager provides the link between the Board and the personnel.

(e)R(os) = Human Resources

Information relating to the adequacy of human resources, in terms of quantity, quality, distribution, availability and training. Once again, the General Manager provides the link.

(er)O(s) = Organisational

The General Manager translates the Board's policies and decisions into operational terms. This determines the managerial structure of the team and the club. This information is part of the ecology of the system, that is to say, it helps maintain an optimum balance between effectiveness, efficiency and the assistance given to personnel whose job description changes or who are transferred. Same mode of transmission as above.

(ero)S = Strategic

This type of information concerns policy and regulatory (legal) aspects of the structure. Top-down information is designed to implement actions that are designed to achieve a policy objective. Bottom-up information tends to influence policy to ensure effective and efficient operation, or a bending of the policy line. The General Manager is the pivot.

All the information transmitted to the Board passes through a series of filters. The General Manager can place an interface between the Board and the personnel. At lower levels, expression is relatively direct. As it moves up the hierarchy, it becomes increasingly censured in order to comply with what is politically correct for the whole hierarchical structure.

Vi: Information vectors at HCMB

The study then focused on the personnel's sentiment that the Board does not take into account complaints and suggestions. In fact, a closer look at this 'primary problem' indicated that information is generally transmitted up the hierarchy informally. There are no specific meetings; however, during discussions up to the General Manager level, the personnel express complaints in terms of shortcomings, dysfunctions and possible solutions ('we should . . .'). At the General Manager to Board level, these complaints are considered at (too rare) meetings, and they are frequently only resolved in principle. They are listened to, but the only response is to look for solutions at a later date. The objective aspect of this situation, which creates non-quality, and its subjective aspect (feelings) lead to de-motivation.

T: time and place

As stated above, complaints and suggestions often emerge outside meetings and in an informal, non-structured way. Times and places for raising these issues are not set aside, except on a purely sporting level, from a 'horizontal' perspective.

Problems

The cause/effects diagram for the processing of complaints by HCMB shows one of the main problems raised by the personnel (Figure 3.31). The diagram includes six domains: economic data, culture, hierarchical and decision-making structure, communication modes and vectors, skills and organisation.

Resolution of problems

For HCMB, this analysis enabled the drawing up of a functional specification for the system to introduce as part of an internal marketing solution (Figure 3.32).

By putting the communication components into a circle, it was possible to identify the functions the system must include to ensure complaints are addressed. For example, the transfer function must allow the General Manager

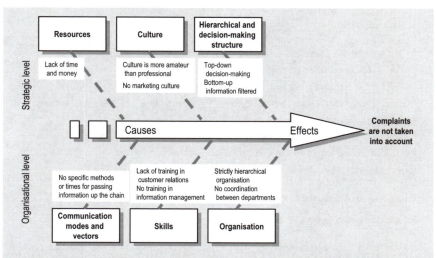

Figure 3.31 Cause/effect diagram for the processing of complaints by HCMB.

to collect information. Considering even the most absurd proposals ensures that no important functions are overlooked. In this way, contact functions, which are part of the information system, can be identified: 'The complaint must be collected without being altered or misinterpreted'.

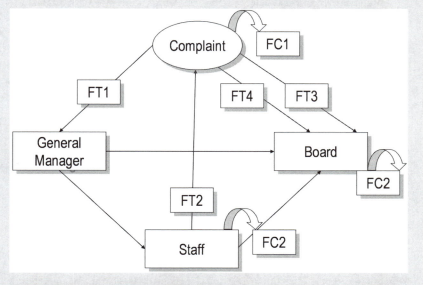

Figure 3.32 Internal solutions envisaged by HCMB.

This showed that:

FT1: The system must allow the General Manager to collect complaints
FC1: Complaints must be collected without being altered
FT2: The system must allow the personnel to express their complaints
FC2: Complaints must be expressed in a way that ensures they can be understood, ranked and used
FT3: The system must allow the Board to take note of complaints
FC3: The Board must be able to understand the complaints
FT4: The system must allow the Board to deal with the complaints.

Recommendations for HCMB

Internal marketing proposed:

- Raising awareness (training) among all the personnel of the need to communicate and of the means available for communication, so the sports organisation can be more 'communicative'
- Structuring strategic information and organising its distribution to ensure the club's policy and the measures taken are well (better) understood
- (Re)structuring the bottom-up and top-down communication systems, combining training for the personnel and the Board (improvement of the information recording system – degree of interest – understanding – of strategic and/or organisational information), and a judicious choice of communication, information gathering and information processing methods.

The next stage is not to draw up an ideal – but probably aspirational – solution from these elements, but to propose several alternative or combinable models. This involves analysing value from economic and multi-criteria points of view.

Solution 1:
Carry out an audit of the sports organisation and engage a specialist firm to reorganise it.

Solution 2:
Do the same thing using trainees.

Solution 3:
Ask the marketing department to work on changing the company culture to a more collaborative one.

Solution 4:

Ask the marketing department to improve the efficiency of the bottom-up and top-down communication systems.

Solution 5:

Ask the marketing department to train all parties in the new communication method.

By weighting social, cultural and duration factors it is possible to allocate values to possible solutions, comparing their cost with their potential benefits. This type of evaluation allows decision makers to be more open about how decisions were made (Table 3.14).

Successful implementation through the application of 'project' logic: identify each action and treat information as a resource

Table 3.14 shows the information flow for each task. The left-hand column shows the transmitters and receivers of the information. The middle column shows the flows ascending towards the marketing assistant (MA). The right-hand column shows the flows descending from the MA (Table 3.15).

1   Collecting information required by the Board
2   Collecting information about the General Manager's wishes and discussion of his/her role at the meeting
3   Collecting information about the personnel's wishes
4   Have the agenda approved by the Board
5   In consultation with the General Manager, fix a date for the meeting
6   Inform the personnel of the meeting's agenda, sub-contract the organisation of the event.

Conclusion

The analysis of internal communication is a valuable tool (and one that is seen as unintrusive) for auditing a structure, revealing its organisational weaknesses and suggesting possible improvements. It can lead to strategic recommendations, at the same time that the conditions for supervising change are integrated into the relational dynamic of the communication system.

Table 3.14 Evaluation of the value of solutions

Solutions	Economic, Financial (/10)	Social, Human change (/20)	Cultural (/20)	Legal (/10)	Logistic, Structure of the space (/10)	Time, Duration (/20)	Risk (/10)	Total, Ratio (/100)	Efficiency (/10)
1	10	18	19	2	8	15	3	75	9
2	2	16	10	8	8	20	5	64	5
3	6	10	10	2	2	5	2	37	2
4	6	10	10	2	2	5	2	37	2
5	6	10	10	2	2	5	2	37	2
3+4+5	8	15	15	2	8	20	1	69	9

Table 3.15 Example of the use of the tool for identifying the communication flows required by an action: 'Drawing up the agenda for a Board-Personnel meeting' by the marketing department

	Marketing Department (MA)	
Board	1	4
General Manager	2	5
Personnel	3	6

Resources

Johnson et al. (2004)
Montagnon (2005, 2006, 2007)

Resource websites

www.hommes-developpement.fr
www.pmi.org

Conclusion

The introduction of a relationship-marketing approach to the market, network and internal sub-systems is an iterative process that allows an organisation to improve its overall performance by learning from cumulative experience. This process requires the implementation of actions to promote the stakeholder focus in order to create and develop relationships with a value constellation. Figure 3.33 shows the components of this framework.

The second issue relates to the assessment of a sports organisation's relationship-marketing strategy in the three sub-systems. To do this, an organisation must choose indicators for each sub-system. These indicators must be relevant to its situation and the necessary information must be available. On a macro level, it is about evaluating performance with respect to the four end goals in the three sub-systems (Table 3.16).

This evaluation can be completed by a more qualitative phase. Then it is possible to determine for each sub-system whether it is simply necessary to maintain the current situation or whether it is necessary to make an effort to improve it. The scores presented in Table 3.16 show that this sports organisation should focus its efforts on the network and on internal sub-systems.

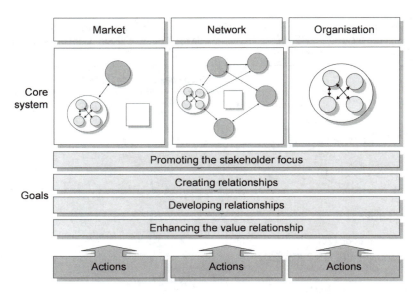

Figure 3.33 Relationship-marketing strategy implementation framework.

Table 3.16 Evaluation of performance with respect to the end goals and sub-systems

	Market	Network	Internal
Stakeholder focus	4	2	1
Strategic stakeholders engagement	3	2	2
Strategic stakeholders relationship development	3	1	1
Value relationship with existing stakeholders	4	2	2
Total	14	7	6

Chapter 4

British Judo case study

Relationship-marketing principles in a national governing body of sport

Introduction

The business of sport is becoming more sophisticated and the need to adopt cutting edge business principles to be successful is universally accepted. The sporting landscape is complicated. The key objectives of a sporting body are unique and can cover quite a wide spectrum.

In business, the key objective is normally to make a profit with a number of secondary objectives that may contribute positively towards the key object-ive. In sporting bodies, the key objectives are less specific and certainly more varied. A national governing body of sport might have a spectrum of key objectives – with largely equal levels of importance. The purpose of a national governing body (NGB) is: to manage the sport; increase participation; improve the profile; generate greater resources; stage world class events; to improve the workforce to deliver the sport; to service a membership base; to strengthen the delivery units; to improve the technical delivery; to secure elite performance success and also to entertain. The over-riding objective would be to move the sport forward in all areas. The common requirement in the pursuit of successfully delivering these objectives is the need for resources and partners.

This is a multi-faceted delivery platform and there is a tremendous need to develop relationship-marketing principles with a large number of constitu-ents to effectively deliver the sport. It is also important to understand that in an environment of limited resources, it is critical to analyse your key object-ives, stakeholders and the dynamic between the two, to identify the most efficient way to deliver significant impact.

This case study will analyse the British Judo Association and the develop-ment of a strategically driven relationship-marketing strategy to enlist the support of a wide range of stakeholders to maximise the potential of the body and ultimately the sport. The study will be comprised of an introduction to set the stage. Judo is a traditional sport and it should be noted that no two sports, or in fact sporting bodies, are alike. Each faces unique challenges and also has unique strengths and competitive advantages.

After setting the stage, we will analyse the stakeholders and key objectives using the MACTOR methodology. This will allow us to determine the key actors and key objectives and devise a strategy to maximise the delivery with the resources available. All sports are resource driven. Those sports that have great resources have the ability to drive the sport forward. It takes resources, both financial and personnel, to deliver a product, whether it is a sport or a commercial venture.

We must identify the combinations of stakeholders and relationship-marketing strategies that will deliver value constellations. By choosing the right path and correct combinations, it is possible to deliver a greater overall return.

Setting the stage

The British Judo Association (BJA) was formed in 1948 and is the recognised national governing body for the sport in the UK. The BJA is affiliated to the European Judo Union and the International Judo Federation, along with the British Olympic Association, the International Olympic Association and the Commonwealth Games Council. The BJA membership is club based and currently, there are over 850 individual clubs located in England, Scotland, Wales and Northern Ireland. The clubs are the voting members of the Association.

The BJA also has a relatively large pool of over 40,000 individual licence holders with 30,000 in England, 6,000 in Scotland, 2,500 in Wales and 1,500 in Northern Ireland. There are also another 10,000 individual members linked to the Association through other affiliated judo organisations, the British Judo Council and the Amateur Judo Association. It is estimated that over 100,000 individuals are actively participating in the sport of judo in the UK at present. One of the key objectives of the Association moving forward is to harness this level of activity and move the individual licence holder total closer to the six-figure mark.

The BJA incorporates home country judo bodies in Scotland, Wales and Northern Ireland and also have nine regional area bodies in England. The general working relationships within British judo are good. Although the HC bodies effectively function as separate limited companies with full autonomy, there is much that binds the bodies and there is much consistency across borders.

The BJA is managed by an elected Board of Directors comprised of a Chairman and seven ordinary Board members. The BJA has a staff complement of 52 full-time employees and an annual turnover of circa £4.5m. Judo Scotland has a full time staff complement of six and an annual turnover of circa £300,000. Welsh Judo is staffed with two full-time and three part-time employees, and has an annual turnover of £200,000. The Northern Ireland Judo Federation staff includes one full-time and two part-time officers, with an annual turnover of £70,000. It is clear that each of these bodies is significantly different in terms of size and resources. It is also clear that each of these bodies deals with different funding partners; each with unique policies, requirements and procedures.

The BJA has benefited greatly from support from the key government funded sports bodies, UK Sport and Sport England, and from the other Home Country sports councils over the years and is well placed to move forward now that the structures are stronger and the body has been dramatically modernised. UK Sport is charged with supporting performance sport across the UK and Sport England is charged with sports development, working through the government bodies and other partners, in England. In recent years, the Association has made numerous senior management appointments, improved corporate governance policies and procedures, strengthened the financial model, introduced many new programmes, formed a commercial division, and generally has become a progressive and modern NGB. The building blocks are in place. The financial position is considerably better and virtually all of the political disputes have been eliminated from the sport. The election of a strong and popular Chairman in 2002, along with the strengthening of the professional staff, both contributed to make the Association a more stable and productive NGB. The time is right for further change and growth.

British Judo was included in the select group of 10 One Stop Plan sports as chosen by UK Sport in 2005. The sports were selected based on the ability to deliver on two main platforms; participation and performance. With regard to performance, the specific target is the delivery of Olympic medals. Judo is well positioned to deliver on both counts and is a sport that can reach the widest possible spectrum of the general public. Judo is highly active in disadvantaged areas and has strong female and ethnic profiles. As noted above, there is a relatively large individual licence holder base and the true number of active participants in the sport in the UK is over 100,000. There is the potential to triple the individual membership numbers in 10 years.

There are over 850 clubs in the UK. The vast majority of these clubs do not own or train in permanent training centres (*dojos*). There are probably no more than 50 permanent dojos in the UK. The average club must rent space in a leisure centre or community hall and lay the mats prior to each session and pick them up at the end. The mats are generally stored in the facility. As the number of permanent dojos increases, so too does the potential of the sport. This is moving in the right direction. A comprehensive Judo Facilities Strategy was completed in 2002 and Sport England has funded some major capital projects for new dojos based on this strategy. Facility development is a key area in which we rely almost exclusively on developing relationships with other funding bodies and partners as the Association has no ability to fund capital projects.

Although judo is often grouped with the martial arts it is a true sport, recognised by the International Olympic Committee, and therefore has a much wider participant base worldwide. Judo is a sport that appeals to the widest possible spectrum of our society at large. The sport teaches young people how to be physical in a disciplined manner. It makes young people more confident and assertive – in a controlled way. Judo provides a fantastic physical workout; providing tremendous core stability work along with balance, coordination, the ability to use the movement and inertia of the opponent's body to positive benefit. It teaches you how to fall correctly and without injury. It is a fantastic vehicle to provide sound training for both body and mind that will be of benefit to the young player for a lifetime – both in sport and in career.

Judo is also a form of self-defence and has a unique ability to make participants more confident and able to handle physical contact in a productive fashion. Today, young people often do not learn how to be constructively 'physical' and this is a skill that needs to be taught to all.

The purpose of this study is to analyse how the BJA can become a more commercially oriented entity with the ability to deliver a world class product. Relationship marketing will play a key role in this transformation. As a starting point and to give a flavour for the sport, a SWOT analysis of the Association was completed and is shown in Figure 4.1. It is clear that the potential of the sport outweighs the actual achievements to date. Judo is a true World and Olympic sport, but the potential to create resources and to improve the profile has not been realised. There are many challenges, not the least of which is that judo is a combat sport and therefore the market for participants is limited. The harsh reality is that it is only a certain percentage

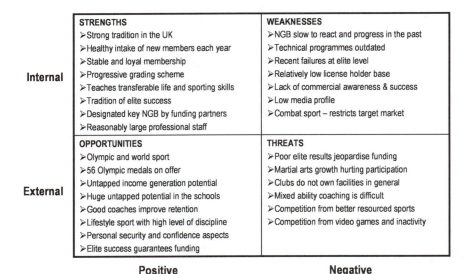

Figure 4.1 BJA SWOT analysis.

of the population that have the desire to enter a mat to undertake physical combat. The physical nature of the sport can also be considered a strength, as young people need a healthy outlet to learn how to be constructively physical.

The results of this study have been utilised to begin the process and the Association intends to use this opportunity to make a dramatic change in the way it delivers the sport of judo. There is little doubt that this is an exciting time for British Judo as the pieces are in place to devise and implement change. By successfully implementing a relationship-marketing strategy the Association will be able to actively compete with the better resourced sports more effectively in the future.

Mission and vision

In order to develop the strategy it is essential to understand the guiding principles. The role of a national governing body of sport is generally two-fold; first to manage and grow a sport within a country, and second to serve as a membership organisation. The mission, vision and values of the British Judo Association are outlined below as a logical starting point.

The BJA mission

To lead, manage, develop, promote, grow and administer the sport of Judo throughout the UK and to ensure the structures are in place to give every individual the opportunity to play, coach, officiate, support, learn and excel at all ages and levels – from beginner to elite.

The BJA vision

The overall vision for the British Judo Association is to become one of the *top five* judo nations in the world and to remain there permanently. This can be accomplished by creating an environment of excellence in the sport of judo by providing:

- *Leadership* – Professional, accountable and visionary corporate leadership with an emphasis on governance and financial stability
- *Quality Deliver Units* – Accessible, well structured clubs and schools to facilitate high level support for players of all abilities
- *Member Services* – Customer focus and engagement to increase membership by a minimum of 5 per cent per annum, year-on-year.
- *Judo for All* – Inclusion at the heart of all activity
- *Technical Excellence* – To ensure the technical programmes are sophisticated and provide for high-level learning, progression and retention to ensure an increasing membership base and create a consistent supply of world class players.

- *Exceptional People* – World class support for members/players by ensuring there is an exceptional workforce
- *Resources* – Income generation schemes to centrally generate the level of resources required to grow the sport
- *Performance* – The UK Plan for progression from beginner to the Olympic podium, incorporating the principles of LTAD planning to allow the elite players to compete with the best in the world on equal terms
- *Drug Free Sport* – Level playing field for all competitors
- *World Class Events* – Improve the quality of all events and attract and stage world events
- *Profile* – A high level communications plan to ensure the sport has sufficient profile to reach full potential.

The Association's world ranking will be judged in two key areas: members and elite success. The target is to have over 60,000 individual licence holders, 1,100 member clubs, and to be consistently ranked in the top five in the world elite rankings by the year 2012.

It is clear that an NGB has a wide-ranging and diversified list of key objectives to deliver an effective service. These ambitious targets cannot be delivered in isolation. The BJA will need to identify the key stakeholders and work with each in a well structured and value weighted programme to maximise the potential.

Values and brand equity – evaluation and enhancement

In early 2005, it was recognised that British Judo had never properly analysed and agreed the 'values' of the organisation. Judo is a traditional sport and many values can be correctly aligned with it, but it was essential to consult with key stakeholders and formally adopt the specific values that are most closely association with the sport and the sporting body.

Figure 4.2   BJA logos.

After a lengthy consultation process involving the Board, Staff and a wide range of stakeholders, which included surveys, focus groups and consultation open days, it was agreed that the core values of the organisation are *discipline, safety, tradition, knowledge, fairness, responsibility, honesty* and *positive outlook*. The British Judo Association logo is consistent with these core values (Figure 4.2).

After establishing the values, the next step was to analyse the brand equity within British Judo. As expected, there was reasonably strong internal recognition and perceived quality but the Association does not really bridge the gap to the general public. This will require much work. The sport has a strong value base that is attractive to children and adults alike. Judo needs to sell this concept as a life-long learning process with a myriad of transferable skills – both physical and mental.

The findings of the analysis are summarised in Table 4.1.

The general perception of British Judo is good. There is a recognition that the Association needs to be more compelling and broaden the technical offerings to attract and retain more members. This can be accomplished by improving the range of offerings and customer service.

The BJA employed a full-time Public Relations Officer in 2003 and has seen a major shift in general satisfaction levels from key constituents. As a National Governing Body it is often difficult to have the reach to be relevant and helpful to the grassroots membership on any kind of consistent basis. The BJA is fighting this battle and winning. Communications must be right to support successful operations. Figure 4.3 provides a sample of some of the BJA publications.

The BJA operates a high-level communications platform with yearly plans and targets. Relationship marketing forms a key element of this strategy – as it must identify, develop and maintain interactive relationships with a large network of media personnel. Judo does not naturally attract heavy media attention. Without a strong presence on television and with limited exposure in the national print media – the sport must work hard to get a message out in a wide variety of other channels.

The key to any successful business is the creative marketing of your product. The public needs to be aware of your brand (Figure 4.4) and products in a positive light to support your company. The British Judo communications strategy aims to achieve the communications objectives and overcome existing challenges through a strategic implementation of stand-alone campaigns and event support, in addition to the core programme. This is described in greater detail later in the chapter.

Stakeholders identification and analysis

The British Judo Association operates within a complicated sporting landscape. In order to focus this process a stakeholders review and survey was

Table 4.1 BJA brand equity

Dimensions	British Judo Association	Comments
• Awareness	Internal awareness is very high External awareness is very low	This would be normal for most NGBs. Only the very large truly bridge the gap into mainstream awareness
• Image	Traditional Successful Not important to the average club or licence holder Political infighting Declining fortunes from 1993–2002	The BJA delivered elite success in the past in spite of the lack of professionalism. Modernisation efforts began in 2002 and the body of today is fit for purpose
• Perceived quality	Mixed – BJA has done some things very well in the past but has suffered from some negativity due to historical mediocrity	The BJA is addressing all of the lingering issues and is now much stronger in dealing with negative perceptions, which are often based on a lack of or false information
• Positive attitude	Strong positive values of discipline, safety, tradition, knowledge, fairness, responsibility, honesty, and positive outlook. Also the perception of stability, integrity, honesty, and tradition	There is much positive energy and optimism about the future within the Association
• Loyalty	Membership retention is poor after the 12 month point. Once a person is in the sport for over 2 years, retention rates are good	Once a player is well established on the grading scheme, learning and enjoying success they have a strong chance of staying in the sport
• Main current stakeholders	Clubs Licence holders Staff Board Players Volunteers UK Sport Sport England Schools	Key asset. The Association has an extensive club base and is strongly supported by key government funding bodies
• Legal protection	Company limited by guarantee, all logos protected by copyright	Secure on this front
• Corporate design	Corporate logo Trading logo Virtual Manufacturer logo	Solid design manual has been produced, which explains how to use the logos. Logos are simple and effective. Will continue with both

Note: The comments are based on preliminary information collected through the stakeholder survey and the observations of the Board and Staff.

Figure 4.3 Judo publications.

completed and specific stakeholder categories were identified to simplify the process. You can see this in Figure 4.5. The British sporting landscape is probably among the most complicated in the world with the advent of governmental devolution and the multitude of traditional governance and support bodies that have evolved over the years.

The Association deals directly with five Sports Councils, nine Sport England

Figure 4.4 Gi Gear logo.

Regional bodies, four Institutes of Sport, etc. There is much to celebrate as the support can be excellent from many sources but there is a prevailing feeling among most sports that it could be simplified. That is another day's work. British Judo must deliver on two main fronts – Excellence and Participation – with an emphasis on excellence from a funding standpoint. The larger direct (from one key partner) resources are available for elite success. Overall, there are greater resources available for sport development and participation but this would be provided by hundreds of regional and local bodies. The larger sports with greater manpower are more successful at engaging at this level. British Judo will ultimately get to this level but must prioritise key resources to ensure the maximum impact is delivered.

All key objectives must support this simple goal. Stakeholders were analysed and grouped into the following units; core elements, funding partners, control bodies, national support bodies, income potential groups and local support bodies. The British Judo Association stakeholders are shown in Figure 4.5.

Figure 4.5 shows the large number and also the diversity of the stakeholders. In order to maximise the potential of the Association it is critical that we can analyse the field and determine which need to be prioritised and key relationships developed. Ultimately, we need to have sophisticated relationships with all but there is a question of focusing limited resources on priorities to build an Association that has the ability to deliver in the short,

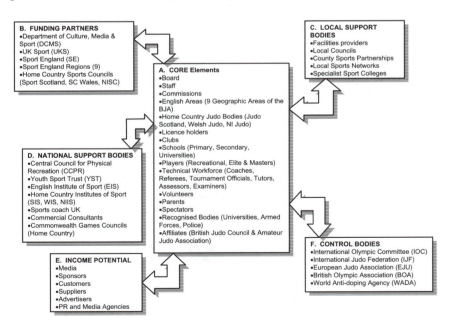

Figure 4.5 BJA stakeholders grouped into categories.

medium and long term. This is complicated and essential. Putting the sport and in this case the BJA in the centre of the relationship process, in relative order of importance (from 1 to 6) the stakeholders would be grouped as shown in Figure 4.6.

The Association has healthy, two-way interaction with all of these individuals and bodies. British Judo is very well supported but this level of support means there are many masters to answer to. This can be time consuming, but the resources gained are well worth the requirements and there is a strong support structure in place.

The next logical step is to identify those stakeholders that are most important to the short-, medium- and long-term objectives of the company and to prioritise the working relationships and marketing efforts with those partners. The MACTOR planning software will be utilised to assist in developing this strategy. This is the challenge. Obviously the Association needs to work with all to deliver a wide range of services – but it can move more efficiently and smarter if it can prioritise and get the order correct.

In 2005, the Association completed a stakeholder survey to gain a better understanding of the key bodies to include licence holders, clubs, customers, suppliers, funding bodies, media, volunteers, technical workforce, parents, schools and others. This simple exercise gave the BJA a clearer understanding of these key partners and the needs and desires of each. This type of questioning is essential to build up a body of research to guide the targeting and planning process. It is crucially important to understand your customers and all of the other interested parties. Business intelligence is a critical component in today's competitive marketplace. You need to understand first hand who and what you are engaging with. Perception often differs significantly from reality on this front.

Briefly, Table 4.2 provides a short description of the role played by each of

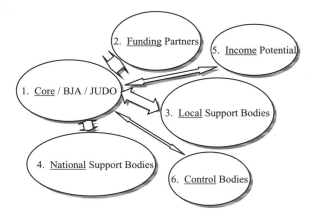

Figure 4.6 Relative strength of relationships with stakeholder groups.

Table 4.2 BJA stakeholders – description and current relationship

Stakeholder	Description of role	Current relationship
1. Players (PLAYERS)	Recreational and competitive players	Medium – generally good but can be improved
2. Clubs (CLUBS)	The voting members of the Association and also the key delivery units for the sport of judo in GB	Medium – generally good but can be improved
3. Technical Workforce (Technical)	The Coaches, referees, table officials, tutors, assessors, verifiers, examiners and all of the technical delivery and support personnel who make the sport function efficiently. Most of these would be volunteers with about 10% being paid professionals	Medium – generally good but can be improved
4. Board of Directors (BOARD)	Lead, manage and control the BJA, therefore the sport of judo in GB	Strong
5. Volunteers (Volunteer)	The thousands of unpaid individuals who dedicate time and resources to make the sport work	Weak – the BJA has very dedicated people but are only recently developing recruitment and support programmes – this is critical area for all of sport
6. Staff (STAFF)	The paid staff of the British Judo Association. Services cover the whole range from strategic management to service provision	Strong
7. UK Sport (UKS)	The government quango charged with the delivery of elite sporting success specifically in Olympic sports	Strong – very strong working relationships with this very supportive funding partner
8. Sports Councils (COUNCILS)	The four Home Country sports councils are charged with supporting NGBs to delivery sport at all levels of the player pathways. Overall sport development is their brief	Strong – very strong working relationships with these very supportive funding partners

Stakeholder	Description	Relationship
9. Sport England Delivery System (DELIVERY)	The English regionalised delivery system which incorporates Sport England Regions, County Sports Partnerships and Local Sports Networks. They are charged with the delivery of local sport	Weak – This presents a tremendous opportunity but the BJA does not have adequate resources to engage at a high level on a regional basis at this point. Improving
10. Institutes of Sport (INSTITUTE)	The four Home Country sports institutes are charged with provided sports science and general support to the elite player pathways to impact on the delivery of elite success	Strong – rapidly developing our relationship with these bodies and the potential of this support is being realised
11. Facilities Providers (FACILITY)	Generally local councils but also others that provide facilities which host judo classes and competitions	Medium – through the clubs
12. Department for Culture, Media and Sport (DCMS)	This is the Government department charged with setting sports policy and also in charge of funding allocations that are directed to sport. Key player in British sport	Medium – the BJA does not really engage at this level, preferring to work through the intermediary funding partners. Considering current size and potential this needs to be developed
13. Schools (Schools)	Primary, Secondary and third level schools who deliver judo in curriculum time and also in after school sessions – utilising their facilities	Medium – the BJA has a strong schools programme but it was only formed in 2005 so it is not having huge impact yet. Private operators dominate this market
14. Local Government Councils (Local Gov)	Key sport supporters in the UK. It is estimated that local government provides almost 66% of the total funding that is directed to sport – largely in the form of local facility provision and programmes	Medium – again, the BJA struggles to engage at this level with the existing resources has trouble engaging with hundreds of bodies
15. Corporate Partners and Advertisers (Sponsors)	Companies who pay a fee for marketing rights or advertising. They may also commit benefit in kind or intellectual support in exchange for an association	Weak – this is an area the BJA has not developed well. It has one true corporate partner, but need to work hard to develop new relationships in this area

(Continued overleaf)

Table 4.2 Continued.

Stakeholder	Description of role	Current relationship
16. British Judo Trust (TRUST)	A limited company with charitable status that was formed to provide a vehicle for fund raising with specific charitable objectives	Strong – under BJA control but in its infancy stage of development. First year income generation target of £25,000
17. Donors (Donors)	Companies, trusts, foundations or individuals who support the sport through the British Judo Trust or other	Weak – the BJA has identified a Patron for the trust who is making a significant 5-year commitment and it has launched a membership scheme and one campaign. This is developing but has a way to go
18. Spectators (Fans)	Paying fans who attend national and international events	Weak – the BJA does not have a huge amount of fan interest. It needs to expand outside of the player/parent base and this is a tough challenge
19. Customers (Customers)	Individuals or companies who purchase goods or services from the BJA	Medium – merchandising sales are relatively strong and the BJA is developing other programmes to engage customers to create resources for the sport
20. Suppliers (Suppliers)	Companies who provide products or services that the BJA is able to resell for a profit	Medium – there are 4–5 main suppliers for merchandising operation but due to the relatively low turnover of £10,000/ month the BJA is not a strong player in the field – yet!
21. Sports Coach UK (SCUK)	Government funded bodies charged with improving the coaching systems across all sports on a GB wide basis	Medium – there is a healthy working relationship with this important body on all levels but the BJA has struggled to deliver the new coaching systems due to technical gaps on the development teams
22. Media (Media)	The local, regional, national and international media. This includes print, radio, internet and television	Weak – there are some healthy personal relationships with the PR person working hard to establish links but at the end of the day the editors are not inclined to write about judo. A work in progress – getting better all the time but slowly

23. British Olympic Association (BOA)	The National Olympic Committee for GB	Strong – there is a healthy and active working relationship with the BOA. The BJA is currently involved in a pilot performance programme with their performance director and the BJA Chair is on the BOA Executive Board
24. European Judo Union (EJU)	The continental control body for the sport of judo in Europe.	Strong – the BJA Chair is on the EJU Exec Board and has a very strong and active relationship with the body, as does the Association in general
25. International Judo Federation (IJF)	The International Federation for the sport of judo	Strong – there are four BJA people in key IJF positions. There are reps on the Planning, Ethics, Protocol and Research Commissions within the IJF. Very well placed to influence and work with this important body
26. Central Council for Physical Education (CCPR)	A support body for National Governing Bodies of sport in GB	Medium – a healthy working relationship with this body
27. World Anti-Doping Association (WADA)	The international lead agency in the battle against performance enhancing and other doping in sport	Medium – The BJA does not have an active direct working relationship with this body but have good links through the GB Anti-doping body – UK Sport. The BJA is strong in this area

the key 27 stakeholders in British Judo. There are actually almost 50 distinct bodies but we have grouped them for the purpose of this exercise.

The stakeholder listing is long and represents many diverse groups. Some are more important than others and some may be less important in the short term and more important in the long term. The purpose of this study is to determine the importance of each and the relevance to deliver a specific list of objectives. In the next section, we will outline the key objectives – then hopefully put it all together to develop a plan to introduce a strategy to move to a relationship-management strategy for the British Judo Association. Part of the plan will be some strategies to develop these relationships for the mutual benefit of all parties.

Key objectives – Priorities and analysis

The BJA has clear objectives and targets. As a National Governing Body of sport, there are a number of key areas that require special focus and a platform of eight business areas that form the nucleus of the business model. The BJA is divided into eight divisions, each with one over-arching objective, supported by a number of sub-objectives. The over-arching objective of the BJA is to make Britain one of the top five judo nations in the world. This is ambitious, but achievable. The key objectives, along with the key partners required to deliver the objective and their roles are outlined in Table 4.3.

The overall objectives of the Association and the *high level* partners that can play a key role in the delivery of the objectives are shown in Figure 4.7.

It is a simplistic grouping that reflects the numbers of desired partners – but there is a heavy planning requirement to get the relationships to the stage where they are functioning effectively and in a cycle of continuous development and renewal. To further develop the concept of 'width' or the broad range of partners required to deliver effectively, Figure 4.8 shows a quick summary or which key stakeholder categories are required to deliver specific key objectives. You will note that each objective requires input from at least two stakeholder categories and the majority required input from five or six of the groups. Of course, not all of the specific stakeholders from each group will be key players – but at least one will be, as noted in Figure 4.8.

We now have the background information on stakeholders and the key objectives of the BJA. In the next section we will analyse the information and develop the plan using a strategic planning tool.

Methodology and analysis

We will now move on to the analysis stage. The stakeholders and objectives will be studied in greater detail and the priority relationships identified. Once we determine the key actors and the convergences, influences and dependencies, we will be better placed to move forward with the planning

Table 4.3 BJA objectives and associated key stakeholders

Objective	Key relationships	Role
1. Participation – to increase participation and licence holder figures year on year to agreed targets.	Sport delivery units (Club/Schools) Sport England (Councils) Membership services Development Team Facility providers – local councils, etc. SE Delivery system Technical Workforce	Deliver quality sport to masses working with BJA Development Team Funding partners for sports development pathways CRM activities and support To strengthen delivery units and promote intake into the sport Facilities Matches facilities with programmes to provide platforms for players To deliver a quality technical experience to enhance retention
2. Elite Performance – to establish technically rich player pathways that consistently deliver multiple Olympic medals	UK Sport Personal and Elite Coaches Institutes of Sport Councils Technical workforce Event Managers (National, Continental, World) Clubs Centre of Excellence	Funding partner WC coaching provision Sports science provision Funding partner at lower levels of the player pathways Preparing young players for further development Provision of player competition pathways for preparation and delivery Provide environments of excellence in which to develop Provides a higher level environment of excellence for further development
3. Technical Excellence – to create programmes and a workforce to deliver the technically rich sport of judo to encourage retention and excellence	Technical workforce (coaches, tutors, assessors, verifiers, referees, competition officials, etc.) Sports Coach UK Sport England (Councils) UK Sport	Provision of technical expertise at all layers of the player pathways – leads to retention and elite excellence. To launch a new platform of coach education, gradings, competition pathways, and workforce development UKCC facilitators and workforce training and qualifications Coach education support and funding Elite Coach training and cutting edge developments
4. Resource Generation – to increase grant support and centrally generated resources to agreed yearly targets	Licence Holders (participant base) Government funding partners (UKS, HC Sports Councils) Customers	Licence fees, gradings, merchandising, etc. Support for elite and specific sport development programmes Merchandise Corporate Training Repeat giving *(Continued overleaf)*

Table 4.3 Continued.

Objective	Key relationships	Role
5. Events – to stage professional and sustainable national and international events	Corporate Customers Trust Donors Corporate Partners Advertisers Event managers (Staff) Facilities Providers UK Sport Major Events City Councils and Development Agencies EJU/IJF Sponsors/Advertisers/Donors	Sponsorship in return for marketing rights Fees in return for advertising space To provide pathways and profile for the sport Venues to stage Funding for major events Funding and marketing support for specific events Devolve hosting rights for major events Provide necessary financial support for all events
6. Profile – to improve the profile of the sport of judo – specifically in the national media	Media Clubs Elite players / coaches Sponsors	To improve the overall knowledge of the sport and generate interest and income potential To work with local media channels and to provide information for central distribution Need heroes to promote the profile of any sport Jointly work with partners to improve profile through paid outlets
7. Governance – to meet or surpass all recommended governance levels for all areas of operations	Elected Officials Staff Professional Service Providers Sport England (Councils) UK Sport	To ensure the highest levels of governance; financial, personnel, contracting, IT, equality, inclusion, etc. Audit and advice, legal, health and safety, HR Assurance Process Mission 2012
8. Top Five Judo Nation in the World	All Stakeholders	This is the over-arching objective of the Association as outlined previously in section 3. To be measured by overall success in the preceding seven objectives

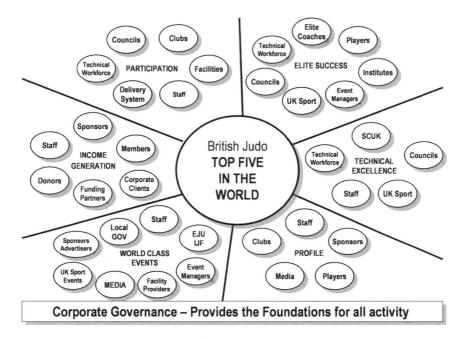

Figure 4.7 Stakeholder groups linked to objectives.

process. We will then discuss building networks to deliver the specific high-level objectives of the Association, which will ultimately deliver the overarching goal of securing status as one of the top five judo nations in the world.

The MACTOR method

As previously discussed in Chapter 2, the MACTOR strategic planning software is extremely useful to determine the relationships between actors and their overall importance in the 'play'. The software can be used by non-experts and once the relevant data is entered the end-user report is very comprehensive and useful. We have singled out two specific charts to incorporate into this study.

The first is the MACTOR analysis of the convergences between actors based on the analysis of the current strengths and weaknesses and the plan for the future. The data on the attributes and relative power of each of the 27 stakeholder groups was entered into the programme and as you will note there were two key areas of convergence. Later, we will introduce a concept of Internal-Network-Market development in this particular study and it is very symmetrical to the findings the first MACTOR findings represented in Figure 4.9. The main convergence centre is in the oval on the right. This

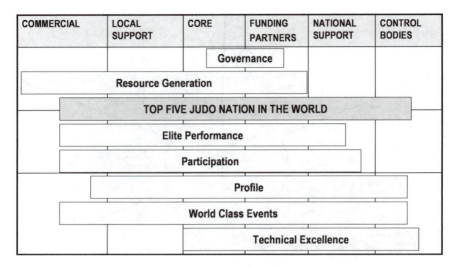

Figure 4.8 Key objectives across stakeholder groups.

grouping incorporates the core elements of the BJA along with the Funding Partners and National and Local support bodies. We would refer to this grouping collectively as the 'enhanced core network', as it includes the core elements and the really critical partners to achieve success. The oval on the left incorporates the income potential partners to include profile bodies, such as the media. This is clearly an accurate reflection of the BJA, as it is certainly one step removed from these key bodies. This is an area that needs great focus if the NGB is to move to the next level.

The only stakeholders that do not fit into the aforementioned groupings are WADA, the BOA, and the CCPR. This is an interesting development and one with which the authors concur fully. These are less critical players in the pursuit of key objectives. The CCPR is a support body that does an excellent job of protecting NGB interests on the political front and also for keeping NGBs informed of the latest developments in the political world that affect sport. It is not a mission-critical body for the BJA. This may change in the future as it develops. WADA is also not mission-critical, as we are more likely to interact with and work with the National Anti-Doping Agency (currently UK Sport – but a NADA will be formed in Great Britain soon). The high level policies set by WADA certainly have a direct influence on the BJA – but the body is once removed. The BOA is a more interesting case. In the past, the body served largely as a support body to take the team to the games but in recent years it has emerged as a multi-dimensional player and is increasing its offerings. The BOA recently appointed a Performance Director and is aggressively moving into the sphere of supporting elite success – working directly with NGBs. In fact, the BJA recently joined a pilot performance

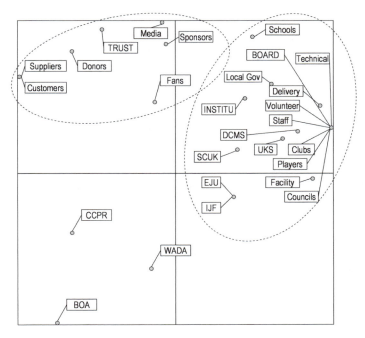

Figure 4.9 MACTOR convergences between the stakeholders.

programme funded and operated by the BOA for a select couple of elite athletes to complement the ongoing high performance support they receive. Both the BOA and possibly CCPR will become more relevant actors in the future and this transition must be managed and developed proactively.

The key objectives going forward would be to clarify the relationships in the right oval and strengthen and develop those that can deliver the best results. The BJA must also work hard to bring the bodies as specified in the left oval closer to the central point of convergence in the upper right quadrant so this key group of constituents can be more effectively utilised in the future.

The next MACTOR chart (Figure 4.10) shows the influences and dependencies between the actors. Again, this has indicated some interesting if somewhat predictable data.

It is seen in Figure 4.10 that there are three clearly defined stakeholders clusters within British judo. There are the enhanced CORE elements as would be expected in the oval in the upper right hand quadrant – reflecting those bodies that have heavy influence and also those that the BJA relies on. There is then a wider network which includes all key support partners and the direct facility and programme providers, which is depicted in the oval in the right hand lower quadrant. These are stakeholders that are not quite as influential but that the NGB is heavily dependent upon. Finally, there is the

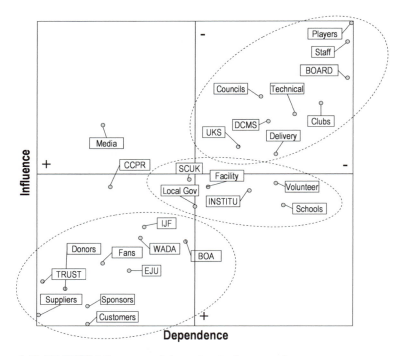

Figure 4.10 MACTOR influences and dependencies between the actors.

control body and commercial grouping, which includes the IJF, WADA, EJU, BOA, sponsors, advertisers, fans, customers, suppliers, etc. This group is shown in the lower left hand quadrant and this means these are bodies that are currently not very influential and also that the NGB is not very dependent on them. Frankly the commercial group are stakeholders that should be very important but in fact have been under-developed to date. This needs to be factored into the plan going forward. The BJA must consolidate the internal group, move the inner workings and interaction within the network up to the next level, and that group must then collectively bring the potential commercial bodies more directly into the fold.

The control bodies have influence through high level policy and major events – but scored low on the influence and dependency ratings due to the fact that they have little day-to-day or operational dealings with the BJA. This is an anomaly in the system. These are obviously important bodies but not as influential on the NGB as they probably should be. This would be judged to be a weakness within the international bodies. We now need to begin the process of strategy creation.

Internal – network – market

The principle of developing relationships by starting with the INTERNAL stakeholders (core), building a wider NETWORK and ultimately moving to a MARKET phase was introduced earlier in this book. The BJA fits neatly into this model. The core elements of the body are shown in the Figure 4.11 in the circle numbered 1 and designated INTERNAL. This is the backbone of the Association – to include the Board, Staff, Clubs, Players, Technical Workforce, Schools and Volunteers. This is the core group that makes it happen. These are the building blocks that need to complete the plans and implement them to move the body forward. The first step the core needs to accomplish is to build the wider NETWORK effectively and in a timely fashion. The wider 'network' is denoted in circle 2 and this is the critical sphere of relationships that must be developed to move the next level.

You will note from the above that once the wider network has been established, the enhanced grouping can then work on the MARKET (circle 3) group to develop this important area. This has been consistently highlighted as the 'weak link' in British judo and it will require a concentrated team effort to have a significant impact in the market area. The figure is designed to show the flow of growing the relationships that will ultimately deliver the objectives. Similar to the sporting arena the art of building and managing a 'team'

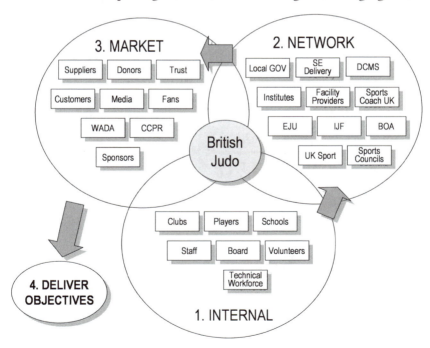

Figure 4.11 Internal/Network/Market Groupings.

is not always straight-forward and this process needs to be carefully planned and executed.

To summarise, it is clear that the BJA needs to consolidate our relationships with those groups in the NETWORK sphere but probably more importantly we need to cultivate and secure more effective relationships with those groups in the MARKET segment. These are the crucial stakeholders that we struggle to engage, largely due to the nature of the sport. In order to progress this must be a priority. Figure 4.12 develops this concept in further detail.

Figure 4.12 is intended to show the growth of a network and also the key drivers and phases of development. The concept of moving from INTERNAL – NETWORK – MARKET is emphasised as we move across the figure. The first section shows the key drivers, which would be the Board of Directors and the Staff of the BJA, as well as the other core stakeholders. This core group is led by the Board/Staff. They must set the policy and strategy, and they are also responsible for the PR, profile and image of the Association. In other words, the body must get its internal house in order to project the right image to attract partners. The National Governing Body is the body that often gives potential partners a first impression of the sport and its potential.

We cannot underestimate the importance of getting the 'house in order' prior to opening the front door. The sports organisation must make sure they are internally fully fit for purpose and have established policies and plans in place to cover all of the key areas such as:

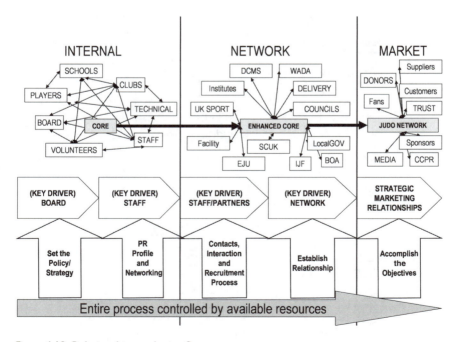

Figure 4.12 Relationship-marketing flow.

- Child protection policy
- Equality strategy
- Disciplinary policy (and a professional enforcement group)
- Financial controls and authorities
- Human resources
- Data protection
- Business contingency planning
- Anti-doping policy
- Strategic plan/operational plan
- Development strategy
- Facilities development policy
- Communications plan (internal and external).

Once these foundation policies are in place, the body then needs to gain credibility by delivering on the ground. All areas of operations must be up to a generally accepted level. Remember, the BJA is a membership body and inevitably the voices of ten disgruntled members can be louder than the sounds of satisfaction from 50,000 others! The NGB must provide a first class service, and have its internal act together before it can look outward with confidence.

Once this is done, the body moves to the second phase of the figure – the NETWORK phase. This is the building of truly mutually beneficial relationships that can be grown and renewed over time. In this phase, the sport body must interact with many key players to identify and recruit the necessary decision-makers to establish a working relationship. Once this is done the 'enhanced network' can be developed and the power of the sporting body is exponentially increased.

For the BJA, the key network players would be the government funding partners (DCMS, UK Sport, Councils) and the national (Institutes, Delivery, SCUK) and local (Facilities, Local Gov) support bodies. The others who form a less interactive and distinct role but still quite important would be the control bodies (EJU, IJF, WADA, BOA) and this is an accepted reality.

Once the enhanced network is built, the MARKET level partners must be brought on-board. These are the potential income generation and profile partners we have discussed earlier. This is an area of great focus – but the body needs to be equipped to have any impact and success here.

Therefore we are developing the relationships along the path shown in Figure 4.13.

Figure 4.13 BJA relationship building.

When the relationship building is complete, the strategic marketing objectives can be delivered. Please pay attention to the note at the bottom of Figure 4.12, the 'Entire process is controlled by resources'. The BJA has a healthy staff complement but does not have the luxury of spending an abundance of staff resources to lobby other stakeholders who may have a role to play. The Football Association would have the numbers and financial resources to pay for lobbyists and other services that may expedite the growth of relationships. Resources are critical and sometimes it seems like the rich are much better positioned to get richer and those that do not have the finance and personnel run the risk of being left behind. This is an area that is particularly crucial to a body the size of the BJA and the organisation is committed to implementing a relationship marketing strategy with the resources at hand.

We will now flesh out some specific examples of relationship building that need to take place to deliver on specific objectives. It is important that the reader has a clear idea of some practical examples of relationship building that will help to deliver specific key objectives.

Participation

At this point we will tackle the issue of participation in sport and specifically judo in the UK. As you will note from Figure 4.14, we see a six-stage process of attracting, training and retaining participants. There are clear steps in the process and also specific partners that are involved in each stage. We intend to analyse the stages and also discuss how to develop the required relationships and involve partners in an effective manner.

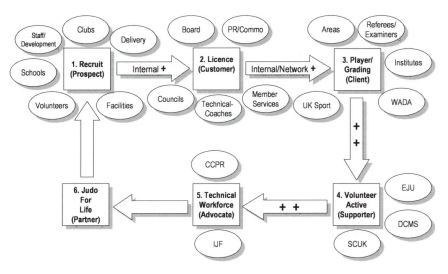

Figure 4.14 Building a team to increase participation.

We have compared the recruitment and retention of participants to the six stages of customer development as originally seen in Table 1.1. Please note that Figure 4.14 is designed to show the building of a stakeholder group from levels 1 to 6 and that the designated stakeholders at each level are the additional ones that come into the picture at that point. It is a cumulative build up of stakeholders so that at point six all 21 listed stakeholders play a major part in the Judo for Life phase.

The business of attracting and retaining participants in sport is a complex and resource-heavy process. At the start of this chapter, we presented a SWOT analysis of the BJA. The key findings of the analysis were that British Judo has a strong history and tradition but probably has not moved with the times and adapted to the challenges and new competition faced by all NGBs. There is fierce competition from higher profile, better funded and more spectator friendly sports but there is equally a serious challenge posed by the new 'docile' activities that have cut into overall sport participation levels. The Playstation, X-Box, increased disposable income levels and many other available forms of entertainment have all conspired to reduce sporting activity in general. Many NGBs would be pleased with British Judo's record of maintaining membership levels at a static level from 1995 to 2005. The Association achieved a strong 22 per cent growth in licence holders from 2005 to 2007.

The Association has a considerable amount of data on current and past individual members in a CRM database and also has the ability to mine this information for specific purposes. This is an important tool for the analysis process and the design of the Relationship Marketing Plan. It is also a key tool in the struggle to develop a customer base. This epitomises the definition of relationship marketing. The BJA must develop the prospects, to the highest possible level but hopefully all the way to the Judo for Life stage, as outlined below.

We will now go on to outline the steps to develop a lasting relationship with participants in the sport so they remain and enjoy the sport of judo for life.

The process

1 *Recruit* (Prospect). The key to recruiting individuals to the sport are the delivery units (clubs and schools) throughout the country. These key segments of the NGB are on the front lines and must be supported, highly trained and motivated, and resourced to deliver this key function. This is an area in which the wealthier sports have a distinct advantage. Football and rugby clubs share the spoils of TV money and broader support and are well positioned to establish actual bricks and mortar facilities. From these facilities they can operate social functions and possibly even have licensed premises to bring external resources into the

sport. This is a distinct advantage. As previously noted – judo clubs do not often have ownership of a club facility and are forced to rely on rental facilities, which can be expensive. Therefore, the NGB needs to invest in the people and personalities that currently drive the sport of judo in spite of the drawbacks. The key stakeholders at this first step of the process would be the Staff, Clubs, Schools, Volunteers, Delivery System and Facility providers. In addition to six key stakeholders, it must be remembered that this process must be actioned throughout the UK. There are excellent local examples of a strong club, supported by a very active County Sports Partnership, based in a great dojo at a subsidised cost by the Local Gov, with a selection of feeder schools, who are actively supported by Staff personnel and have achieved the Clubmark award – therefore qualifying for development grants for additional equipment. These would be highly successful clubs that cater for hundreds of young players and have different pathways for elite players, recreational players, and in fact also support the development of technical personnel such as referees and tournament officials. There are also examples of one coach in a very isolated area who provides a limited service to 10 or 12 judo players who want to get together and have a bit of a practice. The success spectrum is wide and unfortunately very few clubs fall into the first category – those that have a strong and supportive team of stakeholders. This positive environment must be an aspirational target for all of the BJA's clubs – but it is a long way from reality. The club must be the driving force behind the formation of this team – and the driving force behind the club will undoubtedly be an individual who has previously reached level 5 or 6 in this process.

2   *Licence Holder* (Customer). The next step for a recruit who has taken the first step into the sport is to turn that individual into a licence holder (or customer). A player may participate in club activities for a total of four sessions before they need to become a licence holder. The BJA licence provides a range of benefits but the cornerstone of this package is comprehensive insurance coverage. This is the key selling point, and a mandatory requirement. The other member benefits are significant and growing all the time. The licence holder gets the *Matside* magazine quarterly, they get access to coaching and gradings, they get a logon to the BJA website member only areas, and they get discounts on merchandise. One of the key objectives of the BJA is to become more compelling to the membership. NGBs can often be considered a 'necessary evil' instead of an important driver in the development of a specific sport. The BJA has a very active six person Membership Section that is continuously improving service standards and devising new services to increase the relevance of the body to the average licence holder. The database is a key instrument to ensure members are supported and reminded when key renewal dates are imminent. One of the key areas the BJA is exploring to attract

and maintain customers is by changing the technical platform of the sport. Judo is a hard combat sport. Currently, the BJA is in the process of rolling out a Technical Grading Scheme within which a licence holder may progress through the belt system all the way to Black Belt without having to fight for it. This will improve retention dramatically as the sport is the core feature of the platform and by making the systems such as the attainment scheme a little friendlier there is a greater chance of improving retention rates. This move was agreed after much study on licence trends and specific dropout trigger points. It is clear that a Technical Grading scheme will help in this area. The key additional stakeholders in this step of the process are the Board, Public Relations, Councils, Member Services, and the Technical Workforce. Good coaches are the key to retention, supported by a wide variety of other stakeholders.

3   *Player/Grading* (Client). The next stage in the process is for the licence holder to become a player. This would suggest the individual is progressing in the sport and is taking part in competitions. There are various levels of competition so it is not suggested that this is automatically an elite pathway. There are three clear pathways in the sport; elite, recreational and support. The first two are obviously to provide for players of all abilities and the third is to cover those who want to move into other channels, such as refereeing, club administrator, tournament officials, club welfare officers, and other. The BJA employs a Volunteer Manager who is continuously seeking new ways to engage people to get involved in the sport – on and off the mat. Once people get hooked – judo has a great chance to keep them for life. The key new stakeholders at this step would be the referees, examiners, UK Sport, Institutes and WADA (as issues like drug testing become a reality).

4   *Volunteer/Active* (Supporter). The next step on the ladder is arguably the most crucial. Once an individual can be moved to the volunteer/active member status they become a supporter of the NGB. This would be the army of volunteers that generally run all amateur sport throughout the world. People become volunteers for a wide variety of reasons: to give something back, for the social side, for a sense of belonging, for the satisfaction of helping others, for the thrill of helping others to achieve great victories, etc. It is estimated that the BJA has approximately 4,000 individuals who would fall into this category. They run the clubs, organise the competitions and gradings, generate the finance, complete the entry forms and grants applications, and drive the mini-bus. This is the backbone of the sport, and all NGB would do well to take care of this irreplaceable resource. Certainly the BJA could not function without this mass of voluntary support. The key stakeholder groups that are introduced at this point are the EJU, SCUK and the DCMS. The first group because they set the continental policy for the sport and have a significant influence in the retention of person at higher levels. SCUK is the body

responsible for leading the charge to modernise and professionalise coach education in the UK. The DCMS because they directly fund programmes to attract, train and retain volunteers.

5   *Technical Workforce* (Advocate). This is a natural progression from level 4 for those that are on the technical side. In the sport of judo there is a very strong traditional hierarchy dominated by the belt system. A person begins with a Red belt, works through the colours until the coveted Black Belt is achieved, then can achieve advanced levels of Black Belt until the 6th Dan, at which point a Red and White Belt is awarded. For the chosen few who rise to 10th Dan the red belt is awarded again, signifying the new beginning of a lifelong learning process. There would generally only be 1 or 2 individuals in the world with the rank of 10th Dan, so this is a rather lofty perch. The senior judo people are generally coaches and referees and tournament officials. This technical workforce is the glue that keeps the Association together and they are generally high grades and highly respected for achievements to date. At this level, it is critical that the BJA provides support and training and keeps this valuable constituency interested and motivated. The new stakeholders that are introduced at this level would be the IJF and the CCPR. The IJF obviously sets global policy (which is not often changed) and the CCPR provides government level lobbying support across a wide range of NGBs. The individuals that reach this level would truly be advocates for the sport and for the NGB.

6   *Judo for Life* (Partner). Judo is a sport that is more than just a sport. It is a lifestyle and a lifelong learning process that transcends sport. The discipline and confidence that judo instils in young people will be with them for life. It will help in all aspects of personal development. The individuals who reach this level will be true partners to the BJA in the high level development of the sport of judo in the UK. No new stakeholders are introduced at this level as the 21 previously identified will all have significant influence.

This simple six-step process to analyse and hopefully increase retention forms the cornerstone of the BJA's plan to drive up participation levels to hit by very ambitious targets in the run up to the Olympic Games in London in 2012. To attract and retain individuals to sport is challenging. Sport is a great attraction but there is significant competition. The BJA must work with a wide range of stakeholders to provide and inclusive platform for individuals to get involved and stay involved for the long term.

Elite success

To achieve elite success in sport can be one of the most challenging and complicated targets to deliver. Sport is unpredictable. It is decided by a variety of variables – all of which need to come together and spark at exactly the right moment to deliver a result. Five of the Gold medals won by Team GB at the Athens Olympics were decided by 0.545 of a second – collectively! To confirm, over five key events in cycling, rowing and athletics the difference between winning five gold medals or settling for five silvers in the same events was slightly over half a second. In today's competitive environment it is no longer possible to win on athletic ability alone. The athlete needs motivation, determination, desire, and generally the support of a team of experts that ensures that no stone is left unturned in the pursuit of Olympic gold.

This is the same for Premiership football, the National Basketball Association, and all of the professional sporting leagues in the world. The sporting world is now heavily populated with sports psychologists, doctors, vision specialists, masseurs, nutritionists, strength and conditioning experts, and a variety of other support personnel who work with elite athletes. The fact that the richest clubs in the world do not always win the championships in the respective leagues is proof positive that getting the right team in place and delivering athletic performance is a delicate art – that requires much planning, a world class programme, leaving no stone unturned and then possibly even adding a pinch of luck!

The next figure shows the full extent of the stakeholders involved in the delivery of elite success for a judo athlete. This is not comprehensive but a good indication that there are many players involved in the crafting of an elite athlete. Who leads? Who follows? Who directs this complicated equation? Modern thinking dictates that all athlete preparation should be player centred and in fact the player must be at the centre of the 'universe' and central to all decision-making. In reality this probably works for some athletes but others need more direct control and leadership.

In the case of the BJA it is up to the NGB to lead and manage the relationship building process that leads to elite success. Figure 4.15 shows the athlete in the centre, closely surrounded by his personal coach, the BJA National Coach, and the BJA Performance Director. At the highest level this is the leadership team that collectively makes the decisions in consultation with the athletes.

In the second circle, we have identified the key personnel that will work closely with the athlete on a day-to-day basis. The outer ring shows the stakeholders whose resources and decisions influence and assist the athlete – generally from a macro level but also more directly with fans, facility providers, event managers and sponsors playing a more direct role.

It is clear from Figure 4.15 that this complex series of relationships and stakeholders must be managed carefully to achieve success. This is probably the most complex equation in sport – how a team of individuals, each with different roles, skills and motives – combines to produce a champion athlete. In a world where medals are won and lost by hundredths of a second – every possible advantage must be sought out and realised. This requires a team of

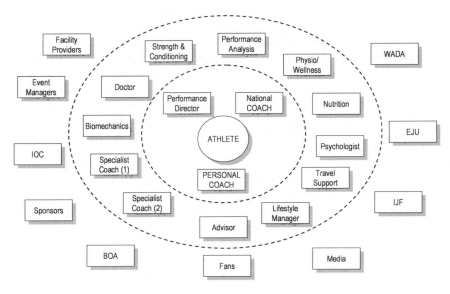

Figure 4.15 Elite athlete support team and service providers.

world-class practitioners who must work with an athlete, which can be complicated. In a sport like judo with a strong personal coach ethos, there are often power struggles between the NGB funded national coaches and the normally club based personal coaches. Personal coaches who nurture the players from a young age to elite levels are understandably 'hesitant' to let players go – even thought they in many cases do not have the skill base to bring a player to the highest level. This dynamic is difficult and when you throw in a team of 10–15 support personnel, it requires a high level of sophistication to ensure all these interdependent and supportive relationships work seamlessly to support one objective – to make the athlete better.

Going back to the beginning, Figure 4.16 illustrates that over the career of an elite athlete there are different stakeholder groups that play key roles in providing the support and platform for the athlete to excel culminating in the final phase of the player's development which is the training to win phase as outlined in the BJA's Long Term Player Development Programme. You will notice that as the player develops there are more stakeholders introduced at each level. The beginner needs a club, coach, facility, and the other stakeholders who support these three (staff, volunteers, technical workforce, councils and SCUK).

When the player hits the Learn to Train phase (age 12) then elite coaches and Institutes (for sports science principles) are introduced. At the Train to Train phase the Event Managers become important as the player needs high level competitive pathways to develop and progress. At the Train to Compete

Elite Player Development

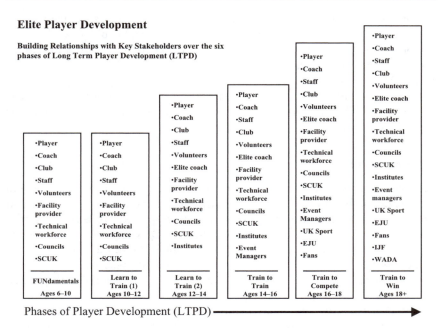

Building Relationships with Key Stakeholders over the six phases of Long Term Player Development (LTPD)

•Player •Coach •Club •Staff •Volunteers •Facility provider •Technical workforce •Councils •SCUK	•Player •Coach •Club •Staff •Volunteers •Facility provider •Technical workforce •Councils •SCUK	•Player •Coach •Club •Staff •Volunteers •Elite coach •Facility provider •Technical workforce •Councils •SCUK •Institutes	•Player •Coach •Staff •Club •Volunteers •Elite coach •Facility provider •Technical workforce •Councils •SCUK •Institutes •Event Managers	•Player •Coach •Staff •Club •Volunteers •Elite coach •Facility provider •Technical workforce •Councils •SCUK •Institutes •Event Managers •UK Sport •EJU •Fans	•Player •Coach •Staff •Club •Volunteers •Elite coach •Facility provider •Technical workforce •Councils •SCUK •Institutes •Event managers •UK Sport •EJU •Fans •IJF •WADA
FUNdamentals Ages 6–10	**Learn to Train (1)** Ages 10–12	**Learn to Train (2)** Ages 12–14	**Train to Train** Ages 14–16	**Train to Compete** Ages 16–18	**Train to Win** Ages 18+

Phases of Player Development (LTPD) ⟶

Figure 4.16 Building a stakeholder support team over the stages of an elite career.

and Train to Win phases, we introduce UK Sport, the EJU, Fans, the IJF and WADA and as the player moves up the competitive pathway, each of these bodies becomes more critical.

We have now introduced the principle of a growing number of stakeholders as players progress through the competitive pathways and also at the pinnacle the extensive team required to propel a single athlete to the ultimate target – Olympic Gold. It is critical that these processes need to be carefully managed and cultivated throughout the life of the player. Successful NGBs put into place a world class delivery network that leaves no stone unturned to support and develop athletic talent. In the UK, the resources and support are made available from UK Sport and the respective Home Country Sports Councils to put these systems in place. To date, only a small handful of British NGBs have fully developed high-level programmes that consistently deliver medals at each Olympiad. British judo has delivered 17 Olympic medals to date but only one in the last three Olympiads, with Kate Howey grabbing a Silver in Sydney. How does it intend to return to the status of consistent producer in an extremely competitive world sport like judo?

Relationship marketing plays a key role in this. The BJA has elected to centralise elite training and this requires a multitude of support from key partners. In order to minimise limited resources it has been agreed that the Association needs to move all key personnel and resources to one location and ask the players to gravitate to this nucleus of excellence at a specified time in their careers. In order to accomplish this, the key stakeholders will be the Performance Director, National Coaches, Personal Coaches, Facility Providers, UK Sport, Sport England, Home Country Institutes, Technical Workforce, Board, Staff, BOA (emerging), and others. All of these groupings must be recruited and sold on the mutual benefits of this type of training delivery. The Performance Director is the key to building the overall network to deliver the required services.

Resource creation

We have repeatedly emphasised that resources drive sport at all levels and those sporting bodies that can generate income are more likely to survive and prosper in the future. The BJA is a very well supported NGB but in fact is not yet delivering on the commercial front. The BJA receives 70 per cent of its total turnover from government sources. This is useful but the ratio needs to be lessened to ensure the body is maximising the potential to centrally generate income. Developing relationships is absolutely essential to the success of this area.

The BJA recently completed a comprehensive review of potential income generation programmes and established a commercial plan that revolves around six main programmes as noted in Figure 4.17. These are Merchandising, Sponsorships/Advertising, the British Judo Trust, Membership/gradings, Corporate training and Funding partners. Figure 4.17 also gives a quick summary of the stakeholders that will be required to deliver on the respective objectives.

Prior to establishing the commercial plan the BJA completed a comprehensive analysis of the market and the potential of the programmes. For a National Governing Body, it is essential to first analyse the core market – which will inevitably be the key consumers of whatever programme the body progresses.

The British Judo core market can be summarised as follows:

Level of involvement

There is a hard core membership group of probably 10 per cent of the total market – or a total of 10,000 out of 100,000. This grouping would virtually dedicate their lives to the sport and would be a receptive audience for all new judo products and services. There is also a high percentage, almost 75 per cent, of juniors in the market group. These are generally motivated young players with a desire to wear the latest equipment and fashion clothing. At least 50 per cent of the total market would be described as very active judo participants.

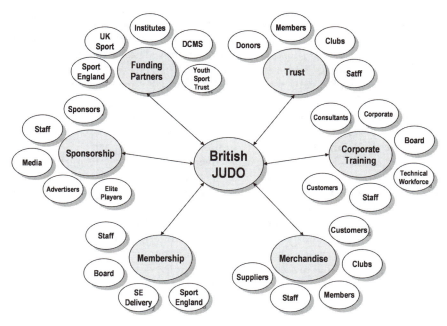

Figure 4.17 Programmes and stakeholder teams required to generate income.

Market segmentation

The market is very clear and very direct. There are the dedicated hard core judo enthusiasts that will form the bulk of the market, and the second tier parents, spectators, friends, etc. who will be more logical buyers of services. As you will see from Figure 4.18, we have segmented our market into six main groups. The *Lifestyle* members are those who are totally dedicated to the sport and spend the vast majority of free time involved in some aspect. Many of these would also work full-time in judo roles, such as coaching. This group would have an extremely strong loyalty to the sport of judo and also a very strong loyalty to the BJA. The next group would be the *Elite* participant who would be almost completely dedicated to performance judo. The members of this group would be extremely dedicated to the sport and dedicated to the BJA. The *Volunteer* group would represent those who dedicate huge amounts of time to the sport through working at club, area, and national level. This category would represent the high level volunteers – and the lower commitment volunteers would be in the member category. The *Member* category would include the average participant, coach, referee, official, volunteer, etc. This would be the bulk of the judo population. The *Sampler* category would represent the thousands of young players who 'test' the sport and get a membership, normally between the ages of 5–15. The *Associate* category would be the final grouping and would include all of those constituents that have a definite interest in the sport, but are once removed from the direct action. This would be parents, siblings, friends, spectators, etc.

The loyalty and involvement of the market segments is summarised in Figure 4.18.

These six categories give the BJA some points of reference to begin to determine buyer preferences and commitment. The relative attractiveness of the respective segments is shown in Figure 4.19.

The BJA has a strong competitive advantage due to its strength and the fact that judo is a niche sport, and it does not enjoy external attention, both in the media and on the high street. It has a strong competitive advantage in all judo markets, for services and products.

The NGB needs to further develop, sustain and defend its competitive advantage by continuously improving service offerings and by becoming a compelling organisation. The feel-good factor cannot be underestimated in the consumer buying process and if a sporting body gets the quality and offerings right, develops a successful relationship-marketing strategy, and

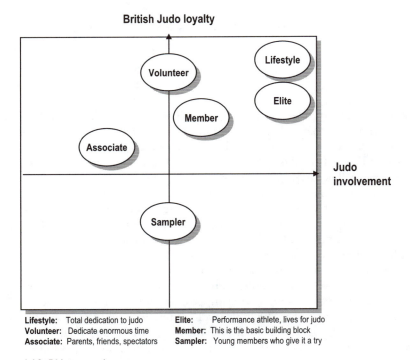

Lifestyle: Total dedication to judo	**Elite:** Performance athlete, lives for judo
Volunteer: Dedicate enormous time	**Member:** This is the basic building block
Associate: Parents, friends, spectators	**Sampler:** Young members who give it a try

Figure 4.18 BJA internal consumer segments.

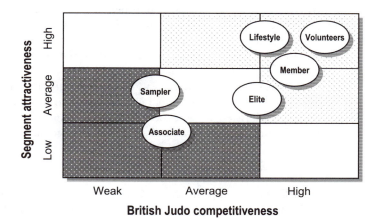

Figure 4.19 BJA consumer segment attractiveness.

follows through with first class customer service – then the fact that all profits from the commercial operations will be re-invested into the sport will be the icing on the cake.

Environmental analysis

Economics

The UK economy is strong and robust, and people generally have disposable income to participate in their chosen sport. Unemployment is low and the average salary is relatively high – with the rate of taxation being one of the lowest in Europe. Although the levels of personal borrowing are at all time highs they are not at a level that need cause undue worry. It is a good time.

Cultural trends

Cultural trends are having an adverse effect on all sports. Young people have become less active and more fixated on video games, TV and other sedentary activities. This pattern obviously makes it more difficult for National Governing Bodies of sport to attract and retain members since the overall pool is smaller but there is much positive activity going on in this regard to address this decline. Sport England and all NGBs are leading the fight to keep young people active and heavily involved in sport by providing enjoyable, safe and well managed sporting activities and competitions. It is important that the judo population is increased for the sake of the preservation of the sport, and also to ensure the NGB's operations can grow unfettered. The sport is definitely disadvantaged by the growing protectiveness of parents toward their offspring. Nowadays, young people do not learn how to be constructively physical and in fact they are largely discouraged from all forms of contact. Judo is a very physical sport, and the harsh reality is that only a certain percentage of the population will be comfortable in this contact environment. To counteract this, the positive aspects of judo to teach young people how to be physical, in a productive and learning fashion, must be emphasised. A strong and confident individual is more likely to succeed in all walks of life. Young people need to be exposed to sports like judo so they learn how to handle the prospect of physical contact with confidence.

Legal

There is strong legislation in place in the UK regarding limited company operations and the BJA is in full compliance with all current legislation. There is a separate limited company, British Judo Competitions and Events, which is the trading arm of the Association. The British Judo trust, formed in 2007, is also a Limited Company that has Charitable Status. The three companies are separate legal entities and each complies with all financial, audit and reporting functions as dictated by the Companies Act and the Charities Commission.

Technology

The Association has embraced technology from the start and continues to look for new ways to utilise this to drive marketing efforts on a low cost basis. The BJA provides weekly e-newsletters, has a hugely active website, and does a great online sales turnover. There is scope to continue to develop in this area by continuously upgrading database capabilities and sales strategies via the net. The BJA is also exploring other new initiatives, such as mobile phone marketing.

After analysing the core market the BJA analysed the potential income generation schemes to rank them based on relative attractiveness and competitiveness. Figure 4.20 represents the findings.

The prioritisation of programmes is a key exercise to ensure success. The NGB has limited resources and cannot establish all programmes at the same time. The old adage that you need to spend money to make money holds true. To create an income producing programme requires significant resources, both personnel and financial, so it is imperative that a body like the BJA must prioritise the programmes that can be started with less upfront capital outlays and that will produce income streams quickly. The BJA has set the priorities and has a clear vision as per Figure 4.20.

The BJA is an evolving organisation that is broadening its remit outside of the traditional roles of attracting and retaining members, delivering member services, and delivering elite success. It is now more heavily involved in issues such as corporate governance, communications, and income generation. Like

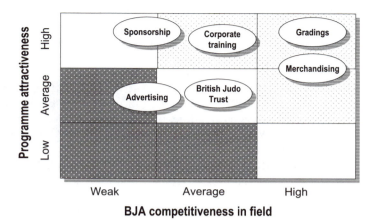

Figure 4.20 Income generation programme attractiveness and competitiveness.

most NGBs, the BJA had a grant dependency mentality and it is not always easy to quickly change this way of thinking. It is also very difficult to manage the progression from an almost fully voluntary sport, with a small admin support staff to a body with significant professional staff resources. There are growing pains as lifelong volunteers are forced to give up operational decision-making roles in favour of the professionals who are involved in multiple aspects of sports management and development.

British Judo has now fully embraced the concept of developing relationships and generating income through non-standard programmes to allow for additional resources to be realised by the sport, for stability and new programmes. There is consensus, and now there is a need to learn new processes and systems to make the Association more commercially active and aware.

Profile

The BJA needs to give complete focus to this important objective going forward. In a sport like judo profile is always going to be a difficult task. There is little consistent televised coverage, with the only dependable coverage coming once every four years for the Olympic Games. It is considered a niche sport – although the number of participants is actually pretty high. It is not particularly easy to understand for outsiders – thereby creating a large void that needs to be bridged to appeal to a wider market.

All of that said – the sport also has tremendous attributes that can attract media attention if properly packaged and sold. For example, a judo tournament generally lasts all day with multiple mats running and hundreds of individual fights. The finals block is the time of heightened interest, but the fans who have sat in the arena all day are often deflated at the point when the excitement should be at its peak – resulting in a subdued environment for what should be the highlight of the day. This is not always the case – but it is all too common. This can be addressed by focusing on 'highlight packages' as opposed to live TV to ensure there is short burst quality content that will leave the viewers with an appetite for more. The Olympics Games does a good job of this by restricting the level of entries and holding only two weight categories per day. Unfortunately, this format cannot be used for all events – but steps are underway to address this issue at all levels. There is a focus group working at BJA level to devise strategies to make events more spectator and media friendly in the future.

The BJA has designed a comprehensive communications plan to address the relative lack of profile and there are two main strands – internal and external. It is critical to get the internal communications of the company working correctly in order to tackle the external market. This is an area where relationship market will be key to the ongoing success. Relationships must be targeted, cultivated, formed and maintained. The BJA must use the entire enhance core network to broaden the profile of the sport.

Figure 4.21 shows the wide range of stakeholder groups that should be actively involved in achieving this objective. Please note that in the lower left hand corner the BJA core elements are reflected. The internal communications plan must ensure that each of these key groups is fully knowledgeable

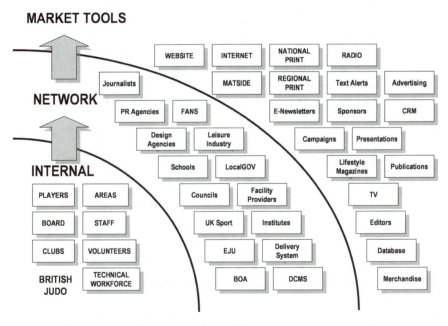

Figure 4.21 Building a team to improve the profile.

and committed to promoting the Association and the sport. Mixed messages from internal sources can have a serious adverse effect on the perception of the potential of the sport.

The INTERNAL elements of the Association need to drive this strategy. The next layer is the NETWORK that needs to be recruited to assist with the objective. Finally, once this network is assembled the final strand would be the MARKET TOOLS required to improve the profile. This is a combination of media outlets, specific tools, and stakeholders that can be used to increase the profile. To recruit and brief such a large network is a challenging task.

This is an area that requires a very personal touch to get non-judo people interested in covering the sport. The BJA is fortunate to have a number of key national journalists who have strong judo backgrounds and can write knowledgably about the sport. On that front the problems begin at the editorial stage where the content is consistently cut back or rejected entirely due to the perceived lack of demand. On the publication side, the BJA needs to crack this editorial block and this needs to be done through the concerted efforts of the network team. This is just one roadblock in a sequence of many. Sustained pressure or, more politely, encouragement is required to improve the media coverage.

The media is just one of the communication channels the PRO/network will use to reach key audiences. For the media to deliver our message, they must value us as a source of information. To achieve this, the PRO will work on a pro-active and re-active basis, supplying accurate information when required and providing usable story ideas on a regular basis to fit their readership.

For the purposes of this external communications programme, the media will be broken down into three tiers:

- *Tier One* – the core media and those who the PRO will be in constant contact with regarding the activities of the Association, the elite athletes and events
- *Tier Two* – will be used regularly but the individual contacts will depend upon the activity taking place
- *Tier Three* – media will be used in conjunction with stand-alone campaigns.

The Association is committed to building a professional and effective PR machine. The profile or public relations strategy is also divided into short-, medium- and long-term objectives. These are outlined below.

Short term (Establish) – Year 1

- Build the INTERNAL network through Staff, Board, Clubs, Volunteers, Technical Workforce and Players to disseminate positive information
- Continually improve communications with members throughout the UK

- Ensure the press office function works with the media throughout the UK
- Support all national competitions and events
- Continually increase the relationship between clubs and the press office in order to increase regional coverage
- Create and launch standalone campaigns on specific issues
- Promote the marketing plan for merchandising operations
- Enhance the British Judo brand.

TARGETS

- To acquire and centrally hold e-mail addresses for 90 per cent of clubs for e-mail communications
- To produce a weekly e-newsletter
- To achieve press coverage to support the identified national competitions across all four Home Countries
- To promote the Marketing Plan with a specific emphasis on merchandising
- To successfully promote the Schools Development Programme and roll out the Enjoy Judo Campaign throughout the country at club level
- To successfully promote the BJA Club Recognition Scheme in the regional media
- To increase broadcast judo features year-on-year
- To ensure *Matside* continues to grow and includes all four Home Countries.

Medium term (Build) – Years 2–4

- To complete the enhanced judo network of promotional bodies to include the National and Local support bodies, fans, control bodies, journalists, and agencies to assist in the production of professional outputs
- To secure regular TV coverage with the GB World Cup – even on a full cost basis to get the ball rolling
- Continue to build relationships with key media and increase the amount of interaction with the tier one and tier two media
- Continue to build up the level of campaigns, which take judo on to the non-sports pages
- Build membership numbers
- Build spectator numbers at events
- Establish regular broadcast coverage.

TARGETS

- For the BJA to hold an e-mail address for 100 per cent of clubs for e-mail communications

- To produce a weekly e-newsletter including news from all four Home Countries
- To design and launch two stand-alone Judo campaigns per year which take judo onto the health and lifestyle pages
- To achieve press coverage supporting all the identified national competitions
- To increase broadcast judo features year-on-year
- To increase regional coverage that includes key British Judo Association mentions to support BJA club level recruitment
- To achieve a regular 'round up' GB World Cup feature within the broadcast media.

Long Term (Expand) – Years 5–10

- Finalise the NETWORK to improve the profile of the sport of judo
- Organise regional training seminars for Areas and Clubs on specific topics
- Move judo to a lower second tier sport in terms of overall national media coverage. Now probably a lower third tier.

In order to deliver these objectives, the BJA needs help. The establishment of a PR network is complicated, and there is a heavy reliance on the goodwill and support of other stakeholders. Incremental improvements in this area depend on many variables, including the success of other key objectives such as elite success and participation gains. The NGB needs to improve the offerings and make sure the internal stakeholders are 100 per cent committed to the concept of selling the BJA. The next step is to identify and build the network, using the previous data to prioritise the stakeholders. Publicity is always available if a body can pay for it. In the case of the BJA, like most sporting bodies, it relies on quality news, contacts and hard work to make an impact.

Technical excellence

In a highly technical sport such as judo, the technical platforms operated by the NGB are arguably the most critical aspect of the operations. The two most visible key objectives – participation and elite success – are underpinned by technical programmes. As you will see from Figure 4.22, judo is a complex technical sport. There are five main strands on the technical front and each must be in sync with all others. The grading or belt system adds a unique dimension as it serves as a parallel competition structure. Players are actually advancing on two parallel fronts: competitions and gradings.

Figure 4.22 shows the key stakeholders that are involved in the delivery of each of these technical programmes. There is, of course, much overlap between

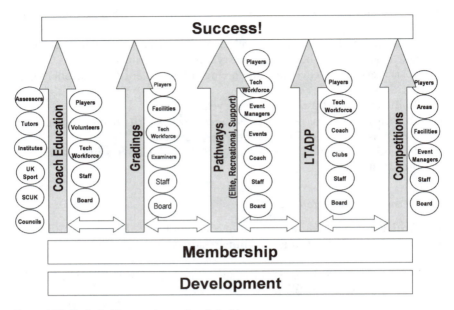

Figure 4.22 Technical integration and stakeholders.

the stakeholders over the respective programmes, and there should be. The BJA sometimes struggles from 'silo' thinking and changes that are made to one technical programme can have serious ramifications to others. The relationship building in this area is further complicated by the fact that the policy on the technical front was traditionally set by volunteer groupings called Commissions of the Association. With the growth of the BJA and the creation of key paid positions – Performance Director, Technical Director, Director of Gradings, Coaching Officer, Director of World Class Programmes, and a complement of six Regional Technical Officers the balance of power has shifted and the paid staff play the dominant role in technical development.

The transition of power from the voluntary sector to the paid sector as key decision-makers is another example of managing stakeholders groups and managing expectations, when working in a relationship strategy. Shifting power is one of the most difficult change management processes to implement. British Judo is not only in the process of changing the leadership on the technical front but has also launched a 'Technical Renaissance' to completely review and upgrade the technical agenda. This goes to the heart of the sport and careful stakeholder relationship building is required to move forward.

Led by the paid staff, the first call is to get full backing from the elected Board of Directors for proposed changes. This goes back to internal synchronisation. The Board is brought into the planning process very early on and contributes significantly to the development of the new programmes. By involving the Board at every step, there is an implicit buy-in and therefore it is easier to send a united message. The Association must plan meticulously to ensure harmony.

In early 2007, the BJA accepted that the key principle that runs through all areas of activity that is critical to success is Retention. This was discussed in the participation section and it has been agreed that the technical platform is the most critical factor in retention. Good coaches teaching strong technical programmes keep young people in the sport. The BJA launched a then ground-breaking coach education and grading system in 1982 and did little to update or change it until the launch of this Technical Renaissance. Even a state of the art system cannot survive at peak efficiency for 25 years without significant updating.

The key changes that are being enacted revolve around the coach education system, the launch of a Technical grading scheme, and the changes to the competitions structures. The first two are extremely emotive issues and the BJA has worked hard to develop a strong team to convince the internal stakeholders that this is the way to go. With a mantra of 'retention' and the introduction of high level technical thinkers to the staff the development of new programmes has been pushed forward at pace.

The Staff/Board team, once in total agreement, then begin a programme of relationship building at the next stage – which would be the Technical Workforce (largely volunteer), Clubs, Volunteers, Players and to a lesser extent the funding partners. Many of the technical changes are funded by funding partners so it is imperative to keep these key stakeholders in the loop. The final stakeholders that must be brought onboard would be the Facility providers and Event Managers. These groups will play a key support role in the delivery of the programmes.

The key formula for success in the Technical area would require the following elements:

- *Quality products* – the programmes must be designed by individuals and groups who have the confidence and respect of the masses
- *Consultation* – the more constituencies that are involved in the development of the programmes the better. To be included in the development group generally assures buy-in to the final product
- *Communications* – successful implementation of these programmes will depend on a strong communications plan to ensure there are no surprises
- *Training* – continuous professional development (CPD) is the backbone of all careers, whether paid or voluntary. The BJA must work hard to ensure the technical workforce is equipped to handle change and is motivated to deliver
- *Implementation* – once the workforce is ready then a deliberate rollout needs to be implemented, with the older programmes cut off almost

immediately. There is no room for uncertainty or indecisiveness that leads to the running of parallel programmes in some instances

- *Support* – after the implementation the support must remain in place indefinitely
- *Renewal* – the Association must ensure there is a process of continuous review and renewal to the technical programmes in the future. This is essential as it is much easier to initiate incremental change than to re-invent the wheel every 25 years

The above process requires a huge team of talented individuals to implement.

World class events

'Major events' is an area where relationship building is absolutely critical to the success of the event. An event begins as an idea or a suggestion, and ends with a large-scale multi-faceted team delivering a major event that thousands of people can enjoy. How successful an event is depends heavily on the quality and range of the final team assembled to make it happen. It can be seen from Figure 4.23 that there are five key stages to deliver an event and a final stage, which refers to legacy and the future. At each stage after the decision to bid for an event, there are multiple stakeholders added, ultimately building to the full team as shown in Stage 5.

In 2005, the BJA decided to bid to host a yearly World Cup tournament. The World Cups are the elite tournaments in Europe that form the backbone

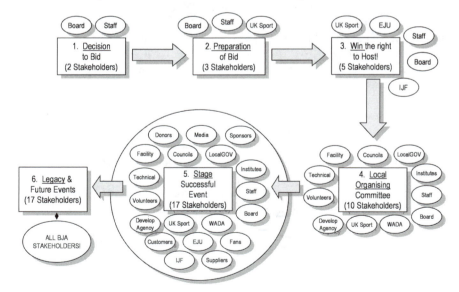

Figure 4.23 Delivering a major event – developing key relationships.

of the Olympic qualification process. They are high level events staged in key European cities, such as Paris, Hamburg, Moscow, Rotterdam and a variety of others. In order to host this event it was imperative that the BJA secured the support of the UK Sport Major Events Panel in order to make the event financially viable in the early years while sponsorship and spectator numbers could be built up.

The Board instructed the Staff to prepare a business plan to be presented to the Major Events panel to secure 'in principle' funding to move the bidding stage. Once financial support was secured, the UK Sport events team then assisted the BJA with the bidding process to the EJU and the licence to stage the yearly event in Birmingham in the National Indoor Arena was quickly secured.

Once the event was secured, the key stakeholders moved to form a local organising committee with representatives from all key stakeholder groups. The local organising committee is the key stage to ensure the event is successful. If a high calibre team representing all key interest groups is assembled at least 10–12 months prior to the event there is an excellent probability of successfully staging a quality event. The BJA also hosted the European Championships in 1995 and the World Championships in 1999 at the NIA so there were already strong ties in place between the BJA and the NIA, Birmingham City Council, the West Midlands development Agency, and the local volunteer base. This pre-existing relationship allowed the BJA to get the LOC organised quickly and efficiently and the first event in April 2006 was a resounding success with a tremendous presentation format, TV and radio partners secured, and a large crowd for a women's event. The first Men's event in September 2007 was universally praised as one of the best in Europe and this event will ultimately grow into being one of the consistently top events in Europe, alongside Paris, Hamburg and Rotterdam. This is largely due to the successful relationship-marketing plan that was implemented – both internally to build the LOC and externally to make the event financially viable and to attract a large crowd and solid media coverage.

You will notice in Figure 4.23 that it takes no fewer than 17 key stake-holders to have a great event. This is a diverse combination of control bodies, internal core elements, National support bodies, local support bodies, and income potential groups. All must come together in a structured and syn-chronised plan to make the weekend run perfectly. The athletes, officials, fans, and media must all be satisfied on the day.

Legacy is an important concept for all events in the future. Events have a powerful impact on the locality and also on the sport and it is imperative that the impetus of a major event is utilised to develop a facility or increase par-ticipation or drive some other positive programme or change. The Olympic Games have in the past been a catalyst for the revitalisation of a city – like in Barcelona 1992. The city used the Games as a major springboard to re-build dilapidated sections of the city and to firmly put itself on the map as a cosmopolitan European capital and a desirable tourism destination. The Great Britain World Cup was a catalyst for a West Midlands development programme that successfully engaged dozens of clubs and hundreds of volunteers. This will provide long-term benefits for the sport – and can be built upon year-on-year going forward.

It is clear from all of the above sections that relationships with a diverse range of stakeholders need to be highly developed to deliver in a sporting organisation. The next section will discuss in greater details some strategies to cultivate and develop those relationships with customers, stakeholders, and anyone else who can be a part of the plan.

Implementation of relationship-marketing plan

Previously in this chapter, we have described the background and present state of the Association to set the stage for this study. We have also clearly defined the mission, vision, high-level targets, stakeholder analysis, and provided a detailed analysis of which stakeholders are critical to which key objectives, and which stakeholders are most important and need priority attention. The BJA has a plan, and a big part of that plan is to create a relationship-marketing strategy that will be successful and ultimately provide much needed support resources to the sport of judo to allow the body to deliver to its full potential. We have discussed the relevant stakeholders that need to be developed and turned into true partners in order to deliver the objectives outlined. We will now outline the steps taken to create and develop relationships in the sporting organisation.

The first topic that needs to be explored is the underpinning reason to establish the relationship between the NGB and the specific stakeholder. This is the key foundation for the process and will direct the nature and scope of the future relationship. There are many reasons why relationships may be formed. Some of these are:

- The sport
- Common objectives (may be sport, health, discipline, crime prevention, etc.)
- Synergies
- Mutually beneficial working relationship
- Commercial objectives
- Corporate social responsibility
- Individual social responsibility (give something back, volunteering)
- Elite performance targets (athletes need assistance)
- Lifelong learning/personal or corporate development
- Necessity
- Government objectives
- Personal relationships.

It is important to note that most relationships will actual involve a number of the above underpinning reasons – but some will be very direct and really only have one key objective and therefore probably one key reason driving the association. Relationship-marketing theory would suggest that part of the strategy is to involve as many of these reasons as possible – thereby making the relationship more comprehensive and compelling. The more comprehensive and compelling the relationship, the further it can be developed, exploited and renewed for long-term productivity.

For the purpose of analysis and planning, it is practical to group these underpinning reasons into a number of categories. They can be grouped into four main categories:

1   *The Sport* – The key factor driving most of the internal stakeholders is the furtherance of the sport of judo. This is achieved by successfully delivering the key objectives of the NGB across a variety of platforms. There are many involved who are in the sport for the sake of the sport alone. The Board of Directors, players, technical workforce, clubs, EJU, IJF, Sport England and the Sport England Delivery System, and spectators would fall into this category.

2   *Excellence* – Judo is a key Olympic sport and World and Olympic medals are an important objective for the BJA. We have previously identified the complex team and relationships required to deliver at the highest level. High level performance targets are one of the key drivers for all of sport. Every athlete wants to compete and ultimately see where that competitive pathway takes him. The journey might end up recreational or it might lead to the Olympic Games. This is one of the basic principles of all sport and forms an important element in the ultimate retention of participants. The key stakeholders that would fall into this category would be Players, Technical Workforce, Clubs, Staff, Board, UK Sport, Councils, Institutes, Spectators, Sports Coach UK and WADA.

3   *Commercial* – There is a very strong business element to sport and it is a multi-billion pound industry in most large countries. Look no further than the Premier League in English football to verify the staggering numbers that are involved when referring to turnover, TV contracts, player salaries, ticket prices, positive impact on the local economy, the valuation of the clubs, and many more. Sport is a big business and getting bigger all the time. Judo in Britain is fast growing but has not been hugely successful to date in the area of resource creation. The foundations have been built and new income generation programmes are taking shape. This is a rapidly developing area and there is interest growing in the commercial side of British Judo. The key stakeholders in this area would be Board, Staff, Customers, Suppliers, Trust, Corporate Partners and Advertisers, Spectators, Facility Providers and Donors.

4   *Social Responsibility* – Sport has a unique ability to deliver on this agenda.

Sport can be used to keep young people off the streets and give them a healthy outlet and a sense of purpose. It can instil confidence and discipline in young and old alike. It can be an important part of a healthy lifestyle and prevent obesity. It can reduce criminal activity by giving potential young offenders a sense of belonging. Sport is a wholesome vehicle that can be used to deliver on a wide range of socially responsible objectives. The role of an NGB is multi-faceted and social responsibility is high on the list of priorities. There are a number of key stakeholders that are interested in this area to include Corporate Partners, Board, Staff, volunteers, EJU, IJF, Councils, Local Gov, Schools, Clubs, the Trust, BOA, and Donors.

Please note that each individual stakeholder is different and distinct. One Club might fall into the first category as above and another Club might fit neatly into all four. The BJA certainly has clubs of both types. A full perform-ance club should certainly be working to objectives in all four of these cat-egories. It would be promoting the sport, producing elite players, creating resources to plough back into development, and delivering on the social agenda by instilling discipline and confidence in young people. UK Sport would be an example of a one-dimensional stakeholder. This government quango was initiated simply to support elite sport and ensure that Team GB delivers at the highest levels. This organisation would be interested in the general health of the sport in Britain, but only in the sense that the sporting body needs to be strong enough to support an elite platform that delivers. They have in the past worked with the NGB to strengthen the structures and governance, but once this was accomplished they reverted to their true objective – which falls squarely into the excellence category.

In Figure 4.24, you will quickly see that there are many stakeholder groups that are underpinned by more than one category. This is natural and as stated above the greater the extent to which the BJA can broaden the interest across these main underpinning categories the better chance of a successful long-term relationship.

Now that we have identified the foundation – what is the next step to build the relationships? There are some identifiable characteristics within each of these categories. In the case of the first category, The Sport, the main justification is probably the fact that they need each other. The internal stakeholders in this category are purely interested in furthering the sport and they simply must engage with the NGB in most cases to participate. In the Excellence category the feeling of success or winning is a powerful motive. Individuals who are involved with winners gain tremendous satisfaction for this association. The bottom-line in sport is often about winning and losing and the 'ecstasy of victory and the agony of defeat' play an important role in the human psyche.

Social Responsibility provides the stakeholders who engage the opportunity

The Sport	Excellence
Board	Board
•Staff	•Staff
•Players	•Technical Workforce
•Technical Workforce	•Players
•Volunteers	•UK Sport
•Clubs	•Councils
•Schools	•Institutes
•EJU	•Spectators
•IJF	•BOA
•Councils	•Sports Coach UK
•Sport England Delivery	•EJU
•Local Gov	•IJF
•Facility providers	•WADA
•DCMS	•DCMS
•Sports Coach UK	•Media
•CCPR	
•Spectators	
Social Responsibility	**Commercial**
Board	Board
•Staff	•Staff
•Volunteers	•Customers
•Corporate Partners	•Spectators
•Technical Workforce	•Suppliers
•Councils	•British Judo Trust
•EJU	•Corporate Partners and Advertisers
•IJF	•Facility providers
•Local Gov	•Donors
•Schools	
•British Judo Trust	
•BOA	
•Donors	

Figure 4.24 Reason categories for stakeholders – Why do they engage?

to support and endorse a healthy and wholesome activity with a wide range of positive outcomes. It is interesting that the first three categories all provide a 'feel good' element about working with a sport and the NGB responsible for that sport. The final category, Commercial, is slightly different and the profit motive is prevalent here. Sponsors and advertisers are less inclined to engage due to personal allegiance to a sport, although it certainly helps! Most sponsors nowadays are continuously analysing and reviewing sponsorships and advertising platforms through a variety of statistical and other evidence. Commercial engagements must be profitable for both parties – or else they are soon terminated.

Once the logic or reasoning behind the potential engagement is clearly understood for all stakeholders the BJA then needs to prioritise the stakeholders to have a clear idea of how to distribute scarce resources. For example, Local Gov is a powerful nationwide player for sport in that they provide most of the facilities and also fund thousands of development programmes. It is estimated that the contribution from this source is up to 66 per cent of the total amount spent on grassroots sport in the UK. UK Sport's annual turnover is in the region of £75m. The Local Gov total contribution would be over one billion pounds per annum. This is an important stakeholder but the reality is there are hundreds of local councils throughout the UK and it is not possible for the BJA to directly engage with even a reasonable percentage of them. Therefore the Sport England Delivery System, which is comprised of nine regions throughout England, is a more likely target for direct partnerships with the NGB. These Sport England regions bring together County Sports Partnerships, Local Sports Networks, Specialist Sports Colleges, and other interest groups to form a regional delivery body. This must be factored into the planning.

For the BJA, the general plan is that national level direct engagement is the most effective based on the current size of the organisation. The largest sports in England have county bodies, generally in up to 40 counties, with paid staff to engage at a high level with most of the County Sports Partnerships and Local Government Councils. This is a long-term target for all sports – but it is not realistic at this point in time. Therefore the BJA's strategy is to engage at a local level through the stronger judo clubs and volunteers. This is a good example of an organisation extending its reach through constituent members with a common objective. There are over 850 clubs in the BJA but unfortunately only about 100 are strong enough to engage actively with local service providers. This is an area that is being addressed aggressively through the Develop Team. This team is assisting clubs in building capacity, largely in the form of volunteers and personnel, so they are better equipped to engage with local stakeholders who may provide invaluable assistance. The BJA works directly with the Sports Councils in each of the Home Countries, specifically Sport England, to strengthen the clubs with programmes like Clubmark. Clubmark is a structured process to ensure that a club is fit for purpose and complies with all of the applicable legislation for running a club. The end result is the receipt of the Clubmark certification and this is a valuable certification to have when seeking grant support or dealing with local support partners.

The ranking of stakeholders is an imperfect science as there are dozens of dimensions to each relationship and they are often overlapping and complicated. In British Judo, the strategy to build the relationships has been staged. It is true to say that all 27 stakeholder groups were engaged to some extent at the beginning of this study but it would also be fair to say that much work and focus needed to be dedicated to this important area.

The following table provides a basic prioritisation of the stakeholders at the time of this study. This is based on the MACTOR findings, and the further analysis in section seven on which stakeholders play an important role to deliver each of the key objectives (Table 4.4).

The relationship building process starts internally, and the BJA Core is the key group to grow the network and establish the relationships that are required to promote the sport. The next step is to grow strong relationships with the key funding partners, which are largely in place but can be improved. The key funders, UK Sport and Sport England are large and complicated

Table 4.4 Prioritisation of stakeholders

1. Core BJA Board Staff Clubs Players Technical Workforce Volunteers	Internal core
2. National funding partners UK Sport Sports Councils Sport England Delivery System	Enhanced core
3. Local support bodies Schools Local Gov Facility Providers	Enhanced core
4. National support bodies Institutes Sports Coach UK BOA DCMS	Network
5. Income potential Media Customers Sponsors/Advertisers Suppliers British Judo Trust Spectators Donors	Market
6. Control bodies EJU IJF WADA CCPR	Network

organisations. There is benefit to be gained by fully understanding all of the nuances and potential support elements in each. This is a key priority going forward. These bodies also have reach into the next two most important stakeholder groups – the Local Support Bodies and the National Support Bodies. The BJA is using this leverage to further relationships at the next level.

The final phase of the process is how to build the relationships. Stakeholder relationships in sporting organisations can be hard to measure, but there is certainly a process that can be followed to ensure all of the bases are being covered. Simply put the NGB needs to CREATE then DEVELOP then

MAINTAIN and in some cases ultimately TERMINATE relationships with key stakeholders. The probability in the case of the BJA is that no stakeholder will need to be terminated, as a basic relationship with each will always be required. That said, a major down-scaling of a relationship can be very close to a termination.

Figure 4.25 gives a simplified process for developing relationships with key partners. It is simple and yet easy to get wrong! Some of the key building blocks are often neglected and this leads to long-term decay and failure.

You will note from the figure that this building of marketing relationships is a multi-stage process and requires much planning and energy. It is critical that the analysis and targeting steps are completely in advance. There is no time to waste on superfluous contacts that cannot deliver to the required agenda of the NGB. The process begins at the bottom of the figure by establishing the foundation for the future relationship. This will be shared values and the potential to establish a mutually beneficial working relationship.

Once this is established then the specific reason why the relationship should be initiated must be established. This may cover a range of reasons over a range of the four categories as previously outlined. The next step is to determine exactly who is the key decision-maker that needs to be recruited to build the relationship. This is not always as clear as it should be. Influence

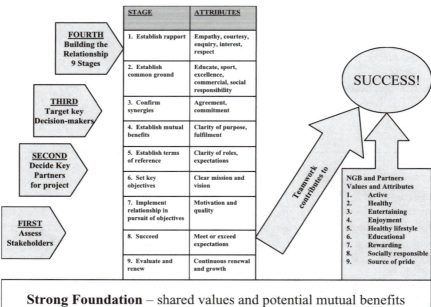

Figure 4.25 Building relationships in the sporting environment.

and budgets may be controlled by some non-standard positions. It is essential to know your potential partners. Once this is done then the nine-step process as outlined in Figure 4.25 provides a fairly comprehensive guide to relationship building, maintenance, and review. It is hard work to develop key contacts and working partnerships and it takes significant additional work to ensure they do not spoil and end prematurely.

The analysis stage is critical to continuing marketing relationships for the longer term. There are eight key points that need to be considered when analysing stakeholder relationships and specifically relationship-marketing principles. These are:

- *Stakeholder status* – the Stakeholder status may be evaluated on a number of scales. Previously we established a six-stage system for ranking participants in the BJA with the descriptors of:
  - ○ Recruit
  - ○ Licence Holder
  - ○ Player
  - ○ Volunteer
  - ○ Technical Workforce
  - ○ Judo for Life

  This scale outlines the depth of the relationship and as the participant moves down the list they are more deeply involved at each subsequent level.
- *Loyalty* – can be functional or emotional and is one of the key factors for a successful partnership. Loyalty schemes play a huge role in all walks of commercial life and this holds true in sport
- *Nature of the exchange* – B to C, B to B or Network (indirect) oriented. Network will be the most effective
- *Trust* – a cornerstone of all working relationships
- *Commitment* – this is critical to build on existing relationships to ensure longevity
- *Resources provided* – there must be a fair commitment from both parties regarding resources to include financial, personnel and technical resources
- *Distance of the Exchange* – the exchange may be direct, through networks or both
- *Benefits linked to the relationship* – there must be clear achievable objectives and these must be beneficial to both partners and measurable.

This analysis is basic and important. Relationships are evolutionary and repetitious. This evolution encompasses the following phases:

- Start by creating a first interaction or transaction or voluntary implication (TO GET)

- Continue by developing an increase in the frequency of the exchanges, involvement and development of trust (TO GROW)
- Establish the relationship in order to reduce demands which ultimately leads to less effort and greater rewards for both parties (TO KEEP)
- Decline which may lead to the gradual deterioration or a sudden exit by one party (TO END).

There are many ways to develop and retain marketing relationships in sporting organisations. The above information is designed to show how a national governing body of sport sets targets and then identifies which stakeholders are essential or useful to achieving these targets. Once this analysis is completed the sporting body must set priorities and then initiate a plan to aggressively work with all of the key partners to form an enhanced network that can deliver in a market environment.

Conclusion and perspectives

There is unlimited potential for the sport of judo to grow and prosper over the next ten years. The BJA is well placed to compete with most sports in the UK in the key areas of participation and excellence. British Judo has a presence in all geographic areas, can deliver on the inclusion agenda, and has traditionally delivered Olympic medals for the GB Team. There are 56 judo medals available each Olympiad, with seven male and seven female weight categories and a gold, silver and double bronze in each. That is a statement worth repeating. Success has been achieved in the past, but the true potential of the Association will be realised in the next decade.

The BJA has embraced this study and sees the potential of what can be achieved by using relationship-marketing strategies in all areas of operation and by exploring new commercial opportunities. Strategic planning for the relationship-marketing strategy is critical. The Association is at a crossroads. It can continue to progress and take measured steps or it can truly push for top five in the world status. This is an achievable goal. Britain will struggle to surpass the Japanese, French, Germans and Koreans; but there is no reason why the BJA cannot sit comfortably with this group and deliver many World and Olympic medals for the UK for the foreseeable future. There is intense elite competition on the men's side from the Japanese, French, Koreans, Chinese, Germans, Dutch, Georgians, Russians, Brazilians and assorted other Eastern European countries. There is also substantial competition on the female side from Japan, France, Korea, China, Cuba, Brazil, Germany, Holland, Belgium and Spain. British Judo is fortunate to have a reasonable gender balance and in fact has a stronger female elite programme than most countries.

There are probably 100,000 individuals participating in judo sport in the UK and the current elite programme is self-judged to be ranked eighth in the world, based on key criteria. It should be possible to capture more of this activity on the individual database, and move both the men's and women's programmes into a top five position – but this is a very ambitious target.

Financial stability and ultimately strength must be achieved to be in a position to take more chances and provide a higher level of professional support to the thousands of judo volunteers. Volunteers are the lifeblood of all sports but in the age of increasing bureaucratic requirements and social options, the NGB must be in a better position to support these requirements or the volunteers will be driven out of the sport. It is a fact that with each passing generation the total hours the average volunteer is willing to commit in a given week is shrinking. This void must be managed and filled – and this costs money.

It is clear that the British Judo Association is a growing and progressive body that is capable of delivering the sport of judo at a much higher level in the future with improved resources. Judo is a traditional sport and the income generation potential has not been fully explored on a worldwide basis. The IJF, currently one of the top ten largest International Federations (IF), based on the number of affiliated countries, employs only three administrative staff to support the elected President. Undoubtedly this is one of the smallest professional contingents at the IF Head Office of a major Olympic sport. This traditional thinking has dominated almost all judo NF's and in the past the BJA was no exception.

British Judo has begun to implement this plan. High-level targets have been set, and the review and evaluation process is in place and will be comprehensive. The BJA has created a major attitudinal shift in both the Board and the Staff and indeed in the membership at large. Fairness, transparency and communications have been the cornerstones of this change management process and this has served the Association well. Due to the quality management of the change hard and sometimes radical decisions have been warmly accepted and embraced.

Tremendous growth has been achieved in the past five years with guidance and support from key partners – specifically UK Sport and the Home Country Sports Councils. Now the sport is poised to really drive to the next level – and move to category one elite status. Like in business the jump from good to great is a big one. Relationship-marketing strategies will be a key role in realising this target. To do this strong marketing partnerships will need to be developed, formed, managed and renewed to increase the reach and resources. This study has identified a clear vision to establish a relationship-marketing strategy in a sporting body.

It is the duty of every sporting body to keep moving forward – or ground will certainly be lost. This is true in all sectors but it is probably most clearly pronounced in sport. On the field of play competitions are won by the narrowest of margins – in the Boardroom of the sporting organisation it is fast becoming equally competitive.

Chapter 5

Conclusion

The reader finishing this book may well find that it has raised many questions and that it has not provided the ultimate solution that will increase marketing efficiency. However, the primary aim of the book was not to suggest ready-made solutions, but to promote a new way of viewing marketing, thus facilitating the change in attitude that is needed if marketing is to be managed and developed more effectively. The book also describes and illustrates a method and tools for defining and implementing a relationship-management strategy within sports organisations. This is a complex process based on the skills of the people involved and their ability to share their acquired knowledge. From this point of view, the book has been designed to give a broad range of ideas and to encourage readers to reflect on their personal experiences in order to improve their marketing skills and thereby achieve their objectives more efficiently.

Application of the principles of relationship marketing

Such reflection will also lead the reader to question whether or not the principles and tools of relationship marketing should be applied to a given sports organisation. The case of the British Judo Association and the illustrations presented throughout the book show that relationship marketing must be adapted to the particular level of resources, skills and the operating environment of the organisation concerned.

The principles of relationship marketing should be applied step-by-step. The first step concerns the organisation itself, within which the foundations of the marketing action must be built. This essential starting point is often overlooked, resulting in many sports organisations attempting to implement a CRM system without taking into account the fact that this also requires introducing internal changes first. Implementing relationship marketing involves much more than installing the relevant software. It requires modifying relations with stakeholders, behaviours, skills, resources and the internal organisation of the body. This is why many CRM systems have failed: they are not the final solution for increasing data-processing capacity and developing new services and software systems do not provide a strategy. The second step concerns the creation and development of relationships with targeted end-users, which involves a second challenge – that of improving loyalty. Many sports organisations favour offensive marketing, concentrating on recruitment, and neglect less costly and more effective defensive marketing strategies. The third step is to introduce the changes needed to allow the implementation of a network-oriented relationship-marketing approach, as it is more difficult to manage the relationships within a network than to manage a one-on-one relationship. It is only when a sports organisation has learned to manage market-based relationships that it will be able to build a collaborative network with its stakeholders.

These three stages are shown in Figure 5.1. The procedure must be seen as an iterative process because it is only when a sporting organisation has established the foundations of relationship marketing, created a relationship with targeted end-users and built a collaborative network that it will be able to define the improvement objectives for the three phases.

Overcome resistance to change

The main obstacle to implementing relationship marketing is resistance to change. In every organisation, change is subject to two opposing forces: one that is favourable, and one that is resistant. Hence, despite the advantages for a sports organisation of applying the principles of relationship marketing,

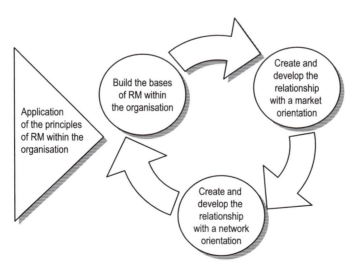

Figure 5.1 The steps in implementing the principles of relationship marketing in a sports organisation.

there is always resistance. The first part of this resistance is related to personal interests, as people tend to see the cost of change (e.g. modifications to processes, pressure for results, etc.) but not the concrete benefits they will gain. In addition, some people have low tolerance for change, which leads them to resist because they think they will not be able to adapt their skills to new systems. Another reason is connected to the fact that change may be beneficial for one part of the organisation and have negative consequences for another. For example, for the management of a club, the introduction of a system for dealing with complaints from its members will allow it to react to problems and improve the quality of its service. This may involve changing the training schedule of the people delivering the service and the communication process with personnel will allow the identification of people who cannot deliver the required quality of service. Sometimes things that appear to be minor issues to one individual or group will seriously affect another person. The people concerned do not always understand the nature of change, and there may be an imbalance between the management and other personnel. This generally leads to a crisis of confidence in the proposed change.

Resistance to change is normal and should be anticipated. It is easier to get change accepted by reducing the strength of this resistance than by increasing the forces driving the change. These forces are mostly internal to the organisation, which further reinforces the importance of internal marketing and of the way change is implemented. As Rondeau (2002: 110) pointed out, 'the success of a transformation is not only a question of the positive disposition of the parties concerned, it is also necessary to develop the individual and organisational capabilities needed to implement that transformation. Empowerment enables the parties to be equipped to carry out the change'.

The future of relationship marketing in sports organisations

Over the last 20 years, relationship marketing has breathed new life into marketing. For certain organisations it has led to a change of paradigm, whereas others are still in the appraisal phase. According to Egan and Harker (2006: 230), 'as a paradigm, relationship marketing is now at the stage of converting theory into tools and guidelines for practice directly relevant to consumer marketing'. It has sometimes produced variable results, as applications such as CRM have been introduced haphazardly, despite it only being a relationship-management tool that facilitates experiential relationships (Customer Experiential Management) and that impacts on all internal and external stakeholders.

The manners in which relationship-marketing strategies are drawn up and implemented by sports organisations are constantly evolving. Given their characteristics and the environment in which they carry out actions to achieve their end goals (i.e. commercial, social and environmental), they are led to produce innovative strategies. Three examples have been chosen to show that the future is firmly rooted in the present. The first example is FC Barcelona, which has developed the concept of 'members for life'. This initiative shows that it is possible for the club to develop a relationship with a supporter throughout that person's life, and even throughout future generations of his/her family. This programme also shows that it is possible to generate large economic resources from a marketing programme whose end goals are mostly social. Second, the Ecomass project, which was designed and set up for the Athletics World Championships in Helsinki in 2005. Ecomass fore-shadowed network-based relationship-marketing programmes aimed at reducing the environmental impact of sporting events. Today, sport is a powerful social phenomenon that can unify and enthuse the entire planet. Sport's uniting spirit, with the catalyst being sporting events, is undoubtedly an effective vector for raising awareness of the importance of protecting the environment. Finally, Sport in Action shows the importance of social marketing programmes in developing countries such as Zambia. This non-government funded project runs workshops for adolescent girls and organises festivals around sport, traditional games and fitness. All of these areas of delivery are underpinned with education about HIV/AIDS, children's rights, and alcohol and substance abuse.

These three cases illustrate the diversity of relationship marketing in sports organisations and prefigure the directions in which it is likely to evolve. According to Coviello and Brodie (2001: 396), 'it is important to understand both similarities and differences in marketing practice across contexts, including when and why different approaches to marketing are being practiced, how multiple approaches can be practiced simultaneously, and how these practices might be influenced by other firms, market or managerial characteristics'.

Case Study: FC Barcelona: 'Members for Life'

Dr Andreu Camps (Director of INEFC)
Special thanks to:
Josep María Fontclara (FCB Social Sector Director)
Francesc Solanellas (Director of FCB's 'tu déportes idel' Sections)
Francesc Cruces (FCB Social Sector Development Department)

Barcelona Football Club (FCB): Facts and Figures

FC Barcelona was founded over 100 years ago. It is run as a non-profit organisation under the relevant sports legislation of the Spanish State and of the Autonomous Community of Catalonia. It owns a large number of sports facilities:

- The 'Camp Nou' football stadium with a capacity of 98,772 spectators
- The 'Mini Estadi' football stadium with a capacity of 15,276 spectators
- A 137,000 m^2 sports city with accommodation for sportspeople and a range of training venues
- The Palau Blaugrana indoor venue with a capacity of 7,235 spectators
- An ice rink with a capacity of 1,256 spectators
- A second indoor venue with a capacity of 1,200 spectators
- Other facilities, such as a museum, a club shop, offices and medical services, etc.

It manages a large range of sporting activities:

- Professional soccer with a team in the Spanish premier league
- Amateur soccer with 15 teams (11 men's, 4 women's)
- 13 different sporting sections:

  - Four are professional: basketball, handball, roller hockey and five-a-side football
  - Nine are amateur: athletics, rugby, baseball, volleyball, field hockey, ice hockey, figure skating, ice skating, and wheelchair basketball in collaboration with the Guttmann organisation.

In total, 115 teams participate in competitions.

FC Barcelona's financial situation is summarised in Table 5.1.

The club has introduced a relationship-marketing strategy aimed at the following stakeholders.

Table 5.1 The financial situation of FC Barcelona

	Consolidated results 2006/2007	Budget 2007/2008
Operating revenue	€290.1 million	€315 million
Operating costs	€270.6 million	€300 million
Operating income	€+19.5 million	+ €15 million
Financial and extraordinary results	€-4.5 million	€0
Net result before tax	€+8.8 million	+ €15 million

Members

Members, of which there are approximately 160,000, are people who have voting rights with the club (except under 18s and new members). Over the last four years, there has been a substantial increase in the number of members from the following groups: young people, women and people living outside Catalonia. In total, 36,000 members are women, 30,000 members are under the age of 18, 65,000 members live in Barcelona, 76,000 live elsewhere in Catalonia and 19,000 live in the rest of Spain or abroad.

There are three categories of member:

- Child Member (up to 6 years old). Subscription of €35 per annum
- Youth Member (up to 16 years old). Subscription of €72 per annum
- Senior Member (16 years old and over). Subscription of €145 per annum (voting rights from the age of 18).

During the last two years, the number of members has increased by 11,500 per year, as 18,000 new members have joined the club and 6,500 have left (5 per cent rotation).

Season ticket holders

As well as membership rights, season ticket holders have a reserved seat in Barcelona's stadium for certain categories of football match. They are also guaranteed seats at basketball and handball matches. Only members can become season ticket holders, of which there are about 88,000 for football matches. Ticket prices depend on where the seat is in the stadium. There are 12,000 people on the waiting list for season tickets but only 600 people fail to renew their season ticket every year.

Because of UEFA regulations for football stadiums, the club does not replace season tickets that are not renewed. However, the club can meet requests for the UEFA Champions League and to extend the VIP areas.

'Penyas'

Penyas are FC Barcelona's supporters clubs. There are 1,828 penyas, of which 1,450 are considered to be active. Some 626 of these penyas are in Catalonia, 679 are in the rest of Europe and 93 are in the rest of the world. Total membership of the penyas is around 250,000.

Sympathisers

Sympathisers are people who have a positive attitude towards the club and a feeling of belonging to it, in the widest sense of the word. It is estimated that 70 per cent of 18–65 year-olds in Catalonia are sympathisers. Throughout the world, there are thought to be approximately 18 million sympathisers.

Partners

FCB was the first club to include 'solidarity sponsors' in its sponsoring programmes. The club will pay its main solidarity sponsor, UNICEF, €1.5 million per year for five years in exchange for the right to put the UNICEF logo on its shirts. UNICEF will use this money in humanitarian projects for children throughout the world. FC Barcelona's partners are listed in Table 5.2.

Structure of the club with respect to its member and loyalty-building programmes

President and Management Committee

The Management Committee consists of 17 members, who are elected by all the club members for a period of four years. It is chaired by a President. The social sector is run by a vice-president and three other members of the Management Committee.

Executive Structure

The head of the executive structure is formed by a Board of Directors, which is responsible for all 11 sectors, or operational departments, as well as for the sporting structure.

The Social Sector is responsible for relations with the club's members,

Table 5.2 FC Barcelona's partners

Official partners	Official providers	Official collaborators	Official media	Other sports sponsors
Nike, Coca-Cola, TV3, Audi, Étoile Damm, La Caixa	Asistencia Sanitaria, Colegial, Hacer, Vueling, Mediapro, NH hotels bwin.com Babybel	Artiplan, Autocares Padros Sacro National-Atesa	El Mundo Sportivo 9 Sport	Basketball (AXA Winterthur); Handball (Llet nostra); Roller hockey (Sorlidiscau and mussap); Indoor football (senseit)

season-ticket holders and all the 'barcelonismo' in general. It also runs the Supporter Services Office (OAB) and the technology and information department, which is in charge of projects involving new technologies.

Supporter Services Office (OAB)

The Supporter Services Office was created in 2003 in order to provide all Barça supporters with a high-quality and efficient information service. It is called the Supporter Services Office, and not the Member Services Office, because its services have been designed to meet the needs of all Barcelona supporters and not just those of the club members.

The Office has a large number of staff, who are in direct contact with the club's supporters. These staff are divided into two teams: one for dealing with members, the other for dealing with the 'Penyas' and other supporters.

The most notable aspects of the service are:

- Telephone services:
    - Call centre with 10 information desks that are open from 9 a.m. to 9 p.m., every day of the year (except for major holidays, such as Christmas Day and New Year's Day)
    - Call centre with three information desks to manage the 'Seient Lliure' (seat free in the stadium) programme
    - Users call a reduced-rate telephone number
    - An easy-to-remember telephone number 902 + the year FCB was founded + 00 (902 1899 00)
    - On average, this service receives 2,300 calls per day and 700,000 calls per year.

- E-mail services:
    - Call centre employees reply to e-mails, as well as to telephone calls
    - Service available 9 a.m. to 9 p.m., 365 days of the year
    - Use of a specific e-mail address: oab@fcbarcelona.cat
    - This service receives and replies to 90,000 e-mails per year.

- Direct personal contact:
    - Eight people are employed to provide face-to-face information to supporters
    - The office responsible for direct relationships with the public is located close to the football stadium, inside FCB's sports complex. It

has nine information desks, which are open Monday to Saturday, from 9 a.m. to 9 p.m. On Sundays and match days the office opens 2 hours before the match

o   This service deals with an average of 6,000 requests every week (information actions or responses to concrete requests from supporters).

The foundations of programmes for members

Studies have shown that Barcelona's links with its members are mostly based on 'socio-emotional components' and that there is no financial end goal. This partly explains why the club has chosen to put the UNICEF logo on players' shirts, rather than the logo of a commercial organisation.

The social programme for members is called *El gran repte* (The great challenge). It has enabled the club to almost double its membership in seven years, with member numbers increasing from 106,000 during the 2001/2002 season to 160,000 for the 2007/2008 season.

This result is linked to the modification of the strategy and the concepts on which the club's relationship with its members is based. Before 2003, it was considered essential for members to be season ticket holders, because season tickets were a vital element in building loyalty. From 2003 onwards, membership was no longer necessarily linked to buying a season ticket and to the sporting spectacle itself. Consequently, it was necessary to diversify the club's loyalty-building programmes.

There was also a change in the mentality of the club's management, who no longer believe that loyalty-building programmes should only be aimed at members, rather they should be aimed at all supporters in order to maintain and develop strong affective relationships between supporters and the club. To achieve this objective, the club has used new technologies to create a direct relationship with supporters through suitable information channels.

Loyalty-building programmes

Loyalty-building programmes are mostly aimed at members and new programmes provide season ticket holders with innovative services (distinction between season tickets and stadium). The services offered to members are based on the principle of 'exclusivity' for the person concerned.

- Direct services:
  These are free services the club offers to all its members, providing added

value compared with other supporters. The most important services are:

- All members (over the age of 18) can vote in the election for club president, which is held every four years. They may also be chosen as a 'socio compromisario' to attend the annual delegates assembly
- Members can choose which of the FCB Foundation's social programmes will be allocated resources
- All members can address complaints to the 'Sindic del Soci' (defender of members' rights) through the club's website, by e-mail, by fax or by letter. Complaints are always dealt with by the OAB
- On joining, every member receives a bronze badge. After 25 years, a silver badge is awarded, after 50 years a gold badge and after 75 years a gold and diamond badge
- *Barça* Magazine is sent, free of charge, to all members. Each bi-monthly issue has 68 colour pages of information about the club
- *Barça Camp Nou* is a match-day newspaper with information about the fixture. It is distributed in the stadium. Between 30,000 and 70,000 copies are printed, depending on the expected crowd figures
- Prize draws in which members can win one of ten seats to watch a match from the Presidential stand at the Camp Nou
- Monthly prize draws for all members. Prizes include Barça merchandising products and trips with Barça to watch away matches
- There are no season tickets for important matches, such as the final of the UEFA Champions League or the *Copa del Rey*. The seats allocated to the club are drawn out of a hat and awarded to members who applied for them (members must then buy the ticket). For the final of the UEFA Champions League in Paris there were 34,000 requests for tickets, representing 75,000 members (each request can include up to four members who want to watch the match together).
- *Seient lliure* (free seat in the stadium) allows season ticket holders to inform the club when they cannot go to one or more matches (the club claims the stadium is always full and to have the best profitability). The club then sells these seats and the member receives 40 per cent of the ticket price. If a member gives the club a seat for an entire season, 90 per cent of the season ticket price will be reimbursed. This system means that the stadium is full for 70 per cent of matches
- Provision of free seats for matches in all sections, except for first-team football and basketball

- Annual season tickets for football and other sections are only available to members
- Free entrance to the museum or for the stadium visit.

- Benefits and advantages:

  - Members who are not season ticket holders have priority over non-members for buying tickets for seats not being used by season ticket holders
  - 20 per cent reduction on ticket prices for matches (for the first ticket)
  - Possibility to travel with the team to away matches at special rates
  - If a season ticket holder does not use his/her seat for Champions League matches, he/she receives a 25 per cent refund on the season ticket
  - 20 per cent reduction for basketball tickets
  - A 25 per cent reduction on online TV
  - A 25 per cent reduction on all mobile phone services
  - A 5 per cent reduction on any item bought from Barça's official shop. A 10 per cent reduction if the purchase is made by internet
  - A 10 per cent reduction for the FCB football school
  - Special price for the 'Exposition time' service
  - Reductions on complementary services, such as room rental, meals etc. (30 per cent reduction for room rental)
  - Special offers and promotions for FCB members (e.g. 10 per cent reduction for articles bought from Bauhaus, 10 per cent at Barcelona Zoo, or 5 per cent at the Book House). Usually, there are no more than 10 or 12 promotions or special offers.

- Other services:
  FCB provides a range of complementary services that are designed to diversify its offer. These services include: VIP areas at the stadium for matches with catering at the stadium, rental of audio-visual rooms, guided visits to the Videomarcador museum, hostesses for events, public relations operations in VIP areas, presence of players at company events, sports goods, football tournaments, medical services, parking, FCB Bus, etc.

- New technology services:
  All members who use the internet to join the club get free and exclusive access to a number of new technology based services:

  - A 100 per cent Barça e-mail account: yourname@mail.fcbarcelona.cat

- ○ An exclusive e-mail newsletter
- ○ Registration with the club's free mobile-phone information service (the club pays the sending costs and registration for the service). Infomembers text message alert system. Members receive at least two messages or reports per week. No more than 10 per cent of the information in messages sent by text message or e-mail is advertising. Commercial messages are mostly connected with sponsoring actions with FCB. Of a total of 160,000 members, around 80,000 receive text messages and 75,000 receive e-mail messages. The club sends a special gift to members who update their personal details or their e-mail addresses, in order to guarantee personalised communication with every member
- ○ Access to card information through FCB's website. Searches for members' cards can be carried out using the membership number and one's personal identification code
- ○ Possible to contact the club directly and to carry out a large number of operations through its website. During the last two years, 65 per cent of new members joined the club through its website
- ○ Members can use the *Seient lliure* (free seat in the stadium) service to inform the club, via internet, that their seat will not be used for one or more matches, or to obtain a ticket for a match that is not included in their season ticket. On average, 5,500 season ticket holders do not use their seats at each match
- ○ In the future, members will have exclusive access to certain parts of the website, thereby allowing further personalisation to meet their expectations and a more individualised relationship with the club.

Special youth programme

The preceding paragraphs have shown that relationship-marketing programmes aimed at members have three significant characteristics: members' relationships with the club are mostly based on the emotional component, the average age of members has dropped significantly in recent years and members' loyalty has greatly increased. The conjunction of these three characteristics has contributed to the creation of a special programme for 'young members' under the age of 18.

The guiding principle is that the club must offer young members a range of activities and services to ensure they retain strong emotional ties with the club throughout their adult lives.

There are two specific lines of action:

1   The creation of a special website for young supporters (not just for members) that has a different format and different content to the main club site: http://www.fcbjunior.cat
2   The introduction of an exclusive programme for young members, which is called *Creix Amb El Barça* (Growing up with Barça). This programme, which is aimed at children and adolescents, offers different products for different age groups in order to create an affective relationship with Barça. It includes 'citizenship' and 'culture' programmes. The idea is that Barça can make a positive contribution to young people's development.

The 'Growing up with Barça' programme has three levels:

1   The 'Baby campaign' has a strong emotional content that will make an impression on children for the whole of their lives.

- Babies are considered members from the day they are born
- Members are sent a range of Barça gifts
- Photographs of new members are published in Barcelona's newspapers to welcome them into the club.

2   The 'Child campaign' provides children with continual reminders that they belong to Barça:

- Members are sent a height chart so they can measure and record their growth
- Every year, members are sent a membership card with photograph that they can collect and place on the height chart. Membership cards, known as *Carte Barça Tonos*, have been designed to be attractive to children. Every year, they have a different design
- With the card, members are sent an exclusive Barça 'pink' every year.
- Members receive a gift on their birthday (exclusive club promotional item) with a congratulations letter from Barça
- Exclusive cultural programmes (theatre and cinema shows) are organised for Barça's young members
- The club organises a Christmas drawing competition for all its young members? The winning drawing is used for the club's official Christmas card
- Possible to watch some of the professional football team's training sessions

- Members under seven can watch matches free of charge if they are accompanied by an adult and they do not take up a seat
- The flagship service gives all young members the chance to come to the Camp Nou on an official match day, dressed in a club strip, and have an official photo taken in the stadium. The waiting list for the photo has been reduced from 2 years to 5/6 months at present (photos can also be taken with the basketball, handball and hockey teams).

3   The 'Youth campaign' provides activities that are adapted to a member's age. In addition to the above programmes (e.g. gifts, congratulations, membership cards, exclusive cultural activities, etc.) it includes:

- For each first team game, a prize draw is used to give members the opportunity to be a ball boy or ball girl during the match (one per match)
- A prize draw for 15–18 year-olds gives ten members the opportunity to watch a match from the 'Presidential Stand'. This is called 'Open Stand'
- On their 18th birthday, members receive a congratulations letter from the club, together with a special gift and the 'Club Statutes'. Members are also informed that they can now vote within the club.

In addition, the club provides a large number of internet-based services, most notably:

- Opportunity to have a 100 per cent Barça e-mail address: yourname@mail.fcbarcelona.cat
- Opportunity to receive an exclusive e-mail news bulletin
- Special members' area in the junior FCB website
- Young members that register for the club's mobile phone service receive free information from the club: match times, results, etc.

1.3 New technologies and FCB's communication

New technologies are an important part of FCB's strategy of building personal relationships with its members, as these technologies allow the club to create strong emotional ties and thereby build loyalty. FCB has also understood the value of new technologies for creating relationships with all its supporters. As such, it offers the following services:

- An official FCB website (http://www.fcbarcelona.cat). On average, 26 million pages are visited by 3 million users. The site has been translated into seven languages: Catalan, Castilian, English, Japanese, Chinese, Korean and Arabic. Some 40 per cent of visitors to the site consult the Catalan or English pages

- A TV channel. *Barça TV* is a subscription-only television channel that is broadcast using Digital Plus and Imagenio technology. It has approximately 50,000 subscribers. Programmes are based around Barça's sports activities and the broadcasting of the club's matches. There are 12 hours of programmes every day
- *TVonline* is an 'on demand' TV channel that can be watched via the internet
- *R@dio Barça* is a radio station that can be listened to via Barça's website. It provides commentary in Catalan, Castilian and English for all Barça's matches
- Show Time allows supporters to have photographs made showing themselves with Barça players or in famous Barça places (e.g. the Camp Nou). Supporters send their pictures to the club's website, choosing the photographs they want their picture to be incorporated into. After a few days, the supporter receives the photo album he has chosen and paid for. This service is used to create presents for people, showing them with their favourite players
- FCB provides an up-to-the-minute information service via text message and e-mail. Free for members
- An on-line FCB shop where supporters can buy all FCB's merchandising products
- Ticket sales via the internet and through cash dispensers belonging to the 'La Caixa' bank, which has branches throughout Spain
- Products and services linked to mobile phones. The FCBMòbil programme offers the following services:

  o   Up-to-the-minute information via text messages. This service is free for members and can be activated by non-members. It provides the following information: the week's headlines, fixture list, goals (as they are scored), match results, important moments in matches

  o   Screen backgrounds. A range of screen backgrounds for mobile phones can be downloaded, including player photo albums, historical photos, Camp Nou, latest photos, backgrounds with the supporter's name

  o   Barça Toons. Cartoons of people connected with Barça can be downloaded

- ○ Logos. Up to four different Barça logos can be downloaded and the Barça emblem can be put on mobile phones.

Future lines of action

In order to improve the management of the member loyalty-building pro-
essential to segment these people and find out more about their
expectations and interests. Hence, the club intends to introduce
ship management system for its supporters and, for the 2008–
new CRM system that will provide more individualised informa-
services demanded and provided.

ECOmass Project – The Helsinki World
ps in Athletics 2005

Case focus:

Major sport events can have a negative impact on the environment due to the construction of infrastructure and facilities, spectator and visitor transport, and waste production, etc. The 2005 World Championships in Athletics was the first in the history of the IAAF to implement environmentally friendly measures. The 'ECOmass' project was designed to reduce carbon dioxide (CO_2) emissions and the amount of waste sent to landfill, and to look for eco-efficient operating methods. It highlighted the importance of a collaborative strategy between the host cities, the Local Organizing Committee (LOC), the international federation, business partners, and not-for-profit organisations.

Case diagnosis:

The IAAF World Championships in Athletics is the third largest sporting event in the world in terms of impact and audience. It is preceded only by the Olympic Games and the Football World Cup. The 10th edition, which was held in Helsinki on 6–14 August 2005, attracted over 400,000 spectators to the Olympic Stadium, and had ticket sales of 340,000. The games brought to the city a total of 2,788 team members from 196 countries, as well as an almost equal number of accredited media representatives (2,753). According to estimates, between 15,000 and 17,000 foreign visitors came to Helsinki to watch the games.

To host this event, the IAAF required a stadium with covered stands capable of accommodating more than 40,000 spectators, with an adjacent stadium for athlete training. The competition should have taken place in London but the IAAF decided to transfer the event to Helsinki because London's new Wembley Stadium was not finished in time. Helsinki's facilities included a village to accommodate the delegations and a transport system capable of conveying tens of thousands of people. The negative impact on the environment (i.e. pollution, energy, air-conditioning, etc.) of hosting such events is becoming a sensitive issue. As a result, the local organising committee and its primary stakeholders used a relationship-marketing strategy to design and implement specific programmes that would promote and develop environmentally friendly practices.

Case development:

The ECOmass project was initiated and coordinated by the Lifelong Learning Institute (TKK Dipoli) at Helsinki University of Technology and funded by the European Commission (Life Environment). The goals were to: promote the benefits of eco-friendly mass sport events, produce practical guidelines on environmental issues for sports organisations and to address eco-efficiency as a strategic tool for implementing environmentally friendly measures, to highlight the best practices from different parts of the world and to introduce ways to protect and preserve the environment.

The project's key strategic stakeholders included the Finnish Athletics Association, the Helsinki 2005 organising committee, the cities of Espoo, Helsinki and Vantaa, Motiva Oy, Skills Finland, Stadium-foundation, WWF Finland, Helsinki Metropolitan Area Council (YTV) and the Ministry of the Environment. Their roles and functions are presented in Table 5.3.

For the first time in the history of the International Association of Athletics Federations, the World Championships included a strategically planned

Table 5.3 Stakeholders involved in the environmental programme

Stakeholders	Involvement
Helsinki Metropolitan Area Council	Mainly responsible for public transport and waste management in the Helsinki metropolitan area
City of Helsinki, host for the world championships	As part of the environmental programme, the City of Helsinki Sports Department implemented the first ever environmental system in Kisahalli, which housed the media centre for the championships

City of Espoo	In charge of the athletics village. The environmental centre and the city's tourist office were heavily involved
City of Vantaa	The location of the metropolitan area's airport. The city's environmental department was involved in the implementation of the environmental programme
Skills Finland	Partner in identifying relevant areas and practical solutions for measuring and reporting
Finnish WWF	Identified solutions for reducing CO_2 emissions and creating a practical, internet-based CO_2 calculator
Motiva Ltd	Organisation promoting the use of renewable and efficient energy sources. Their knowledge was essential for the CO_2 calculator and for traffic and logistics eco-efficiency
Stadium Foundation	The foundation runs Helsinki's Olympic Stadium. It also initiated its own environmental activities as part of the environmental programme
Ministry of the Environment	National sponsor of the environmental programme
Ministry of Education	Financed the functions of the environmental programme and verified the results
IAAF Finnish Athletics	Event organiser
Helsinki 2005 Organising committee	Partner when executing the ECOmass environmental programme at the championships
Helsinki University of Technology Lifelong Learning Institute Dipoli	Project leader
European Commission	Life Environment funded the programme

environmental programme. The success of this programme was based on col-laboration between the event's primary stakeholders, who also provided resources (i.e. human, financial, technical, etc.). Helsinki Metropolitan Area Council played a central role. The marketing campaign targeted mainly the IAAF, the host city, the participants and the general public.

Programme characteristics

The project was carried out during the period 1 August 2004 – 31 July 2006. Stakeholders collaborating in this programme engaged resources in order to provide innovative and eco-friendly solutions. These resources affected three main areas:

1   Helsinki 2005 LOC volunteer and partner training and communications, in order to increase the awareness of sustainability issues among all the stakeholders of the Championships:

- The 'Walk the Green Helsinki' map was distributed at Helsinki 2005 information desks. The map included seven walking routes, finest nature sights and pick-up points for city bikes
- Daily eco-tips were distributed to teams (Village newsletter), the media (daily bulletin), volunteers (*Viestikapula* newsletter in Finnish) and the public (daily programme and Stadium TV)
- The City of Helsinki and Helsinki Metropolitan Council installed an air-quality indicator close to the Stadium
- ECOmass infodesk in Dipoli. Drawings by pupils at Espoo Martinkallio elementary school brought attention to the importance of environmental thinking and action
- The United Nations International Year of Sport and Physical Education was represented at the ECOmass infodesk, as well as at the Finnish development aid organisation's bus located by the Main Press Centre from 6–14 August
- Helsinki 2005 LOC: all 3,200 volunteers and some national partners and suppliers received training on environmental issues.

2   Traffic and logistics created by the Championships in order to reduce total CO_2 emissions by 10 per cent:

- Free public transport in Helsinki Metropolitan area for accreditation holders
- 25 per cent reduction on Helsinki City Transport tourist tickets on presentation of a ticket for that day's events (sold at the Stadium)
- Toyota Prius hybrid cars used as the lead cars at marathon and walking races
- Helsinki city bikes available for a €2 deposit
- Bicycle stands at Accreditation Centres

- Signposted walking routes between the stadium and Helsinki city centre and between the Athletes' Village and Tapiola shopping centre
- Shuttle bus service between the car park in Helsinki Fair Centre and the stadium.

3   Constructions using alternative energy and water sources in order to increase the use of renewable energies by 5 per cent:

- Use of wind-generated electricity at the stadium during the Championships
- Athletes' Village mainly used existing infrastructure
- Stadium Foundation, 'Kisahalli' Main Media Centre and TKK Dipoli improved an environmental management system already in use, as part of the preparations for hosting the Championships
- Temporary constructions (tents, fencing, electrical appliances, etc.) were mainly rented
- Fitted carpets were generally re-used after the Championships
- Temporary toilets were connected to Helsinki's sewer system, thus avoiding the unnecessary use of chemical substances

Results

Helsinki 2005 and ECOmass will pass on the legacy of the environmental programme to IAAF, and to future organisers and host cities. This will take the form of an easy-to-use manual and a UN seminar entitled 'Sports Events Implementing Sustainable Consumption and Production Patterns'. The IAAF decided to get involved in a sustainable development policy and to set up the 'IAAF Green Project' in order to find ways of contributing to the global environment through events such as the IAAF World Championships in Athletics. It started its work at the 11th IAAF World Championships in Athletics, in Osaka in 2007.

The IAAF belongs to the club of sustainable sports that cooperate with the United Nations Environment Programme (UNEP) and contribute to the International Olympic Committee's third pillar – the environment – through their actions and commitments. The IOC recognised a particular responsibility towards promoting sustainable development and it regards the environment as the third dimension of the Olympic ideal, alongside sport and culture. In 1995 it decided to create the Sport and Environment Commission. Reducing costs while protecting the environment is a key issue.

Resource websites

www.dipoli.tkk.fi/ymparisto/ecomass/
www.dipoli.tkk.fi/ecomass
www.iaaf.org
www.jeux-mondiaux-environnement.org
www.olympic.org

Case Study: Sport In Action (SIA) – Child Empowerment through Sport (Psychosocial support programme)

Clement Mubanga Chileshe – Sport In Action Executive Director

The Strategic Issue

Sport in Action (SIA) is a non-governmental organisation whose aim is to use sport and recreational activities to improve the quality of life for children and adults. Formed in 1998, SIA was the first Zambian sports NGO to be registered. Its membership comprises administrators and former sportsmen and sportswomen who felt the need to share their experiences of the impact sport can have on individuals.

Sport In Action is based on two concepts, namely the sport development programme and the development through sports programme. SIA aims at providing sports programmes that will change all aspects of people's lives.

'Every day has a newness about it, it is never a carbon copy of yesterday', said one writer.

The dwindling numbers of Zambian children and youth taking part in sporting activities is of grave concern. A 2006 survey conducted by the programmes department of SIA revealed myriad reasons for this drastic turn of events and for the erosion of Zambia's sporting culture. Prominent reasons include the downturn in the economy and the after effects of the privatisation of the economic powerhouse, Zambia Consolidated Copper Mines (ZCCM), who were the major sponsors and providers of various sports activities for children. The poor economy has had a chain effect that has hit the schools system, resulting in a major reduction in funding for school sport and physical education (PE). Local authorities have abandoned their sports and recreation facility roles, leading to community sport and recreation facilities for children being leveled up for residential and business construction.

While such good opportunities for children were going down the drain, AIDS was also taking its toll, depriving many children of their loving and providing parents. The frustrations of poverty were increasing the culture of child neglect and abuse. More and more children were reduced to one or less meals a day, leading to a devastating rise in the number of street kids. Zambia had never seen a time so distressing to its children as this.

The rise of intervention programmes by government, international development aid partners and civil society is a welcome sound to the ears of those who care for the welfare of children. A call to action against the effects of this stressful environment was sounded and many have answered from different perspectives. The role of sport and play in providing a child-friendly environment can never be over emphasised. In 1998, SIA was formed to take up this role through a project called Child Empowerment Through Sport (CETS).

Project development

The goal of CETS was to empower orphaned and vulnerable children in distress with life skills for better living and positive futures. SIA defined *Child empowerment* as a process of enabling children through knowledge, skills and resources and providing an environment that will allow them to cope with life's challenges and attain a better lifestyle.

The *objectives* of the programme were to:

1   Mobilise children in distress to take part in sport and psychosocial support activities and life skills
2   Lobby stakeholders and obtain their support and engagement for a child friendly environment that upholds children's rights and needs
3   Create relevant capacities and sports facilities for developing community and school sport and PE programmes

To do this there was need for a road map that would effectively identify, mobilise, and engage children in distress. More importantly, once the road map was drawn, there was a need for sustainable support belts to be established. The programme was set up in and out of schools, and it established partnerships with schools, community clubs, faith-based institutions, government departments and local authorities, including traditional village chiefs.

Public awareness campaigns and media (TV, radio and newspaper) programmes were developed to market the programme. Meetings with stakeholders were held to lobby their support and guidance; young leaders and teachers were mobilised and trained as coaches/activity leaders; PE sessions were reintroduced in selected schools; community sport for children's clubs were established with members drawn both from distressed and non-distressed children under the age of 15; and competitions were held to increase publicity, stakeholder appreciation and participant motivation.

The school and community programmes gained ground very quickly, with participant numbers and frequency of activities proportionately increasing in size. While the number of children participating was increasing, the number of girls remained very small, especially in the out-of-school programme and particularly in rural villages. A survey found that more than any other reason, the parents were the biggest negative influence on girls' participation. While the biggest challenge was identified, mitigation was not easy, as there was a realisation that the participants' parents and family members were not part of the stakeholder circle and programme partnership. This provided a great wake-up call, which meant going back to the drawing board and reconsidering the gaps in the plan.

A workshop was held to advise training-programme officers and activity leaders on how to execute a door-to-door campaign with the families. The campaign did not work well due to parents' resistance and cultural challenges. It was discovered that families did not relate to the project in any way, that they were unaware of the programme's benefits, and that they felt that the only effects were to expose their girls 'indecently' and to take them away from their household chores.

In order to involve families in the programme, a *Parents' Forum* project was introduced, through which children's adult relatives attended workshops and meeting sessions facilitated by influential members of the community who supported the programme. In addition, sport and family-health education sessions were held for women. It did not take long for women to enjoy their participation and appreciate the health and culture education the programme offered. They gave personal testimonies on how it improved their lifestyles. It was then that families started to identify with the programme and started responding positively to requests for their support, including allowing their female children to participate in the sport and life skills programme.

Within a year of the Parents' Forum project, the number of girls participating rose more than 150 per cent. From 400 children in two districts in 1998, participation in the programme's daily activities rose to more than 65,000 children in 24 districts in 2006.

In spite of all the efforts and successes of the CETS programme, the SIA continually has to deal with challenges such as:

- Early marriages of girls
- Homelessness
- Poor sports facilities and equipment
- Long distances to sports facilities
- Too many household chores for children
- Poor support from some guardians.

Funding partnerships

In successfully implementing and sustaining the programme, the SIA has had to identify child-welfare and development stakeholders at both national and international levels. Two segments, Organisations for children's sport and Organisations for children's growth and development, were formed and proposals were made to potential partners. It was easier to sell the programme to sports organisations than to non-sports organisations, as this was a new concept not understood by many. The fact that sport was sold as a right and a need made the project attractive to non-sports organisations.

The programme has managed to attract funding partners such as Save the Children Sweden, whose interest is in the programme providing children's rights and protection education to both children and their families. UNICEF has also been supportive, with the aim of providing psychosocial support to children while also engaging them in HIV/AIDS and reproductive health life-skills education. The Ministry of Education has supported the programme with the aim of strengthening integrated physical education and life-skills education in schools. The Norwegian Olympic Committee has supported the programme with the dual aims of developing sport by providing child-centred sport programmes and of providing positive sporting experiences to children for positive futures. The private sector (for-profit organisations) has supported periodic events, such as one-off tournaments, but it has not yet provided the much needed daily and weekly activities.

Outcome

- As a result of the CETS programme and progressive collaborations with both funding and implementing partners, the number of children participating in daily and weekly life skills and psychosocial support through sport and physical education activities has reached 75,000
- More than 600 volunteers and teachers working in the programme at various levels and roles

- More than 1,500 families actively take part in parents' forums and support their children and programme
- More than 100 schools have re-introduced physical education classes and have integrated them with life-skills education for child protection and HIV/AIDS
- More than 400 children have progressed to participate in district, regional and national select teams of various sports
- There is an increase in the number of children being sent to school by parents who have become aware of the importance of educating their children and that education is a right
- Standards of personal hygiene and general cleanliness have improved, thereby reducing the incidences of cholera and other diseases
- The majority of children have come to know and understand their basic rights and have therefore become more responsible individuals who are also able to demand their rights
- Cultural, religious and economic barriers to better childhood have reduced
- Early marriages of minors, especially girls just after puberty, have reduced
- Learning achievements in academic work have improved for most children attending sport and PE sessions
- Fifteen sport and PE facilities have been repaired and/or created in schools or communities within walking distance of the children.

The value of our SIA minds is in our hearts made of children's lives – if 10 minutes of sport means 5 minutes of real happiness in a child's otherwise distressed day, then it's worth it . . .

Resource websites
www.sportinaction.org
clementchileshe@gmail.com
sia@sportinaction.org

These three case studies cite specific examples of the principles of relationship marketing having a powerful effect on the development, growth and success of sporting bodies, events and programmes. In each case, the synergies created by developing relationships proved to be crucial to the success of the venture.

The sporting landscape is complicated and challenging. Cutting edge business principles must be embraced and employed to ensure success. Relationship marketing is a growing force in the sporting world and we hope this book has provoked the reader to consider the issue and decide how it fits into future plans.

In relationship marketing, there are no 'one size fits all' solutions. There are no universally right or wrong answers. The most important step is the first one. Hopefully this book has provided some thought provoking theory and case studies to allow the reader to develop an informed and progressive plan to harness the power of the relationship in its many forms in the sporting environment.

Notes

1 Relationship marketing for sports organisations

1 Gummerson (2006) has pointed out that the marketing equilibrium is created by three market forces: collaboration, competition and regulation, and institutions.

2 Strategic analysis for relationship marketing

1 The Olympic Games and the Olympic rings are protected for all these classes.

3 Issues in implementing a relationship–marketing strategy

1 The Henley Centre survey of 1,000 consumers reveals that fear and suspicion of company motives make relationship marketing appear to be just 'another way of selling'.
2 'Four out of ten respondents, about 78 million Americans, believe they have been victims of consumer privacy invasions. Eight in ten American adults (158 million) feel they have lost control over how companies collect and use their personal data' (Reidenberg, 1999).
3 Guinness World Records (2007).
4 E.g. country with the highest number of participants; country whose participants cover the largest number of kilometres to reach the venues, etc.
5 This fee depends on where the event is held and on the exchange rate between the host country and the participant's country.

References

Aaker, D. A. (1991) *Managing Brand Equity: Capitalizing on the Value of a Brand Name*, New York: The Free Press.

Aaker, D. A. (2001) *Strategic Marketing Management*, 6th edn, Hoboken: John Wiley and Sons.

Andreasen, A. R. (1994) 'Social marketing: definition and domain', *Journal of Marketing and Public Policy* 13(1): 108–14.

Andrioff, J. and Marsden, C. (1999) Corporate Citizenship: what is it and how to assess it? *Personalführung* 8: 34–41.

Arndt, J. (1979) 'Towards a concept of domesticated markets', *Journal of Marketing* 43: 69–75.

Bagozzi, R. P. (1975) 'Marketing as exchange', *Journal of Marketing* 40(June): 17–28.

Ballantyne, D. (1997) 'Internal networks for internal marketing', *Journal of Marketing Management* 13(5): 343–66.

Berry, L. L. (1983) 'Relationship marketing', in L. L. Berry, G. L. Shostack and G. D. Upah (eds) *Emerging Perspectives on Services Marketing. Proceedings of Services Marketing Conference*, Chicago: American Marketing Association, pp. 25–8.

Berry, L. L. and Parasuraman, A. (1993) 'Building a new academic field – The case of service marketing', *Journal of Retailing* 69(1): 13–60.

Bowen, H. R. (1953) *The Social Responsibility of the Businessman*, New York: Harper and Brothers.

Bruhn, M. (2003) *Relationship Marketing: Management of Customer Relationships*, Englewood Cliffs, NJ: Prentice-Hall.

Bukowiz, W and Williams, R. (2000) *The Knowledge Management Fieldbook*, Edinburgh: Prentice-Hall.

Buraud, L. and Boyer, D. (2000) *Le marketing avancé: Du One to One au E-business*, Paris: Editions d'Organisation.

Calvani, V. (2007) *Coni Servizi Brand Equity and Services Platform: a Proposal of Relationship Marketing Strategy Applied to Sport Facilities*, MEMOS Project. Lausanne: IDHEAP – Université Claude Bernard Lyon 1.

Cegarra, J. J. and Michel, G. (2001) 'Co-branding: clarification du concept', *Recherche et Applications en Marketing* 16(4): 57–69.

Chappelet, J. L. (2004) 'Strategic management of Olympic Sport Organisations', in J. L. Chappelet and E. Bayle (eds) *Strategic and Performance Management of Olympic Sport Organisations*, Champaign, IL: Human Kinetics, pp. 1–42.

Christopher, M., Payne, A. and Ballantyne, D. (1991) *Relationship Marketing: Bringing Quality, Customer Service and Marketing Together*, Oxford: Butterworth-Heinemann.

Christopher, M., Payne, A. and Ballantyne, D. (2004) *Relationship Marketing: Creating the Stakeholder Value*, Oxford: Elsevier.

Cova, B. and Cova, V. (2001) 'Tribal aspects of postmodern consumption research: The case of in-line roller skaters', *Journal of Consumer Bahaviour* 1(1): 67–76.

Coviello, N. E. and Brodie, R. (2001) 'Contemporary marketing practices of consumer and business-to-business firms: how different are they?', *Journal of Business and Industrial Marketing* 16(5): 382–400.

Crié, D. (2002) 'Rentabilité des programmes de fidélisation avec carte de fidélité dans la grande distribution', *Revue Française du Marketing* 188(3): 23–42.

Crozier, R. A. (2006) 'Internal branding: Employer branding', in *The IABC Handbook of Organisational Communication*, New York: Jossey Bass, p. 271.

Detrie, J. P. (2005) *Strategor*, 4th edn. Paris: Dunod.

Donaldson T. and Dunfee, T. W. (1999) *Ties That Bind: a Social Contracts Approach to Business Ethics*, Harvard: Harvard Business School Press.

Donaldson T. and Preston, L. E. (1995) 'The stakeholder theory of the Corporation: concepts, evidence and implications', *Academy of Management Review* 20(1): 65–91.

Donaldson, W. G. and O' Toole, T. (2000) 'Classifying relationship structures: relationship strength in industrial markets', *Journal of Business and Industrial Marketing* 15(7): 491–506.

Dunmore, M. (2002) *Inside-out Marketing: How to Create an Internal Marketing Strategy*, London: Kogan Page.

Egan, J. and Harker, M. J. (2006) 'The past, present and future of relationship marketing', *Journal of Marketing Management* 22(1–2): 215–42.

Elo, J. (2007) *A Proactive Operation Model to Improve Media Relations of the Finnish National Olympic Committee*. MEMOS project. Lausanne: IDHEAP – Université Claude Bernard Lyon 1.

Ferrand A. and Chanavat, N. (2006) *Guidebook for the Management of Sport Event Volunteers*. Lausanne: Sentedalps – IDHEAP (www.sentedalps.org).

Ferrand, A., Torrigiani, L. and Camps i Povill, A. (2006) *Routledge Handbook of Sports Sponsorship: Successful Strategies*. Abingdon: Routledge.

Ferrand, A. and Torrigiani, L. (2004) *Marketing of Olympic Sport Organisations*, Champaign, IL: Human Kinetics.

Flipo, J. P. (1999) 'Activité de service et relations interentreprises: vers une gestion stratégique des facteurs relationnels et des éléments d'interface', *Revue Française du Marketing* 171: 63–76.

Frederick, W. C., Davis, K. and Post, J. E. (1988) *Business and Society. Corporate Strategy, Public Policy, Ethics*. New York: McGraw Hill.

Freeman, R. E. (1984) *Strategic Management: A Stakeholder Approach*, Boston: Pitman.

Friedman, A. L. and Miles, S. (2002) 'Developing stakeholder theory', *Journal of Management Studies* 39(1): 1–21.

Friedman, A. L. and Miles, S. (2006) *Stakeholders: Theory and Practice*, Oxford: Oxford University Press.

Godet, M. (2001) *Creating Futures: Scenario Planning as a Strategic Management Tool*, Paris: Economica.

Godin, S. (1999) *Permission Marketing: Turning Strangers into Friends and Friends into Customers*, New York: Simon and Schuster.

Gordon, I. (1999) *Relationship Marketing: New Strategies, Techniques and Technologies to Win the Customers You Want and Keep Them Forever*, Hoboken: John Wiley and Sons.

Grönroos, C. (1990) *Service Management and Marketing: Managing the Moment of Truth in Service Competition*. Lexington, MA: Lexington Books.

Grönroos, C. (1994) 'Quo Vadis, marketing? Toward a relationship marketing paradigm', *Journal of Marketing Management* 10: 347–60.

Grönroos. C. (2000) *Service Management and Marketing*, Chichester: John Wiley and Sons.

Grönroos, C., Gummerson, E. (1985) *Service Marketing – Nordic School Perspectives*, Stockholm: Stockholm University, School of Business, Research Report.

Gummerson, E. (1987) 'The new marketing – developing long-term interactive relationships', *Long Range Planning* 20(4): 10–20.

Gummerson, E. (1999) *Total Relationship Marketing*, Oxford: Butterworth-Heinemann.

Gummerson. E. (2006) *Total Relationship Marketing*, 2nd edn, Oxford: Butterworth-Heinemann.

Hakansson, H. and Snehota, I. (1995) *Developing Relationships in Business Networks*, London: Routledge.

Heilbrunn, B. (2003) 'Modalités et enjeux de la relation consommateur-marque', *Revue Française de Gestion* 29(145): 131–44.

Hinde R. A. (1979) *Towards Understanding Relationships*, London: Academic Press.

Hinde R. A. (1995) 'A suggested structure for a science of relationships', *Personal Relationships* 2: 1–15.

Holbrook, M. B. (1999) 'Introduction to consumer value', in M. B. Holbrook (ed.) *Consumer Value: A Framework for Analysis and Research*. London: Routledge, pp. 2–12.

Johnson, J., Scholes, K. and Whittington, R. (2004) *Exploring Corporate Strategy: Text and Cases*, London: Prentice Hall.

Kapferer, J. N. (2000) *Strategic Brand Management*, 2nd edn, London: Kogan Page.

Kempeners, M. and Van Der Hart, H. (1999) 'Designing account management organisations', *Journal of Business and Industrial Marketing* 14(4): 310–55.

Kotler, P. (1992) 'It is time for total marketing', *Business Week* Advance Executive Brief 2: 1–7.

Kotler, P. and Armstrong, G. (2001) *Principle of Marketing*, 3rd edn, Harlow: Financial Times Prentice Hall.

Lambin, J. J. (2002) *Le Marketing Stratégique: Du Marketing à l'orientation-marché*, Paris: Dunod.

Le Gallou, F. (1992) 'Présentation de concepts de la systémique, 2ème école européenne de systémique', *AFCET*, octobre.

Levine, J. (1993) 'Relationship marketing', *Forbes 152*, 20(14): 232–4.

Lewi, G. (2005) *Branding Management. La Marque, de l'idée à l'action*, Paris: Pearson Education.

Little, E. and Marandi, E. (2003) *Relationship Marketing Management*, London: Thomson.

Marion, G., Azimont, F., Mayaux, F., Michel, D., Portier, P. and Revat, R. (2003) *Antimanuel de Marketing*. Paris: Editions d'Organisation.

Martinet, A. C. (1984) *Management Stratégique: Organisation et Politique*, Paris: McGraw Hill.

McConnell, B. and Huba, J. (2004) *Creating Consumer Evangelists: How Loyal Fans can Become a Volunteer Sales Force*, downloaded on 2/7/2004 from: http://www.mialiareport.com /jul04_story5.cfm

McCubbrey, D., Bloom, P. and Younge, B. (2005) 'USA swimming: The data integration project', *Communication of the Association for Information Systems* 16(10): 299–316 [e-journal].

McKenna, P. (1998) *En temps réel: S'ouvrir au client toujours plus exigeant*, Paris: Village Mondial.

Melero, V. and Durand, E. (2005) *Sport et médias, Conférence introductive du cours sport et médias*. Paris: Institut d'études politique.

Mercier, S. (2006) 'La théorie des parties prenantes: une synthèse de la littérature', in M. Bonnafous-Boucher and Y. Pesqueux (eds). *Décider avec les parties prenantes: Approche d'une nouvelle théorie de la société civile*. Paris: La Découverte, pp. 157–72.

Mintzberg, H., Ahlstrand, B. and Lampel, J. (1998) *Strategy Safari: A Guided Tour through the Wilds of Strategic Management*, New York: Free Press.

Minvielle, A. (2004) 'Qu'est-ce qu'une partie prenante?', *Working paper*, Paris: CNAM.

Möller, K. and Halinen, A. (2000) 'Relationship marketing theory: its roots and direction', *Journal of Marketing Management* 16: 29–54.

Mongillon, P. and Verdoux, S. (2003) *L'entreprise orientée Processus – Aligner le pilotage opérationnel sur la stratégie et les clients*, Paris: AFNOR.

Montagnon, S. (2005/2006/2007). *Working papers*, Université Claude Bernard Lyon 1 (Online).

Morgan, R. M. (2000) 'Relationship marketing and marketing strategy: The evolution of relationship marketing strategy within the organisation', in J. N. Sheth and A. Parvatiyar (eds). *Handbook of Relationship Marketing*. Thousand Oaks CA: Sage, pp. 481–504.

Morgan, R. M. and Hunt, S. D. (1994) 'The commitment-trust theory of relationship marketing', *Journal of Marketing* 58(July): 20–38.

Mullin, B. J., Hardy, S. and Sutton, W. A. (2007) *Sport Marketing*, 3rd edn, Champaign, IL: Human Kinetics.

Muniz, A. M. and O'Guinn, T. C. (1996) 'Brand community and the sociology of brands', in K. P. Corfman and J. L. Provo (eds) *Advances in Consumer Research* 23: 265–6.

Normann, R. A. and Ramirez, R. (1993) 'From Value Chain to Value Constellation: Designing Interactive Strategy', *Harvard Business Review* 71(July/August): 65–77.

Normann, R. A. and Ramirez, R. (1998) *Designing Interactive Strategy: from Value Chain to Value Constellation*. Hoboken: John Wiley and Sons.

Palmer, A. (1994) *Principles of Services Marketing*, London: McGraw-Hill.

Peelen, E. (2005) *Customer Relationship Management*. Harlow: *Financial Times*/Prentice Hall.

Peppers, D. and Rogers, M. (2004) *Managing Customer Relationships: a Strategic Framework*, Hoboken: John Wiley and Sons.

Pesqueux, Y. (2006) 'Pour une évaluation critique de la théorie des parties prenantes', in M. Bonnafous-Boucher and Y. Pesqueux (eds). *Décider avec les parties prenantes: Approche d'une nouvelle théorie de la société civile*. Paris: La Découverte, pp. 19–40.

Pitts, B., Stotlar, D. K. (2007) *Fundamentals of Sport Marketing*, 3rd edn, Morgantown, West Virginia: Fitness Information Technology.

Porter, M. E. (1985) *Competitive Advantage*, New York: Free Press.

Pride, W. M. and Ferrell, O. C. (1997) *Marketing*, 10th edn, New York: Houghton Mifflin Company.

Reidenberg, J. R. (1999) 'Restoring Americans' privacy in electronic commerce', *Berkeley Technology Law Journal* 14(Spring): 771–2.

Ries, A. (1998) *The 22 Immutable Laws of Branding*. New York: Harper Business.

Robinson, L., Camps I Povill, A., Henry, I., Vandeputte, L. and Clark, M. (2007) 'Organising an Olympic Sport Organisation', in J. Camy, L. Rosinson (eds) *Managing Olympic Sport Organisation*. Champain: International Olympic Committee – Olympic Solidarity, Human Kinetics, pp. 1–60.

Rokeach, M. (1973) *The Nature of Human Values*. New York: Free Press.

Rondeau, A. (2002) 'Transformer l'organisation. Vers un modèle de mise en œuvre', in R. Jacob, A. Rondeau and D. Luc (eds). *Transformer l'organisation*. Montréal: HEC, Collection Racines du Savoir, pp. 91–112.

Rowley, T. J. (1997) 'Moving beyond dyadic ties: a network theory of stakeholder influences', *Academy of Management Review* 22(4): 887–910.

Samu, S., Krishnan, S. and Smith, R. E. (1999) 'Using advertising alliances for new product introduction: interactions between product complementarity and promotional strategies', *Journal of Marketing* 63(1): 57–74.

Scardamalia, M. and Bereiter, C. (1994) 'Computer support for knowledge-building communities', *Journal of the Learning Sciences* 3(3): 265–83.

Shani, D. (1997) 'A framework for implementing relationship marketing in the sport industry', *Sport Marketing Quarterly* 6 (2): 9–15.

Shank, M. D. (2005) *Sports Marketing: A Strategic Perspective*, 3rd edn. Upper Saddle River, NJ: Prentice Hall.

Sheth, J. N. and Parvatiyar, A. (2000) *The Handbook of Relationship Marketing*, Thousand Oaks: Sage Publications.

Slack, T. and Parent, M. M. (2006) *Understanding sport organizations: The application of organization theory*, 2nd edn, Champaign, IL: Human Kinetics.

Smith, S. and Wheeler, J (2002) *Managing the Customer Experience*, London: Prentice Hall.

Sport North Federation Strategic Business Plan 2004–2009. Unpublished paper.

Tabatoni, P. and Jarnioux, P. (1975) *Les systèmes de gestion, politiques et structures*, Paris: PUF.

Vermeulen, F. (2006) *Le marketing de Swiss Olympic: vers une augmentation de la valeur pour les parties prenantes*. MEMOS Project. Lausanne: IDHEAP – Université Claude Bernard Lyon 1.

Waddock, S. A. and Graves, S. B. (1997) 'The corporate social performance – Financial performance link', *Strategic Management Journal* 18(4): 303–19.

Wilson, B. and Cole, P. (1997) 'Cognitive models of teaching', in D. H. Jonassen (ed.) *Handbook of Research in Instructional Technology*, New York: MacMillan.

Zeithaml, V. A. and Bitner, M. J. (2003) *Services Marketing, Integrating Customer Focus Across the Firm*, 3rd edn, Boston: McGraw Hill.

Index

Note: *italic* page numbers denote references to Figures/Tables.